CW00969491

A History of Gaelic Football

A HISTORY OF GAELIC FOOTBALL

Jack Mahon

GILL & MACMILLAN

Gill & Macmillan Ltd
Hume Avenue, Park West, Dublin 12
with associated companies throughout the world
www.gillmacmillan.ie
© Jack Mahon 2000
0 7171 2876 8

Print origination by O'K Graphic Design, Dublin
Printed by
ColourBooks Ltd, Dublin

This book is typeset in 10.5/12 pt Berkeley Book

A CIP catalogue record for this book is available from the
British Library.

1 3 5 4 2

CONTENTS

ILLUSTRATIONS

Between pages 184 and 185

The Galway team which played in the All-Ireland semi-final of 1966.

James McCartan of Down.

Dermot Earley of Roscommon.

The Offaly team of 1971 which brought the Sam Maguire Cup to the Faithful County for the first time.

Sligo's Mickey Kearins tussling with Mayo's Ger Feeney.

Cork's winning captain, Billy Morgan, climbs the steps in the Hogan Stand in 1973.

The Dublin All-Ireland champions of 1974.

Tony Hanahoe of Dublin in action in the 1974 All-Ireland final against Galway.

Brian Murphy of Cork challenges Pat Spillane of Kerry in the Munster final of 1976.

The Kerry team of 1977: NFL champions.

The Dublin-Kerry All-Ireland semi-final of 1977.

Seán Walsh of Kerry and Brian Mullins of Dublin rise for the ball.

Jack O'Shea, one of the all-time greats, demonstrates the art of fielding.

The Offaly team that denied Kerry their bid for a historic five-in-a-row in the 1982 All-Ireland final.

Two views of Séamus Darby's goal that won the 1982 title for Offaly.

The Kerry team that completed a three-in-a-row in 1986.

The Meath team of 1990, winners of the Leinster title and All-Ireland runners-up.

Seán Boylan who has piloted Meath to almost twenty years as a major force in the game.

September 1992. Anthony Molloy becomes the first — and so far the only — Donegal captain to lift the Sam Maguire Cup.

The Leitrim team that won the Connacht championship in 1994.

Peter Canavan of Tyrone, one of the very finest footballers of the 1990s.

Ulster teams dominated the championship in the first half of the 1990s. Donegal and Derry (shown here) won in 1992 and 1993, respectively.

Kildare and Dublin in action in the Leinster championship of 1998.

The Galway team that bridged a 32-year gap by bringing the Sam Maguire Cup back across the Shannon in 1998.

1

THE ORIGINS OF GAELIC FOOTBALL

Gaelic football is by far the most popular of Irish sports today and is played in virtually every town and village throughout the country, regularly attracting huge attendances, as well as being played by Irish exiles abroad. The organising body of the sport, the Gaelic Athletic Association, has more than two thousand registered clubs, most of which cater for several teams in various competitions. Organised championships date back to 1887, three years after the founding of the GAA in Thurles.

Gaelic football cannot claim anything like the antiquity of hurling. The Statutes of Galway (1527) give us the first direct reference to football. They ordered citizens not to play 'the hurlings of the littill ball with hockie sticks or staves, nor use no hands ball to play without the walls but only the great footballe.' Everyone found guilty of transgressing this law was liable to a fine of eight pence. Citizens were encouraged to participate in shooting with longbows and short crossbows, and hurling darts and spears.

Just why football was not prohibited is a mystery. But it was not long before it too was included among the prohibited sports. The Sunday Observance Act (1695) prescribed a fine of twelve pence for any 'person or persons whatsoever, that play, use or exercise any hurling, commoning, foot-ball playing, cudgels, wrestling or any other games pastimes or sports on the Lord's Day ...' But these statutes failed to suppress the prohibited sports, and football of sorts was widespread in Ireland, as elsewhere, long before the foundation of the GAA in 1884.

There are other references to football in the seventeenth and eighteenth centuries, specifically in poems, which give a good idea of the rough-and-tumble nature of the game as it evolved over the years.

The first of these is by the north Leinster poet Séamas Dall Mac Cuarta, who, in a twelve-verse poem called 'Iomáin na Bóinne', described a football match played at Fennor, on the south bank of the Boyne close to Slane, about 1670. The men from the Nanny River played the men from the Boyne Valley, who were the victors. Wrestling challenges after the game were provided for; and it is clear that snatching and carrying the ball were features of the play. Meath's great football tradition is firmly rooted!

The term *iomáin* may be confusing, as it includes in its meaning both hurling and football, with *iomáin le camán* to denote hurling. The English writer John Dunton, who travelled around Ireland in 1677, wrote in a letter: 'They do not often play at football, only in a small territory called Fingal near Dublin where the people use it much and trip and shoulder verie handsomely.'

Perhaps the earliest description of an Irish football game to appear in print, and one of the earliest in Europe, is the epic poem by Matt Concannon the Elder, which describes a football match played in Fingall in 1720. The teams, six a side, hailed from Lusk and Swords, and were played onto the crowded green by a piper. Bent sally-rods formed the goals. The ball, of oxhide stuffed with hay, could be caught overhead and kicked along the ground or in the air; it could also be carried. Tripping and wrestling were allowed—indeed skill in these tactics was necessary. Getting the ball over the end line was termed an 'advantage', but it had to be driven 'through the adverse goal' for victory.

Lusk got 'advantage' in the first half, but Swords scored the winning goal. The trophies were 'six Holland [linen] caps with Ribbons Bound' for the winners, and 'six pairs of gloves' for the losers, with a 'Cask of Humming Beer' for all.

> Ye champions of fair Lusk and Ye of Soards,
> View well this ball, three folds of Bullock's Hide,
> With leathern thongs fast bound on every side:
> A mass of finest hay concealed from sight,
> Conspire at once to make it firm and light:
> At this you'll all contend, this bravely strive,
> Alternate thro' the adverse goal to drive;
> Two gates of sally bound the spacious green,
> Here one and one on yonder side is seen.

Paddy Mehigan, alias Carbery, whose *Carbery's Annual* brought so much joy to us in the Christmases of our youth, is one of my chief sources for Gaelic football's origins. In the booklet *Gaelic Football*, published in 1941, he recalls another poem, 'Léana an Bhábhúin' by Redmond Murphy an tSléibhe, describing a football match in Omeath, County Louth, in 1740. Twelve men from each of two rival parishes participated. Snatching and running with the ball were permitted, and the game lasted from midday till evening. The poet describes how a relative of his own, Patty an tSléibhe, was injured in a wrestling match during play after being thrown on a heap of stones beside the meadow; he died sixteen days later.

Football was played in County Kildare too, and Edward Fitzgerald watched a game between Meath and Kildare in 1797, where 'Kildare's tall strong twenty men wore white linen shirts.' In the same year Wogan Browne, a popular County Kildare gentleman, threw in the ball to start a football game; for so doing he had his name removed from the list of magistrates by 'Black Jack' Fitzgibbon, Lord Clare.

As was the custom in hurling, big football games for high wagers were played throughout Ireland in the eighteenth and nineteenth centuries. In 1731, at Dangan, County Meath, 'a grate match at footeball was played between married men and bachelors'—a frequent entertainment. Oxmantown Green and Merrion Fields near Dublin were used as football grounds. In 1741 a game was played on the frozen River Liffey after a spell of heavy frost. Forty years later, according to the poems of Ned Lysaght, football was played every evening in College Park by the 'pensioners' and 'commoners' of Trinity College. Drumcondra was a football venue in 1774 and was still one of the top venues after the founding of the GAA in 1884.

In parts of County Kerry, especially in the Dingle Peninsula, a form of football known as *caid* became popular in the nineteenth century, before the Famine, as evidenced by Father W. Ferris of Glenflesk, who wrote a thesis on the then traditional game. There were two forms of the game: 'field caid', in which boughs of trees in the form of an arch were used as goals, and 'cross-country caid', in which the object was to take the ball from one parish to another.

The word *caid* essentially refers to the ball used, which was made of animal skins with an inflated natural bladder inside, which resulted in an elongated rather than a round ball. In 'cross-country caid' the ball was thrown in on the parish boundaries, the battle for supremacy lasting through the daylight hours of a winter Sunday, from after Mass till dusk. The time for pastimes then was after the crops were saved. Young and old participated. Wrestling and holding were allowed, as was carrying the ball; speedy runners, craftily placed on the outskirts of the ruck, often gained considerable ground and sometimes took the ball all the way home for a win.

In time, 'caid' gave way to a slightly more sophisticated form of football, which became loosely known as the 'rough-and-tumble game' and which was the immediate precursor of 1884. These games were often as boisterous as the name suggests. A leather ball stuffed with hay was used; wrestling, tripping and tumbling were permitted. There were few or no rules, and this of course led to rows, ructions, and often bitterness.

This was the scene in the post-Famine era before the coming of the GAA. The native games of hurling, football and handball came close to extinction with the coming of rugby to Ireland, by way of Trinity College, and the arrival of association football or soccer in the late eighteen-seventies; the pneumatic bladder, which came in the eighteen-sixties, made a huge difference All these factors influenced men such as Cusack and Davin in the formulation of the first playing rules of Gaelic football. Rugby was the first of the organised football games to catch on in Ireland, and Michael Cusack, from Carron, County Clare, played it in his youth, as well as cricket while attending school in Dublin.

In 1884, Ireland was on its knees. Three rebellions had failed. Famine and disease had ravished the country; emigration was rife. Irish culture, in the shape of its language, music, dancing, and games, was in danger of oblivion. Then Michael Cusack sounded the clarion call, and the nation rallied. The culture that seemed dead was only 'in slumber deep.' Despite much opposition, poor organisation, and bad management at times, the GAA came into being in 1884, and Gaelic games spread like wildfire. The nation found new heart and spirit, which led on to the growth of the greatest amateur sporting organisation in the world.

The GAA is now a powerful weapon for sporting involvement in the life of modern Ireland. The reconstructed Croke Park is a monument to the GAA's founders, and the popularity of Gaelic games is a source of pride to all involved. Gaelic football as a game evolved into a popular sport played in almost every parish in the land, though at the moment it is suffering from what might be called an identity crisis. Playing rules are being changed too often, perhaps; tactics are tending to destroy skill and self-expression. Time will see the game find its true identity. It has come a long way since the 'rough-and-tumble' days and retains many great skills of fielding and kicking and such native skills as the toe pick-up on the run and of course the solo run. Much indeed has happened since Séamas Dall Mac Cuarta wrote 'Iomáin na Bóinne' in the seventeenth century.

2

THE 1884 RULES AND SUBSEQUENT CHANGES

1. There shall not be less than fourteen or more than twenty one players aside.
2. There shall be two umpires and a referee. Where the umpires disagree the referee's decision shall be final.
3. The ground shall be at least 120 yards long by 80 in breadth, and properly marked by boundary lines. Boundary lines must be at least five yards from fences.
4. The goal posts shall stand at each end in the centre of the goal line. They shall be 15 feet apart, with a cross-bar 8 feet from the ground.
5. The captains of each team shall toss for choice of sides before commencing play, and the players shall stand in two ranks opposite each other until the ball is thrown up, each man holding the hand of one of the other side.
6. Pushing or tripping from behind, holding from behind, or butting with the head, shall be deemed foul, and the players so offending shall be ordered to stand aside, and may not afterwards take part in the match, nor can his side substitute another man.
7. The time of actual play shall be one hour. Sides to be changed only at half-time.
8. The match shall be decided by the greater number of goals. If no goal be kicked the match shall be deemed a draw. A goal is when the ball is kicked through the goal posts under the cross-bar.
9. When the ball is kicked over the side line it shall be thrown back by a player of the opposite side to him who kicked it over. If kicked over the goal line by a player whose goal line it is, it shall be thrown back in any direction by a player of the other side. If kicked over the goal line by a player of the other side, the goal

keeper whose line it crosses shall have a free kick. No player of the other side to approach nearer 25 yards of him 'till the ball is kicked.

10. The umpires and referee shall have during the match full power to disqualify any player, or order him to stand aside and discontinue play for any act which they may consider unfair, as set out in rule 6.

No nails or iron tips on the boots. (Strips of leather fastened on the soles will prevent slipping). The dress for hurling and football to be knee-breeches and stockings and boots or shoes. It would be well if each player was provided with two jerseys, one white and the other some dark colour. The colours of his club could be worn on each. Then when a match was made, it could be decided the colours each side should wear.

This draft, dating from the GAA's foundation years, was the first codification of the playing rules of Gaelic football. The wording is less sophisticated than in later times, but these rules laid the basis for the game we have today, despite many changes over the intervening years. The first recorded game under the GAA rules was that between Callan and Kilkenny on 15 February 1885.

Changes in the playing rules came fast and plenty. In 1886 wrestling and hand grips between players were prohibited. Five overs were allowed to count as a point. Beside the goal-posts, point posts were introduced (which still obtain in Australian football). Points were to count only if no goals, or an equal number of goals, were scored, so that a team scoring one goal won against a team scoring ten or twenty points but no goal. Balls going into touch or over the sideline (as it came to be called) were to be thrown in by the umpires or referee.

In 1888 the Convention—or Congress, as we now know it—'recommended' that referees provide themselves with a whistle. In the early days, forfeit points were allowed when a defender put the ball over his own end line, for which a 'forty-five' is given now. These forfeit points were abolished in 1888 also and the fifty-yard free or 'fifty' introduced.

Three important changes in the playing rules were made in 1892. The maximum number constituting a team was reduced from twenty-one to seventeen. The county champions, who hitherto represented only their county in the All-Ireland championship, were now given the right to select players from any other club in the county for the championship. Five points were declared to be the equivalent of one goal.

In 1895 the value of a goal was reduced from five points to three, and at the 1896 Convention the cross-bar was lowered from 10½ feet to 8 feet. In 1910 the point side-posts were abolished, and the present-day scoring area was introduced. That year too saw the introduction of goal nets.

In 1913 a change of great importance took place when the number of players was reduced from seventeen to fifteen, which obtains to this day. The move was mooted by Harry Boland, the republican revolutionary and close friend of Michael Collins who was later Sinn Féin TD for South Roscommon and who was to die tragically in the Civil War. It is significant that the first game played under the new rule was the magnificent drawn Croke Memorial Final of 1913 between Kerry and Louth in Jones's Road on 4 May 1913, an epic game watched by a record crowd.

The new scoring area was generally regarded as making for greater skill in attack. Backs were in their place before the ball was thrown in at midfield—another huge improvement. The game was developing.

As rules and styles of play developed, so too did the organisational structure. There were new competitions, new grades, and the introduction of the game to universities and secondary schools. The Railway Shield for interprovincial competitions was introduced in 1906, the Croke Cup for the defeated provincial finalists in 1909, and the Sigerson Cup for the inter-university championship in 1911. A Leinster Colleges Committee was formed in 1910, and the junior all-Ireland championship began in 1913.

From 1914 the all-Ireland finals were to be played in Croke Park on the first and fourth Sundays in September—hurling on the first Sunday, football on the fourth Sunday. The national football league began in 1925, and the first national football league tie took place on 11 October 1925, with Laois becoming the first champions. The first Railway Cup final took place on 17 March 1929, and the minor football championship was also sanctioned in 1927.

A scheme for the compensation of injured players was introduced in 1929. In the same year Pádraig Ó Caoimh succeeded Luke O'Toole as general secretary of the GAA, a position he was to hold with distinction until 1964. By 1934, the golden jubilee year of its foundation, the GAA had reached a pinnacle that Cusack and Croke would have found unbelievable. It was well on its way to becoming the dominant sporting organisation in Ireland and a wonderful influence on the lives of Irish people. The 1934 Congress was held in Thurles, the birthplace of the GAA, an event marked by both the *Irish Independent* and the infant *Irish Press*—whose GAA correspondent

'Green Flag' made such an impact on the popularisation of the GAA—
with the production of wonderful commemorative supplements.

3

THE EARLIEST ALL-IRELANDS AND THE DOMINANCE OF DUBLIN CLUBS

Michael Cusack, the visionary from County Clare who helped in such a decisive way to found the GAA, consulted leading football players from different parts of Ireland before drafting the first rules of Gaelic football. High fielding was even then a characteristic of the traditional game. Wrestling (one fall) was allowed in those first rules; tripping, catching and tackling above the knees were all permissible in 1885, when the first big tournaments started. A goal was the only score recognised, and forfeit points were allowed when the defending side put the ball over their own line (which results in a 45-metre free today). Wrestling was prohibited in 1886.

The all-Ireland championships did not begin until 1887. There was much confusion in the beginning, with few entries, many objections and disputes, and a certain lack of control.

The Parnell split in the eighteen-eighties and nineties almost sounded the death knell of the GAA. Many clubs disbanded. The GAA officially backed Parnell, and when he died, in 1891, the organisation was represented at his massive funeral in Dublin.

But Gaelic football survived; and with rule changes, better organisation and facilities, an increased awareness of discipline, and contrasting styles, the game began to spread and prosper. Dublin were the first to perfect the 'catch-and-kick' game; then to Kerry and Kildare is attributed the development of the hand-pass and other skills. Louth were the first to perfect the use of ground football. Connacht was slow to become involved. Cavan led the way in Ulster, but it took some time for many of the other Ulster counties to participate.

There were just twelve entries for the first official all-Ireland title in 1887. The draw was an open one, and counties were represented by their top club. On 29 April 1888 the first all-Ireland final— technically that of 1887—took place in Clonskeagh, Dublin, and in this historic game Limerick Commercials defeated Dundalk Young Irelands by 1-4 to 0-3. The winning team was captained by Denis Corbett, who played in goal.

The all-Ireland of 1888 was not completed, because of the 'American invasion'—the incursion of Irish hurlers and athletes. Despite chaos in 1889, in the end Bohercrowe (Tipperary) easily defeated Maryborough (Laois) in the final by 3-6 to nil. Midleton (Cork) easily defeated Blues and Whites (Wexford) in 1890 by 2-4 to 0-1.

Now followed the great dominance of Dublin in the all-Ireland series, which saw them win eight all-Ireland titles between 1891 and 1902, much of this due to good club organisation in the city. Dublin Young Irelands won three titles in all (1891, 1892, and 1894), their first captain in 1891 being John Kennedy, 'a man who could keep going all day, and anything that hit against him went down.' Then in 1897 came the Kickhams, a team drawn mostly from drapers' assistants in the city, captained by Paddy Walsh, a native of Bandon. They were followed by the Geraldines, who won two successive titles, in 1898 and 1899, captained by a very polished player in Matt Rea, who believed in having his team as fit as a fiddle. Isles of the Sea won in 1901, captained by Dan Holland. In 1902 the first real hero of Dublin football emerged when Jack Dempsey led Bray Emmets (now a County Wicklow club) to all-Ireland success.

Other clubs to win all-Irelands in those early years include Wexford Young Irelands in 1893, Arravale Rovers (Tipperary) in 1895, Limerick Commercials (their second win) in 1896, and Clonmel Shamrocks (Tipperary) in 1900.

There was very little documenting of GAA events at that time. Still, the pioneers deserve eternal credit for beginning the process and maintaining it through turbulent times of political upheaval. Competitions often ran very late. Even in those early years great efforts were made to expand the GAA, with a continuing improvement in the rules; among notable firsts were the introduction of London to the all-Ireland scene in 1900, with the playing of a 'home final' in Ireland beforehand. Sam Maguire, after whom the all-Ireland cup is named, was a playing member of that first London team of 1900.

Tuam Krugers (Galway) were the first Connacht team to reach any final; they were beaten in the home final of 1900 (played in 1902) by

Clonmel Shamrocks (Tipperary), 2-17 to 0-1. The GAA celebrated the centenary of the 1798 Rising throughout the land with a number of special tournaments and the unveiling of monuments to the men of '98. Gaelic football was establishing a firm footing. Greater days lay ahead.

4

KERRY'S FIRST ALL-IRELAND, 1903: A KERRY V. KILDARE SAGA

Football was popular in County Kerry long before the foundation of the GAA in 1884, the ancient game of 'caid' having been played throughout the county for centuries.

The first Kerry club team in modern times to make an impact was Laune Rangers of Killorglin, captained by J. P. O'Sullivan, the noted athlete and footballer. In those early years the winning club team in the county final represented its county in inter-county competition; and in 1892 Laune Rangers first defeated Clondrohid (Cork), and then Dungarvan, to become Munster champions, qualifying to meet Dublin Young Irelands in the all-Ireland final. This was the first all-Ireland in which the number of players was fixed at seventeen (reduced from twenty-one) and in which a goal was equal to five points (following a Kerry motion at the Congress in January).

The 1892 final was played in Clonturk Park, Dublin, on 26 March 1893. With the rather haphazard organisation of those early years, the hurling all-Ireland between Redmonds (Cork) and Faughs-Davitts (Dublin), refereed by Dan Fraher of Dungarvan, didn't finish, being abandoned after fifty minutes. In the second game, also refereed by Dan Fraher, Young Irelanders won by 1-4 to 0-3. Laune Rangers were dissatisfied with the unsporting attitude of their rivals' supporters; the club subsequently challenged their Dublin conquerors to a return game on neutral ground for a set of gold medals, but this never came about. But it was Laune Rangers who really started the ball rolling in Kerry.

There followed a decline in the fortunes of the club, but at the turn of the century the organisation of Gaelic football improved with the rise of Dr Crokes of Killarney to win the Kerry county title. Austin Stack and Maurice McCarthy got things going in Tralee with the emergence of the Boherbee John Mitchels, thus initiating the wonderful rivalry between Tralee and Killarney and the ensuing rapid improvement in standards. A combination of Dr Crokes and John Mitchels, aided by Denny Breen of Castleisland and and Rody Kirwan, a native of County Waterford, represented Kerry in the 1903 championship. Under the captaincy of Thady O'Gorman (John Mitchels), Kerry, with the young Killarney maestro Dick Fitzgerald in the forwards, defeated Clare and Cork to become Munster champions.

The All-Whites of Kildare had qualified in Leinster, and these sides met in the all-Ireland final in Tipperary on 23 July 1905. Kerry was stricken with big-match fever, and a huge crowd thronged the Sunday morning train from Tralee—so much so that it broke down between Ballybrack and Killarney, and a relief train had to be sent from Tralee. The team were taken on a brake supplied by the Quane brothers to the venue after a further delay at Limerick Junction. Kildare also had a huge following in a crowd estimated at twelve to thirteen thousand, in a venue with no stands or embankments. There were many encroachments; still, it was a great exhibition of football, Kildare favouring the passing game and leading by 1-3 to 0-4 with five minutes remaining. Then followed a disputed Kerry goal when the Kildare goalkeeper, Jack Fitzgerald, in fielding a Dick Fitzgerald free was adjudged to be behind the line. The game was abandoned in pandemonium and a replay ordered by the Central Council for Cork on 27 August, with Mick Crowe replacing Pat McGrath as referee. The receipts were £123 13s 4d, then a record gate, and the Kerry train didn't reach Tralee until 4:30 a.m. on Monday.

Another wonderful game took place in Cork, heralding a rebirth of Gaelic football with another huge crowd. This time it was a draw, 0-7 for Kerry to Kildare's 1-4, with Joyce Conlon of Kildare getting the all-important drawing goal at the end. These were the games that introduced the now well-known GAA shouts of 'Up Kerry' and 'Up Kildare'—exclamations never used hitherto.

Kildare were considered lucky. The third game of the first real GAA saga was fixed for Cork again on 13 October, when all attendance records were broken on an extremely wet day, and gate receipts were £270. Kerry won the toss and played with the aid of a slight wind to lead by 0-3 to 0-2 at half time. They went on to win convincingly by 0-8 to 0-2, gaining for the county its first all-Ireland (home) title. So the great marathon was over; but Kerry had still to beat London Hibernians (captained by Sam Maguire) in the final at Clonturk Park on 12 November 1905. This they did, by 0-11 to 0-3, to become Kerry's first champions.

The gallant Kildare men were not forgotten, the Central Council fittingly deciding to present them with a set of gold medals in recognition of the three epic games of the home final and a bonus for both county boards of £25 in excess of ordinary expenses.

The victorious Kerry 1903 team was:

Thady O'Gorman (captain), Jim Gorman, Denny Curran, Maurice McCarthy, John Buckley, Con Healy, John Thomas Fitzgerald, Austin Stack, Dick Fitzgerald, Paddy Dillon, Billy Lynch, Dan McCarthy, J. Myers, D. Kissane, Rody Kirwan, Denny Breen, Ned O'Neill. Substitute: F. O'Sullivan (Killarney) for Ned O'Neill.

The two premier GAA fields in County Kerry today—Dick Fitzgerald Stadium in Killarney and Austin Stack Park in Tralee—are named after two of the 1903 heroes. Dick Fitzgerald, known then in his native county as 'Dickeen', was a mere seventeen years old in 1905. In all he played in nine finals, winning five all-Ireland medals; he was described by Paddy Mehigan as 'among the greatest Gaelic football forwards in the history of the game.' Fitzgerald, who wrote one of the earliest books on Gaelic football, described the three-game series thus: 'Football took a turn for the better around this period. Both counties gave Gaelic football a fillip that marked the starting point to the game as we know it.'

Kerry went on to win two titles in a row in 1904 under the captaincy of Austin Stack, who was described by Mehigan as 'very clean in act and word; he did much in turn for Gaelic football, Gaelic culture and Irish Nationality'—a reference to his contribution to the rising of 1916 and Ireland's fight for freedom.

The Kerry-Kildare contests popularised Gaelic football beyond all expectations. Gates improved in a huge way. Kerry won the 1904 Munster title in a replay with Waterford at Dungarvan on 7 January 1906, by 2-3 to 0-2. (They were lucky enough to draw in Cork on 10 December 1905 with a score of 0-3 each.) Kildare were beaten in Leinster, where Kickhams (Dublin) won out.

In the 1904 final, at the Athletic Grounds in Cork on 1 July 1906, Kerry defeated Kickhams 0-5 to 0-2 with fourteen of the 1903 team, the missing players being Thady O'Gorman, Denny Breen, and Willy Lynch, the newcomers being P. J. Cahill, J. O'Sullivan, and T. O'Sullivan. This was the winning start of Kerry's litany of football successes, which has run now to thirty-one senior titles. Certainly the 1903 team, which first led the way, is held in deep regard in County Kerry.

5

THE KERRY V. LOUTH EPICS AND THE PURCHASE OF CROKE PARK

When we enter Croke Park today and feel so proud of the wonderful development over the years, we may wonder how it all began. It's an interesting story.

The first football final, that of 1887, was played in Dublin on a pitch called Byrne's field at Beech Hill, half way between Clonskeagh and Donnybrook. Beech Hill was then the home ground of the Benburbs of Donnybrook, one of whose playing members, Luke O'Toole, later became secretary of the GAA (1901–29) and had an important role to play in the purchase of Croke Park.

The 1889 final was played in the grounds of St Patrick's GAA Club at Inchicore, where the Tyrconnell Park housing estate is today.

Several of the early football finals, beginning with that of 1890, which was won by Cork, were staged in Clonturk Park in Drumcondra. Long before the foundation of the GAA, Gaelic football of a sort was played in Drumcondra beside the Tolka River. Many famous athletic events were held at this venue, now the Clonturk Park housing estate, opposite St Patrick's Training College, which itself moulded many outstanding footballers over the years and won a number of Dublin senior football championship titles in its time.

The 1893 final was played on the Nine Acres in the Phoenix Park, where many footballers train to this day.

The first final to be played at Jones's Road was that of 1895, played on 15 March 1896 and won by Tipperary. This became the standard venue for finals from 1909 and is the site on which Croke Park stands today.

The Jones's Road grounds, consisting of 14 acres and 17½ perches under a lease of 1829, had been put up for auction in 1906. By a deed of 17 December 1908 the property was sold to Frank Dinneen for

£3,250. Dinneen, a native of Ballylanders, County Limerick, worked for the *Freeman's Journal* and wrote the GAA column in its weekly magazine *Sport*. He was a lifelong member of the GAA, serving at various times as vice-president, president and secretary of the fledgling association. He was a noted athlete in his time and served as handicapper and president of the Athletic Council, which was an integral part of the early GAA until the NACAI took over the jurisdiction of athletics and cycling in 1922.

Dinneen's purpose in buying Jones's Road, for which he was obliged to borrow some of the money, was a selfless one: to hold it for the GAA he loved; and he deserves credit for his great foresight. At that time the GAA's finances were meagre. In 1910 Dinneen was compelled to dispose of a section of the ground (4 acres and 2 roods) to the Society of Jesus for £1,090 together with a rent of £20 a year. This was to be the sports ground of Belvedere College for many years.

In 1913 the Central Council of the GAA promoted an inter-county competition in hurling and football, to be called the Croke Memorial Competition, in order to raise funds for a memorial to Archbishop Croke in Thurles. The competitions, especially the football final and replay, were such a financial success that it was decided to buy the Jones's Road ground from Dinneen, and to rename it Croke Park. Dinneen was agreeable, and by a deed of 18 December 1913 he conveyed his interest to the trustees of the GAA for a purchase price of £1,500 in cash. The purchasers also had to assume liability for £2,000 charged on the premises, the amount of the mortgage Dinneen had taken out with the Munster and Leinster Bank. The trustees of Croke Park were Dan Fraher (Dungarvan), Michael Crowe (Dublin), Luke O'Toole (Dublin), Alderman J. J. Nowlan (Kilkenny), Tom Kenny (Galway), J. J. Hogan (Dublin), Patrick Whelan (Monaghan), John Malone (Ennis), and John Collins (London).

Various reasons contributed to the financial success of the Croke Memorial football final and replay of 1913, but the principal one was the first meeting for some time of the two top teams of the time, Kerry and Louth, after a certain amount of acrimony between the counties. Louth had won their first Leinster senior football title in 1909 and, after defeating Antrim, qualified to meet Kerry in the final at Jones's Road on 5 December 1909 (the first time a championship was completed within the same year). Kerry, captained by Tom Costelloe and including Dick Fitzgerald in their line-out, defeated Louth by 1-9 to 0-6. Louth were captained by the legendary Jack 'Sandman' Carvin, described by Paddy Mehigan in his book *Famous Captains* of 1946 as 'Louth's greatest footballer'. Louth and Kerry duly qualified to meet again in the all-Ireland final of 1910. But the game never took place.

At this time the management of the Great Southern and Western Railway was regarded as being hostile to the national games; and when Kerry were refused certain travelling facilities for their team, officials, and supporters, they refused to travel. At a subsequent meeting of the Central Council, Louth were awarded the title and duly accepted it. This caused much acrimony in County Kerry, where it was felt that titles should be won on the field of play; but Kerry's refusal to play was not of Louth's making. A serious split in the GAA appeared likely for a while; but time is a great healer, and the crisis was averted. The publicity also generated better travelling facilities for teams on long train journeys, though for Kerry the giving away of a great chance to win another title was a heavy price to pay.

Cork won the 1911 title, easily defeating Antrim; and in 1912 Louth (Tredaghs) defeated Antrim (Shauns) to win the title for the second time in three years. Kerry, after their 1909 'stand-down' (as it came to be called), lost to Waterford in 1911 and to Antrim in the semi-final of 1912, the latter loss especially being a great disappointment. So when Kerry and Louth qualified to meet in the final of the Croke Memorial Tournament in 1913 a great showdown was expected, regarded as settling the question of who deserved to win the final of 1910. A wave of enthusiasm swept the country, and both counties looked forward with fervour to the game, which was fixed for Jones's Road on 4 May 1913. The attendance of 25,000 (gate receipts £750) witnessed an epic game that ended in a draw, Louth 1-1 to Kerry's 0-4. Kerry's captain was Dick Fitzgerald, while Louth's was the centre-half-back Jim Smith. To add further excitement to the game, played in sunny conditions, this was the first major game with fifteen a side, and it certainly justified the rule change.

Gaelic football as a spectacle reached a new plane, and the clash of styles between the high-catching and long-kicking Kerrymen and the slick footwork and clever play of the Louthmen created great excitement. Phil O'Neill ('Sliabh Ruadh') in his History of the GAA wrote: 'Both teams were trained to the ounce and gave a display that established Gaelic football for all time amongst the plain people.' The Croke Memorial Fund had now swollen to £1,200.

The replay was fixed for Jones's Road for 29 June, another sweltering day of brilliant sunshine. There was even more interest after the drawn epic, and both teams undertook special training in the first collective training of teams, which helped to engender more local support and created the norm for many years afterwards. Kerry trained in Killarney and Tralee under Jerry Collins and Bill O'Connor, while Louth called on the expertise of George Blessington of Belfast Celtic (a former Scottish soccer player) and James Booth.

The game turned out to be another classic, and an estimated forty thousand paid a record gate of £1,183, the first time receipts for a GAA game exceeded £1,000. The score was level at half time: Kerry 1-0, Louth 0-3. Kerry pulled away in the thrilling second half to win by 2-4 to 0-5, with goals from Paddy Breen and Johnny Skinner. One brilliant sally upfield by the Louth captain, Jim Smith, is still talked about in County Louth; but the final whistle saw Kerry fans carry their heroes around Jones's Road in triumph. The Louth team also received deserved plaudits for their contribution to the two classic games. The game of Gaelic football has never looked back.

On 22 December 1913 the Jones's Road grounds became Croke Memorial Park, later to be known as Croke Park. There was some displeasure in County Tipperary and in Munster generally that the original intention, to erect a monument to Dr Croke in Thurles, was left to one side with the buying of the grounds; but eventually, on 17 May 1920, the foundation stone for the Croke memorial was laid in Liberty Square, Thurles, and on 4 June 1922 the impressive statue of Dr Croke was unveiled.

The 1914 Congress decided that all future all-Ireland finals be played in Croke Park, a decision that has been adhered to save for three occasions: the 1937 senior hurling final (the building of the Cusack Stand caused the game to be transferred to Killarney); the 1947 senior football final (played in the Polo Grounds, New York); and the senior hurling final of 1984, the GAA's centenary year (played in Thurles).

There were to be many changes in Croke Park after it was named in 1913. In 1924 the embankment now known as Hill 16 was built up from the rubble of O'Connell Street left after the destruction of 1916. The old Cusack Stand was built in 1937, and terracing at the canal end was carried out in 1949. The old Hogan Stand, demolished in 1999 and now under reconstruction, was opened on 7 June 1959, replacing the previous Hogan Stand, which had been opened in 1924 on the occasion of the first Tailteann Games—a week of hurling, football, camogie, and other competitions—and named in memory of Michael Hogan, the Tipperary footballer shot dead by British soldiers during the game between Tipperary and Dublin on 1 November 1920. The Nally Stand was completed in 1952, and the terracing underneath the old Cusack Stand was replaced with seating in 1966. The Headquarters Building behind the now-demolished Hogan Stand

and the impressive entrance to the grounds were completed in 1982. Hill 16 was rebuilt to provide better-quality terracing in 1989.

All these changes took place gradually over the years, whereas the changes now taking place in Croke Park, launched on 11 February 1992, are part of a massive four-phase redevelopment plan. The New Stand, which replaces the old Cusack Stand, a proud feature of the modern stadium, was officially opened on 5 June 1996 to mark the end of the first phase of the plan. At the time of writing, the second phase—the building of a similar stand at the canal end—is well under way. This will be followed by the building of a similar structure to replace the old Hogan Stand; and the final phase will be the redevelopment of the Hill 16 and Nally Stand end. When work is complete, three sides of the ground will consist of a continuous horseshoe-shaped stand, in three tiers. The bottom and top tiers will provide the main facilities for spectators, while the centre tier, in effect two mini-tiers, will provide facilities for 'corporate hospitality' and holders of season tickets, as can be seen in the New Stand today.

6

Wexford's Golden Era

I t is almost impossible to imagine now that there was a time when Wexford footballers dominated to the extent that they could win six Leinster titles in a row (1913–18) and four all-Ireland senior titles in a row (1915–18). Nowadays football is very much a poor relation to hurling in the county. Still, there has always been a keen interest in Gaelic football at the grass roots, no doubt a legacy of that golden period.

Wexford's first senior all-Ireland was won by the footballers when Selskar Young Irelands beat Dromtarriffe (Cork) in the Phoenix Park by 1-1 to 0-1 in an unfinished final played on 24 June 1893. Teams had been cut down from twenty-one a side to seventeen a year before. Clubs represented counties then, and the organisation of games was pretty haphazard. Still, there was a fine reception in Wexford for the county's first senior champions, and when they returned the team were carried shoulder high to attend a special Mass in Rowe Street. Later, four barrels of porter were consumed in the Temperance Hall, headquarters of the club. But the golden era had still to come.

It began innocently enough in 1913 with a fortuitous victory over Laois by 1-4 to 1-3 in the Leinster first round. Gus O'Kennedy seemed sure of a goal before being fouled in the closing stages, and it seemed Wexford's chance had gone; but the Wexford free-taker, having mis-kicked completely—his toe stuck in the sod and barely touched the ball—watched in astonishment as it rolled under the legs of the defenders and into the net. Success is often born on the bounce of a ball or a lucky stroke.

Now interest in Gaelic football, which had waned after Wexford's hurling success in the 1910 all-Ireland, grew in leaps and bounds, especially after the team went on to beat Dublin in Wexford Park by 2-3 to 1-0, both goals being scored by Aidan Doyle of Ballyhogue. The game was now played by teams of fifteen a side, and the county team was representative of all clubs in the county. Wexford had evolved a fine passing style and in Seán O'Kennedy, brother of Gus, had a leader of great quality.

Wexford now had to face Louth—regarded as Ireland's top team—in the Leinster final. This was the big test. Wexford seemed beaten when Louth led by 2-2 to 1-1 with seventeen minutes to go; but a point by Frank Furlong, another by Aidan Doyle and finally a goal by Jemmy Rossiter after a fierce shot by Seán O'Kennedy left it 2-3 to 2-2, and the first of six Leinster crowns in a row went to Wexford. Paddy Mackey was Wexford's star; Aidan Doyle played for most of the game with a broken jaw.

Wexford's displays were attracting both notice and fans, and the team now went on to defeat Antrim easily in the all-Ireland semi-final by 4-4 to 0-1. Football fever rose high in the Model County, and there was a huge response to an appeal for the training fund for the final against Kerry. Wexford's trainer was a famed boxer of that era, Jem Roche. Some injuries were incurred in training, but Father Ned Wheeler was back again at full-back for his first game since the first round, played under the false name 'E. Phelan'. A crowd of twenty thousand was present at the final on 13 December 1913, but hard as Wexford tried, they lost in the end by 2-2 to 0-3. Dick Fitzgerald, the Kerry captain, was loud in his praise of Wexford's new football team. All Wexford lacked was experience. The best was still to come.

Ultimate success was not achieved overnight. Kerry were beaten twice by Wexford in friendlies at New Ross and later in Tralee, humbling Kerry by 3-2 to 0-2 before their own supporters. The 1914 campaign was eagerly awaited. First Meath were beaten, 2-4 to 1-1, then Kilkenny at New Ross by 1-5 to 0-3; then Dublin by 4-6 to 1-1, and on to another Leinster final against Louth. They too were trounced, 3-6 to 0-1, as were their Ulster opponents, Monaghan, in the all-Ireland semi-final. Now another test faced Wexford with the all-Ireland champions, Kerry. Here disaster struck with an injury to Dick Hanrahan; and Father Ned Wheeler was unavailable.

The final was a thriller. Wexford led at half time by 2-0 to 0-1 after two goals by Seán O'Kennedy and seemed set to triumph. The second half was even more thrilling than the first. Kerry, now backed by the wind, bounced back and seemed certain to win, but Wexford held out and led by a point with seconds remaining. Kerry got a free out near the corner flag. Dick Fitzgerald took it; it struck the post and rebounded into play. Wexford conceded an easy free, and Kerry lived on to fight another day.

Dick Hanrahan was back for the replay but was quickly injured and was never to play again, a damaged knee ruining his chances of recovery. P. D. Breen, later to become president of the GAA, replaced him. Wexford led Kerry 0-6 to nil at half time; but you never have Kerry beaten, and they proceeded to dominate the second half and to win by 2-3 to 0-6.

Ultimate success was getting closer. Some newcomers had joined the team in place of the Doyles, Johnny and Tom, Tom Murphy and Dick Hanrahan, as Wexford set out after the 1915 title, defeating Kilkenny by 0-9 to 0-4 and Offaly by 1-7 to 0-2, with John Wall scoring the goal to qualify to meet Dublin in the Leinster final at Croke Park. A wonderful game watched by ten thousand people resulted in a draw: 2-2 each.

The former Wexford star Johnny Doyle, now working in Dublin and playing for his adopted county, had proved a stumbling-block in the drawn game. But in the replay on 11 October, John Crowley shadowed the former Wexford man, this time to good effect, and Wexford won, 2-2 to 1-3.

Excitement ran high in County Wexford after the third Leinster title in a row and was added to when Cavan were easily disposed of in the semi-final by 3-7 to 2-2. So for the third year in a row the stage was set for another all-Ireland tilt with Kerry. Would it be 'third time lucky'?

There were no injuries in the Wexford camp, and 'James Furlong' (another alias for Father Ned Wheeler) was available for the first time that year. Great was the build-up: the game was billed as the 'game of the century', and it lived up to this description, attracting a crowd of thirty thousand. Wexford led at the break by 1-2 to 1-0, thanks to a great goal by Gus O'Kennedy. It was level pegging, 1-3 to 2-0, with twelve minutes to go; then Wexford were awarded a thirty-yard free, and Seán O'Kennedy, the captain, called on Jim Byrne, the left-corner-back, to take it. Jim's strong shot flew into the Kerry net just under the cross-bar. Wexford fans went wild; hats and coats were flung into the air.

Four minutes later Wexford were awarded a fifty, which Jim Byrne also took. The ball sailed between the posts for a wonderful point; hats and coats went skywards again. Kerry fought back, but Wexford held on to win by 2-4 to 2-1. The historic date was 7 November 1915.

Wexford fans swarmed the pitch, and Seán O'Kennedy, Paddy Mackey and the hero, Jim Byrne, were carried shoulder high before O'Kennedy held aloft the Great Southern and Western Railway Silver Cup—the Railway Cup, donated by the same railway company that had been at the centre of the 1910 dispute. Wexford were now regarded as the stylists of Gaelic football.

Great was the welcome given the team on its return to County Wexford. The team was: Seán O'Kennedy (captain), Gus O'Kennedy, Paddy Mackey, Tom Mernagh, Aidan Doyle, Tom Murphy, Ned Black, Frank Furlong, 'James Furlong' (Father Ned Wheeler), Martin Howlett, Jim Byrne, Tom McGrath, Rick Reynolds, John Wall, and Tom Doyle.

The political upheaval of 1916 was reflected in sport too. Dublin failed to field a team against Wexford in the first round of the senior football championship at Wexford Park; but worse was to follow when Kerry withdrew from the championship because of a dispute with the Central Council over money. Wexford crushed Meath by 6-5 to 1-2 before winning their fourth successive Leinster crown, easily defeating Kildare on a rainy day by 1-7 to 1-0. Wexford sportingly travelled to Carrickmacross to play Monaghan in the all-Ireland semi-final, where they received a champions' welcome and a hard-fought game with the home side before Seán O'Kennedy inspired his team to win by 0-9 to 1-1.

Wexford were unbeatable now, and Mayo were their opponents in the final on 17 December before a small crowd of three thousand. The return of Father Ned Wheeler meant that Wexford had fourteen of the previous year's winning team, with Ned Black's place going to John Crowley. Croke Park was rock-hard with frost, but Wexford were undeterred and won easily by 3-4 to 1-2. Title number 2 had been annexed.

Wexford's dominance as a football power was severely tested in 1917. With only three minutes to go in the Leinster final against Dublin, the champions were being led by 1-1 to 0-3 and were resigned to defeat when that man again, Jim Byrne, sent in a free from midfield that was punched on by Seán O'Kennedy and gathered by Aidan Doyle, who turned and goaled to gain for Wexford their fifth successive Leinster crown. It was close. Earlier Wexford had beaten Wicklow 6-4 to 0-2 and Westmeath in Croke Park by 1-7 to 0-1, with Gus O'Kennedy scintillating. Kerry were still not competing. This time Monaghan, the Ulster champions, travelled to Wexford Park but lost heavily by 6-6 to 1-3, with Seán O'Kennedy and Dick Reynolds starring.

Clare, trained by Dick Fitzgerald, had come out of Munster and beaten Galway in the semi-final; in a rough enough final they fell to Wexford by 0-9 to 0-5. The three-in-a-row was now achieved—a feat previously accomplished only by Dublin (1897–9 and 1906–8). The great Seán O'Kennedy had captained all three winning teams. Would this team go on to become the first to win the all-Ireland final four times in a row?

In 1918 Wexford first beat Kilkenny, 2-6 to 0-1, at New Ross. Four weeks later came the clash everyone wanted to see, Wexford against Kerry, in a tournament game to raise funds for the Kerry County Board. A crowd of twelve thousand turned up at Croke Park to see a low-scoring game, with Wexford leading 0-1 to nil at half time. In the second half Wexford proved to be worthy champions, but the wonderful Gus O'Kennedy picked up a knee injury, the beginning of the end of a great career. The championship was delayed for three months before Wexford beat Carlow, and a further four months elapsed before Wexford won their sixth successive Leinster title, against Louth in Croke Park on 19 January 1919, by 2-5 to 1-4, with Aidan Doyle, Gus O'Kennedy and Dick Reynolds the stars. Wexford's march continued with a win over Tipperary in the all-Ireland final by 0-5 to 0-4.

These were troubled times. A virulent 'black flu' swept through Ireland, causing thousands of deaths, and Wexford did not have to play a semi-final. Tipperary had beaten Kerry and Mayo. A crowd of ten thousand turned up at Croke Park on 16 February to see the final. Wexford had to field without their leader, Seán O'Kennedy, who was undergoing surgery, and his brother, Gus, was virtually a passenger with his damaged knee. Father Ned Wheeler had retired, and both Tom Mernagh and Frank Furlong were injured. Tipperary led at half time by 0-3 to 0-2. Experience now stood to Wexford. The sides were level with ten minutes to go, and Jimmy Redmond sent over the winning point just before the end. The first four-in-a-row had been achieved.

Seven months later, on 31 August 1919, Wexford's reign ended when Dublin defeated them thoroughly by 0-11 to 1-1 in the Leinster final at Croke Park. Seán O'Kennedy was back after his operation for this defeat. The great run was over, and Wexford's most successful team, which had played in six successive all-Ireland finals, became a memory.

Kerry were to twice equal the four-in-a-row feat (1929–32 and 1978–81). Kildare equalled Wexford's six Leinster titles in a row in their golden period of 1926–31. Dublin repeated that feat, 1974–9.

It was a momentous time in County Wexford. Nine players appeared in all four all-Ireland triumphs: Jim Byrne, Gus O'Kennedy, Martin Howlett, Dick Reynolds, Aidan Doyle, Tom Doyle, Tom Murphy, Tom McGrath, and Paddy Mackey. Five players won three medals: Seán O'Kennedy, Frank Furlong, Tom Mernagh, John Crowley, and Father Ned Wheeler. Two men—John Wall of Bunclody and Willie Hodgins—won two all-Ireland medals, and five more won one each: Ned Black, N. Stewart, J. Doran, Jimmy Redmond, and Dr T. Pierse. Two men—Seán O'Kennedy and Paddy Mackey—also won all-Ireland senior hurling medals with Wexford in 1910.

Since that time Wexford won in Leinster senior football twice: 1925 and 1945. The year 1925 was an extraordinary one, while in 1945 Wexford easily defeated Offaly by 5-9 to 1-4 but subsequently fell to Cavan. Many great Wexford footballers, such as Jack Fane, Willie Goodison (a wonderful centre-half-back), Jackie Culleton, Des O'Neill, Nicky Rackard, and John Morris, played for Leinster but never won a Railway Cup medal, though men like Martin O'Neill and Nick Walsh did in the early days of that competition.

The great team of the golden era of Wexford football is still remembered with pride. I have often wondered why there is no memorial in bronze or stone to the wonderful leader of that band of heroes, the great Seán O'Kennedy.

7

Bloody Sunday, November 1920

As the year drew to a close, the War of Independence was at its height. The reign of terror by the Black and Tans, the infamous auxiliary force, was in full spate. Very few GAA games took place in those war-torn times; only a month before, Cork's noble son Terence MacSwiney died in a London jail after seventy-four days on hunger strike. How the GAA continued to run its competitions at all during those turbulent times is a mystery. Bloody Sunday, 21 November 1920, was the darkest day of all.

In a dawn swoop, Michael Collins's team had wiped out the Dublin ring of the British Secret Service, known as the Cairo Gang, knowing that they were on the point of doing the same to the Republican leadership. That Sunday morning, word of the shooting spread like wildfire. Everybody knew there would be reprisals, and fast.

The fury of the British forces on learning of the shootings was uncontainable. As they looked around for opportunities for reprisal, it was to Croke Park they turned. A football game between Tipperary and Dublin, two of the leading teams of the time, had been fixed for Croke Park in aid of the Republican Prisoners' Dependants' Fund. The general secretary of the GAA, Luke O'Toole, consulted two other senior officials, Jim Nowlan and Dan McCarthy, about the possible cancellation of the match, but all agreed that cancellation might be misinterpreted by the British authorities and that as a consequence Croke Park and the GAA could be prime targets for reprisals.

The Tipperary team travelled to Dublin by train on the Saturday and stayed in the well-known GAA establishment of then and later, Barry's Hotel. On the morning of the game they too heard of the shootings before they made their way to Croke Park in time for the match at 2:45 p.m.

A crowd of about eight thousand was in attendance for this eagerly awaited game. The Tipperary team played in the colours of the Grangemockler club. Dublin were captained by the great Paddy McDonnell of O'Tooles, whose brother Johnny, who used to wear a soft hat while playing, was in goal. Seven other members of O'Tooles were playing for Dublin.

These were the teams that marched out onto the field:

Tipperary

Frank Butler

Mick Hogan	Ned O'Shea (*captain*)	Jerry Shelley
Bill Ryan	Jim Egan	Tommy Powell

Tommy Ryan   Jim Ryan

Bill Barrett	Jimmy McNamara	Jimmy Doran
Gus McCarthy	Jack Kickham	Jackie Brett

Dublin

John McDonnell

Patrick Hynes	Patrick Carey	William Robbins
John Synnott	Christy Joyce	John Reilly

William Donovan   John Murphy

John Carey	Paddy McDonnell (*captain*)	Frank O'Brien
Joe Synnott	Stephen Synnott	Frank Burke

The game began with Tipperary to the fore, when suddenly a British military plane droned overhead, then emitted a red signal flare. Immediately groups of RIC and Black and Tans entered Croke Park at the canal end and began shooting into the crowd and at the players on the field. There was an immediate stampede of spectators and players away from the shooting and towards the railway end and Hill 16. Some fell to the ground and were trampled. When the shooting stopped, the body of the Tipperary corner-back Mick Hogan lay on the pitch. Twelve spectators were shot dead, among them a young Wexford man who had been tending to Michael Hogan, and three Dublin boys aged ten, eleven, and fourteen. Almost a hundred more were injured.

The following are the names of the thirteen people killed in Croke Park on Bloody Sunday:

Jane Boyle, Lennox Street, Dublin

James Burke, Dundrum, Dublin

Daniel Carroll, Templederry, County Tipperary

Michael Feeney, Gardiner Place, Dublin

Michael Hogan, Grangemockler, County Tipperary

James Matthews, North Cumberland Street, Dublin

J. O'Dowd, Buckingham Street, Dublin

Jeremiah O'Leary, Blessington Street, Dublin

William Robinson, Little Britain Street, Dublin

Thomas Ryan, Viking Road, Dublin

John Scott, Drumcondra, Dublin

James Teehan, Green Street, Dublin

J. Traynor, Clondalkin, County Dublin

That night the Tipperary team and officials were accommodated by the O'Tooles club, and on the Monday both teams visited Jervis Street Hospital to pay their respects to Michael Hogan. His body was brought home to County Tipperary on the Wednesday amid displays of unprecedented grief and national pride. A massive crowd followed the coffin from Clonmel to Hogan's native Grangemockler, where he was laid to rest next morning dressed in his football outfit, with all his team-mates at the graveside.

The Hogan Stand in Croke Park was a constant reminder of Michael Hogan and Bloody Sunday. It carried a plaque that listed both the teams and the names of all the people murdered on the day. The Hogan Cup for the all-Ireland senior football colleges championship is named in memory of Michael Hogan's brother, Brother Thomas Hogan, who was a great lover of the GAA when teaching in Westland Row Christian Brothers' School and who died in 1945 at the early age of forty-five.

GAA games were suspended for a time after Bloody Sunday, but eventually they got going again, and the 1920 all-Ireland fittingly saw Tipperary and Dublin qualify, with Tipperary winning the game on 11 June 1922 with the score 1-6 to 0-2. The ball on that occasion was thrown in by the great Dan Breen, renowned in song and story as Tipperary's foremost patriot. Dublin, powered again in part by the O'Tooles, went on to win the next three all-Ireland titles. That particular challenge game on 21 November 1920—a date never to be forgotten in Irish sporting history—was not just any game but one between the top two teams in Ireland at that time.

8

THE STRANGE YEAR OF 1925 AND GALWAY'S FIRST ALL-IRELAND

This was the strangest year of all. Despite all the troubles arising from the First World War, the Rising of 1916, the War of Independence, the Treaty, and the Civil War, the GAA's all-Ireland championships were never abandoned. They were run late at times, and were often carried over to the following year; but by 1925 the situation had almost returned to normal. Almost!

The unprecedented began in Connacht, the province yet to win an all-Ireland senior football crown, and it finished in that province too. The all-Ireland of 1924 had been decided on 26 April 1925, Kerry defeating Dublin by 0-4 to 0-3 in Croke Park. It was expected that the 1925 senior football championship would be finished within the year.

The drama began on 17 May, when Sligo and Roscommon lined out in Boyle for the first round of the championship. It was a closely contested game, and with time running out, R. Dalton (Roscommon) scored a goal to leave the score Roscommon 2-3, Sligo 2-2. Sligo objected and were granted a replay; this took place in Roscommon on 5 July and ended in a draw, 1-5 each. It was another game of swaying fortunes, and a late goal by Mick Noone of Sligo evened the scores.

Meantime, Galway and Leitrim began to provide their share of drama by finishing level in their senior football championship clash at Castlerea on 28 June, with the score 1-1 each. Leitrim on that occasion refused to play extra time. Just two weeks later in Sligo came the third meeting of Sligo and Roscommon and yet another draw: Roscommon 1-3, Sligo 0-6. This time 'Click' Brennan—still a legendary figure in Sligo football folklore—swung over the equaliser in this continuing saga.

Game number 4 took place at the same venue a week later, only to result in yet another draw: Roscommon 1-3, Sligo 2-0. It was a game of phases. Roscommon led 1-3 to nil at half time; two golden Sligo goals evened matters, and Sligo refused to play extra time.

Sunday 2 August was a gala day in Roscommon, with Galway facing Leitrim in their first replay, followed by game number 5 in the Sligo v. Roscommon marathon. The Galway v. Leitrim game ended in yet another draw: Galway 1-4, Leitrim 2-1; but later on Sligo eventually disposed of Roscommon by 2-5 to 0-5. But it wasn't over yet. Roscommon now felt aggrieved and objected to the result, and the Connacht Council granted another replay.

So to Roscommon again on 13 September came the most persistent rivals that Connacht, or indeed all Ireland, had ever known for game number 6 in the series; and for good measure Leitrim and Galway were there in their supporting role for round 3 in their own dramatic sequence. Galway and Leitrim settled with a score of 1-4 to 0-5 in favour of Galway, and it was 5:50 p.m. when the well-known referee Stephen Jordan of Athenry set Roscommon and Sligo on their way. In an even first half the score was an ominous 0-1 apiece, but Sligo went on to win by 2-3 to 0-2. The greatest marathon in GAA history was over.

At this stage Mayo, the Connacht senior football champions of 1924, had been nominated to represent the province in the all-Ireland series and had successfully beaten the Leinster champions, Wexford, in the all-Ireland semi-final at Croke Park on 23 August by 2-4 to 1-4, while on the same day Kerry controversially defeated Cavan in Tralee by a single disputed point, Kerry 1-7 to Cavan's 2-3. Cavan County Board lodged an objection because of the alleged illegality of the Kerry captain, Phil O'Sullivan. The Central Council upheld the objection and awarded the game to Cavan. Kerry then counter-objected to Cavan on the grounds that J. P. Murphy had been ineligible to play. The Central Council upheld this objection also, with the result that Kerry and Cavan were now both out of the championship. Mayo could now in effect lay claim to the all-Ireland title, even though they had not yet kicked a ball in the 1925 Connacht championship and had now qualified to meet Sligo in the Connacht semi-final, a game they duly won by 1-6 to 1-4. Thus they qualified to meet Galway in the Connacht final in Tuam on 18 October.

For a time after Mayo had defeated Wexford in the all-Ireland semi-final, and had survived an objection by Wexford (winning a Central Council decision by a single vote), they were widely acclaimed as all-Ireland champions. But in the Connacht final, with Stephen

Jordan of Athenry refereeing, Galway came from behind with a late goal by Michael 'Knacker' Walsh to beat Mayo, 1-5 to 1-3. The way Galway won that game in the dying moments was one of my late father's favourite stories; I can still see the twinkle in his eye as he recalled the feat of the great 'Knacker' Walsh.

Everything was now in turmoil. Even Connacht Council officials of the time felt that only the Connacht title was at stake; but the morning after the Connacht final the newspapers were asking, 'If Galway are champions of Connacht, then who are all-Ireland champions?'

The issue was not long in doubt. At the next meeting of the Central Council, Galway were declared all-Ireland champions; but because of the great loss in income as a result of there being only one all-Ireland semi-final and no final, it was decided to play a special tournament between the four provincial winners for another set of gold medals. Kerry refused to participate, and Galway went on to beat Wexford on 6 December by 3-4 to 1-1 and subsequently Cavan on 10 January 1926 by 3-2 to 1-2, both games being held in Croke Park.

On the eve of the Wexford game a long discussion arose in Dublin regarding the all-Ireland senior football championship, but the chairman of the Central Council, P. D. Breen, said that he had ruled that Galway were all-Ireland champions, and he stuck to his decision. Kerry's appeal for an all-Ireland congress to decide the issue was turned down. So ended what must be the most bizarre of all-Irelands. It is nevertheless an all-Ireland title cherished by Galway, despite all the draws, objections, and counter-objections.

And a further twist to the story reveals Galway very nearly pulling out of the Connacht final altogether because of a dispute with the Connacht Council over the date and a further request for £50 towards the training of the team. The date for the Connacht final coincided with that of the Ballinasloe Horse Fair in October; and as the Galway team was almost a Ballinasloe selection (as the club selected the team), the fair had a large bearing on the team's preparations. The Connacht Council refused a postponement, and it took three special meetings in Ballinasloe on the week of the game before the team decided to play. In fact on the eve of the game against Mayo, J. J. Nestor, Mick Donnellan (also of Dunmore) and Harry Burke (of Moylough), who, like Mick Donnellan, was selected to play for Galway, travelled to Ballinasloe to beg their comrades to play. It was not until 6:15 p.m., after a long meeting, that it was agreed to travel to Tuam, and only then on condition that Nestor would guarantee that the Connacht Council would agree to the £50 grant. The rest is history. (I am indebted to the late Father Paddy Bruen, parish priest of Aughrim, for research in the minutes of the Ballinasloe club on the details of the pre-match wrangling.)

At a subsequent meeting of the club in February 1926 it was decided that the following team members would receive Connacht and all-Ireland medals: Tom Molloy (captain), Michael 'Knacker' Walsh (vice-captain), Gilbey Jennings, Denis Egan, Thomas 'Trixy' Leeche, John Egan, William Smith, Paddy Roche, Paddy Ganley, Harry Burke, Mick Donnellan, Frank Benson, Laurence McGrath, Leonard · McGrath, and Mick Bannerton. This was the team that turned out in Tuam, together with Father Ned Hughes, Pat Jennings (former parish priest of Killererin), and Josie Walsh, who had played earlier in the games against Leitrim.

For many years afterwards, whenever I visited the Donnellan home, Mick—father of John and Pat and grandfather of Michael, one of Galway's heroes in 1998—showed me his collection of medals and took great pride in showing the 1925 all-Ireland medal and the special gold medal for the subsequent tournament. It has always intrigued me how Mayo agreed to the Athenry man Stephen Jordan as referee; but the late Brendan Nestor, the former Galway star, assured me that Stephen was a highly regarded official selected by the Connacht Council of that time and that even though there may have been rumblings afterwards, it was highly significant that Stephen continued to referee games involving Mayo, and in particular the 1930 Connacht final in Parkmore, Tuam, when Mayo beat Sligo by 1-7 to 1-2.

Galway then played in blue and gold; it was not until 1934 that the maroon-and-white jerseys with the well-known Galway badge were introduced.

Many of the 1925 heroes are part of County Galway folklore, men like Tom Molloy of Corrofin, later a trainer of renown; Leonard McGrath, a dual all-Ireland star; Mick Donnellan, later a noted man of politics; Michael 'Knacker' Walsh, the great character of the wonderful Ballinasloe team of that era; and the Egan brothers from Ballinasloe. These were the men who won Galway's first football all-Ireland, and I suppose they were the ones who really started the wonderful Galway v. Mayo rivalry that reached its intensity in the thirties and lasts to this day.

9

KERRY'S GOLDEN ERA AND FIRST FOUR-IN-A-ROW, 1929–32

After winning the 1903 and 1904 all-Irelands, Kerry remained a dominant force in Gaelic football through every decade, right up to the present time, generating different rivalries along the way. After the two initial triumphs, further all-Ireland success followed in 1909 against Louth—the start of a great rivalry between the counties; and there followed another two-in-a-row in 1913 and 1914, when Wexford provided the opposition. These were the years when Dick Fitzgerald was in his prime as captain. In 1914 he wrote the first book on the game, *How to Play Gaelic Football.* In truth, he was a man apart.

Then came what is known in County Kerry as the golden age of Kerry football: 1923–33. During these years Kerry won six senior, three junior and three minor all-Irelands, four National Leagues, and the Railway Cup twice with all-Kerry teams, as well as participating in three American tours. The highlight of it all was Kerry's first four-in-a-row, 1929–32. A never-to-be-forgotten era had dawned in County Kerry; yet before the dawn it seemed very inauspicious, and hopes of a return of Kerry's greatness looked gloomy.

These were the turbulent years in the wake of 1916, the years of insurrection and Civil War, which in some cases put brother against brother and in County Kerry former team-mates on opposite sides. In fact Gaelic football was the medium in Kerry that healed former feuds, and the all-Ireland triumphs of the golden age are a testament to this. One of the stars of that period, the great full-back Joe Barrett, was one of those involved in that great healing process, and the story of that time is brilliantly recorded in the book by his son J. J. Barrett, *In the Name of the Game,* published in 1997.

Imagine the scene. In the summer of 1923 the thud of a football was not to be heard in County Kerry. Many of the county's young footballers were either interned or on the run. Yet a mixum-gatherum team was fielded to beat Limerick and then Cork in the Munster final. In the latter game only twelve turned out, with three followers coaxed from the sideline to don the green and gold. Yet Tipperary, who had won the 1920 title—played in 1922—were overcome. Shortly after this came a general amnesty and the release of internees. Those who had whiled their time in captivity playing football brought a quick resurgence in the game. The former internees challenged the Munster champions; they drew in the first game, and in the replay the challengers won by a whopping twelve points.

In April 1924 a mixture of former internees and the Munster championship team met and defeated Cavan in the 1923 semi-final, Kerry just edging it by 1-3 to 1-2. Cavan was now becoming a force in football; but the really strong exponents of the game at this time were the Dublin O'Tooles selection, which had won the two previous all-Irelands, men like the McDonnells, Paddy and John, Joe Stynes, Larry Stanley and Frank Burke, the Synnotts, Joe and John—a team that had perfected the passing game.

As some GAA members were still in prison, including the president of the Kerry County Board, Austin Stack, the team decided to 'stand down' and not travel to play in the final. Eventually the game was fixed for 28 September 1924, but the O'Tooles selection proved superior in the end on a two-point margin.

For the 1924 championship the same teams met again in the final, played on 26 April 1925, Kerry having defeated Mayo in the semi-final and Dublin being victorious over Cavan. Paul Russell made a wonderful debut, and Kerry won by 0-4 to 0-3. The great era of Con Brosnan, Bob Stack, John Joe Sheehy, Joe Barrett and Paul Russell had begun. 1925 was a bizarre year, as we have seen; but Kerry, captained by John Joe Sheehy, were back for another title in 1926, for the first of many great battles with the Lily-Whites of Kildare. Sigerson Clifford, that wonderful poet from south Kerry, captures the mood of the times:

> These the men your fathers spoke of
> > in the games your fathers loved,
> These the men who blazed the trail and made it fair,
> In my dreaming now I see them as I saw them long ago,
> Green and Gold, and white limbs leaping
> > when our Kerry played Kildare.

The old days of 1903 were recalled and those hectic battles in Tipperary and Cork. Thirty-four special trains helped to swell the attendance to 37,500. The Lily-Whites used sweeping passing movements up the field; the score at half time was Kildare 0-2 to 0-1 for Kerry. Larry Stanley's catching at midfield for Kildare was impeccable. Jack Higgins shone at centre-half-back, while Paul Doyle was Kildare's danger man up front. But Kerry, who had introduced Johnny Riordan in goal as well as Joe Sullivan and Bill Gorman, were inspired by the greatness of Johnny Murphy. Still Kildare led by 0-6 to 0-3; but with three minutes to go, Bill Gorman got the equalising goal from a Con Brosnan centre. The game ended in a draw, 1-3 for Kerry to 0-6 for Kildare.

Fifty trains travelled for the replay on 17 October. Another great game on a beautiful day saw Kerry win, 1-4 to 0-4. J. M. Collins (Dublin) trained Kerry for the drawn game, but Dr Éamonn O'Sullivan of Killarney took over for the replay. Kerry won the replay without the services of the star of the drawn game, Johnny Murphy, who had taken ill. He died a few days after the replay, at the tender age of twenty-two. His funeral in Cahersiveen was one of the largest ever seen there.

Then followed success with an all-Kerry team in the first Railway Cup competition of 1927, and Kerry's first trip to America in May of that year. Kerry got a hammering from New York in the Polo Grounds before thirty thousand, the score 3-11 to 1-7. They were not invincible after all.

The Kerry team that defeated Kildare in the replay was:

Johnny Riordan

| Pat Clifford | Joe Barrett | Jack Walsh |
| Paul Russell | Jerry Moriarty | John Slattery |

Con Brosnan   Bob Stack

| Jackie Ryan | J. J. Sheehy (*captain*) | Denis O'Connell |
| Tom O'Mahony | Bill Gorman | Jim Baily |

Kerry's prolonged American tour didn't help them in 1927. Against Leitrim in Parkmore, Tuam, they were hard put to win by 0-4 to 0-2, and in the final, on 24 September 1927, Kildare beat Kerry in Croke Park before 36,000 people by 0-5 to 0-3. Special training grants had been denied to the finalists since the previous Congress, and Kerry felt this militated against their more widely scattered team. But giving excuses for defeats has always been part of GAA lore.

1928 was another year of mixed fortunes for Kerry. They won

their first national football league final on 28 April at Croke Park, defeating their great rivals and all-Ireland champions, Kildare, by 2-4 to 1-6 in yet another exciting contest. One quotation from the *Leinster Leader's* report of the game tells it all: 'In the keen sporting rivalry between these two counties lies the best guarantee for the future of Gaelic football.' Later, when Kerry were expected to go all the way, they came a cropper in Tipperary to the home team, who won in the end by 1-7 to 2-3 in one of the most sensational results of all time. Kildare went on to win a second successive title and the Sam Maguire Cup in its initial year, defeating Cavan in the final by 2-6 to 2-5.

1929 was the start of Kerry's four-in-a-row, with Kildare still the team to beat. In the same year, Pádraig Ó Caoimh, the young Cork county secretary, was elected general secretary of the GAA in succession to Luke O'Toole, a man who, like his predecessor, was to serve his association nobly.

Kerry were leaving nothing to chance. After coming out of Munster, Mayo were beaten easily enough in Roscommon by 3-8 to 1-1, while Kildare easily beat Monaghan in the other semi-final. Excitement was sky-high, with the prospect of another epic game and a record attendance of 44,000. Earlier in the year Kildare had travelled to Tralee to play Kerry in aid of the Rock Street football team, but on the eve of the game the great Austin Stack died, and the game was called off. The Rock Street team were to become known later as Austin Stacks.

Into the Kerry team had come three newcomers in Tim O'Donnell, Ned 'Pedlar' Sweeney, and Miko Doyle, and all three helped in no small way to fashion a half-time lead of 1-5 to 0-2 for Kerry, with the elements favouring them in the second half. But back came Kildare, spearheaded by the master forward Paul Doyle, and tension rose as Kerry led by 1-6 to 1-5 with ten minutes to go. But, as often happened since with Kerry teams, they rose to it when needed most. First J. J. Landers pointed, and then John Joe Sheehy sealed victory with a final point to leave it 1-8 to 1-5 at the end. There is a fine photograph of a famous trio taken before that game: Joe Barrett, Kerry's captain, on the left; Dr Cullen, Bishop of Kildare and Leighlin, who threw in the ball; and Jack Higgins, the Kildare captain, on the right. Two GAA fields now bear the name of two of those photographed: Dr Cullen Park in Carlow, and Jack Higgins Memorial Park in Naas.

In 1930 Kerry reached the final again with victories over Tipperary and Mayo (in Roscommon), the latter game being more closely contested than the previous year's at the same venue.

Monaghan surprised Kildare in the other semi-final. Both Kerry and Monaghan did special training for this unique final; but on the Friday morning before the event County Kerry was devastated by the death of the legendary Dick Fitzgerald in his native Killarney. It took all Pádraig Ó Caoimh's diplomatic and persuasive powers to get Kerry to travel at all while Dick Fitzgerald's body lay in repose in Killarney. Travel they did, reluctantly, once they knew that Dick's memory would be suitably acknowledged. And so it was, first by a commemorative Mass in the Jesuit Church in Gardiner Street, Dublin, with thousands kneeling on the street outside, then before the game when the Artane Boys' Band played the haunting Funeral March by Chopin.

As to the game itself, Kerry seemed buoyed up by the ghost of Dick Fitzgerald and won easily by 3-11 to 0-2. John Joe Sheehy, when presented with the Sam Maguire Cup, spoke first of Dick Fitzgerald's great contribution to the game in County Kerry. There was no big welcome home for the team and the cup: instead all Kerry converged on Killarney for the burial of one of its greatest sons. Years afterwards, when Pádraig Ó Foghlú, doyen of County Kerry writers, was asked which was Kerry's greatest team, he included the 1930 one with his best. It was:

Johnny Riordan

Des O'Connor   Joe Barrett   Jack Walsh

Paul Russell   Joe O'Sullivan   Tim O'Donnell

Con Brosnan   Bob Stack

Jackie Ryan   J. J. Sheehy (*captain*)   Éamonn Fitzgerald

Ed Sweeney   Miko Doyle   J. J. Landers

A well-known writer of that time, Phil O'Neill ('Sliabh Ruadh'), wrote these lines of tribute to the great man from Killarney:

> Through the mist of years his name will gleam,
> When he blazed the trail with his Kerry team,
> And brought to the 'Kingdom' name and fame
> In the greatest tests of the Gaelic game;
> Kildare and Wexford and Louth can tell
> Of his deeds, and now his requiem swell,
> And tribute pay to a gallant foe,
> Who played the game as we Gaels know.

Kerry continued on their winning ways, adding the national

football league title to their laurels with wins over Kildare (semi-final) and Cavan (final), the latter by 1-3 to 1-2. Cavan football was coming close to the top. Then followed another highly successful American tour under John Joe Sheehy's captaincy, with Kerry dominating New York in a four-game series before huge crowds at Yankee Stadium (three times) and Comiskey Park, Chicago. Crowds of between 45,000 and 60,000 attended all four. Kerry were feted as world champions and received wonderful welcomes on their return in Killarney and Tralee. John Joe Sheehy retired; and even though some of the team remained on in America, such as Ned Sweeney and J. J. Landers, Kerry easily defeated Tipperary in the Munster final by 5-8 to 0-2. It was much closer in the semi-final in Parkmore, Tuam, when Mayo, like Cavan, showed that they were catching up but lost after a brave battle by 1-6 to 1-4.

A great character from Tuam, Christy Mannion, famous in Connacht for selling favours, rosettes and dolls over the years, told me that his first day out selling was for that semi-final. 'I'll never forget the crowds. I was only a gasúr, and even then Mayo had a wonderful following.' On the same day that Kerry got the close call at Tuam, Kildare just edged out the rising force of Cavan by 0-10 to 1-5. Another Kildare v. Kerry final whetted the appetites of all, and an attendance of 42,000, ferried by seventy-five special trains, thronged Croke Park. It was Kildare on top for the first half, and the score stood at 0-7 ten minutes into the second; but the turning-point came when a long centre from Paul Russell finished up in the Kildare net, and Kerry went on to win by 1-11 to 0-8. The three-in-a-row had been achieved.

Paul Russell had proved too good for the great Paul Doyle, who in the period leading up to the final had scored at will. It was the end of a wonderful rivalry, which didn't really surface again until 1998. Kerry were captained by Con Brosnan, an honour conferred on the great Moyvane man by Joe Barrett though they fought on opposite sides in the Civil War. This wonderful gesture to a friend required massive courage but was one of the great cementing links provided by friendship and football following the wounds of the Civil War.

> Hats off to Brosnan, that midfield wonder;
> He's *par excellence* with feet and hands.
> Where is the Gael can bring down the number
> Of Kerry's idol from Newtownsandes!

Could Kerry now equal Wexford's great four-in-a-row

achievement of 1915–18? A new-looking Kerry team easily defeated Tipperary by 3-10 to 1-4 in the Munster final but almost came a cropper against Dublin in the semi-final on a dreadfully wet day and, after a scoreless first half, just held on to win by 1-3 to 1-2. Again it was a lucky enough goal from Paul Russell that turned the tide. The *Irish Independent* described it as 'one of the greatest displays of Gaelic football ever witnessed.' Mayo qualified for the final by beating Cavan 2-4 to 0-8. Kerry were odds-on favourites for the final.

There was a relatively poor attendance, less than 26,000. Johnny Walsh of Ballylongford was brought on at midfield to partner Bob Stack, with Con Brosnan in the attack. Mayo took over at the start and led by three points to nil; but in the eleventh minute Miko Doyle levelled matters with a piledriver goal. Mayo fought back, and a punched goal by Gerald Courell saw Mayo lead at half time, 1-4 to 1-1. A surprise now seemed on the cards; but just after half time Tim Landers, with a goal, levelled again. Kerry took over and won in the end, 2-8 to 2-4, despite a rousing finish by Mayo in the final five minutes. Joe Barrett was back as captain, winning his sixth all-Ireland medal in the company of Con Brosnan, Bob Stack, Jack Walsh, Paul Russell, and Jackie Ryan.

This was the Kerry team for the 1932 all-Ireland final:

Danno Keeffe

Dee O'Connor   Joe Barrett (*captain*)   Jack Walsh

Paul Russell   Joe O'Sullivan   Paddy Whitty

Johnny Walsh   Bob Stack

Miko Doyle   J. J. Landers   Tim Landers

Con Geaney   Jackie Ryan   Con Brosnan

Substitute: Bill Landers for Con Geaney

The Wexford achievement had been matched; but despite winning a fourth successive national football league title and yet another Munster title, after yet another extensive American trip, Kerry fell to Cavan on 27 August 1933 in Cavan's own Breffni Park by 1-5 to 0-5. The huge attendance of seventeen thousand was a record for an Ulster venue. The dawn of a power in Ulster saw the demise of the first great Kerry era.

> I am Kerry like my mother before me
> And my mother's mother and her man;

Now I sit on my office stool remembering
And the memory of them like a fan
Soothes the embers with flame,
I am Kerry and proud of my name.
(Sigerson Clifford)

10

THE HALCYON ERA OF THE LILY-WHITES OF KILDARE

There's something romantic about the name 'Lily-Whites': it conjures up visions of sporting men from storied all-Ireland finals of the past—loose-limbed athletic heroes who perfected the art of fielding and set a standard in superb hand-passing and combined play.

The sporting public have a great affection for Kildare football, somewhat akin to their extraordinary love of Wexford hurling. It's a legacy richly earned. Huge crowds have always followed Kildare footballers, beginning with those epic games with Kerry in 1903. That all-Ireland saga marked the real establishment of Gaelic football as a leading spectator sport.

Where did the lily-white jersey story begin? The Kildare county secretary, Richie Whelan, told me that flour-bags provided the material for the early Clane football jerseys! In the famous 1903 final series, Kildare, as was the custom, wore the colours of the champion club; and the display of the Kildare team captured the public imagination to such an extent that it was decided to stick with the white in inter-county contests. It was a wise choice.

Kildare had to wait until 1919 to win their second all-Ireland senior football crown, a club era in Kildare dominated by Caragh, with only two members of the 1905 team, Larry Cribben and Frank Conlan, spanning the years. The team was led by the incomparable Larry Stanley, a champion high-jumper of international renown, described by Carbery in his *Famous Captains* as 'estimated by many as the most brilliant Gaelic Footballer the game has known.'

Kildare's 1919 race to glory began with wins over Laois, 3-5 to 2-5, and Westmeath, 4-3 to 1-5 (Jim O'Connor scoring all four goals), and then a much talked-of encounter with Dublin, conquerors of the mighty Wexford men, in the Leinster final. Paddy McDonnell was Dublin's star. Would Larry Stanley prove his master at midfield? This the Kildare hero did emphatically, making the one-handed catch his speciality as he soared to majestic heights in a wonderful display. Kildare triumphed by 1-3 to 1-2 in Croke Park. A week later Cavan fell by 3-2 to 1-2 in Navan; then two weeks later Galway, who had shocked Kerry in a replayed semi-final, had no answer to Kildare's combined power and skill, losing by 2-5 to 0-1. Larry Stanley was again inspired, and at left-half-back the newcomer Paul Doyle was outstanding. The winning team was:

Larry Cribben

Jim Conlan   James Moran   Tom Goulding

Mick Buckley   Joe Connor   Paul Doyle

Mick Sammon   Larry Stanley (*captain*)

Chris Flynn   Father Jim Stanley   George Magan

Jim O'Connor   Frank Conlan   Bernie McGlade

The great period of Kildare football dominance began in 1926 with six Leinster title successes in a row, including five appearances in the all-Ireland final and successive all-Ireland titles in 1927 and 1928, with Bill 'Squires' Gannon being the first to raise the Sam Maguire Cup aloft in 1928. This equalled Wexford's achievement of six Leinster crowns in the previous decade and was not to be matched until Kevin Heffernan's famous Dubs of the seventies won a similar string of six Leinster championships, 1974–9. Six Leinster crowns in a row in any decade is quite an achievement; and Kerry were now to be among Kildare's greatest rivals also.

Naas had taken over the Kildare club spotlight from Caragh, winning no less than five titles in the period 1920–28. Larry Stanley was still to the good, but he was joined now by Jack Higgins of Naas at centre-half-back, a player described by Carbery as 'the greatest centre half-back I've seen play in fifty finals.' Paul Doyle was now at left-half-forward and Matt Goff at full-back, with Mick Buckley, uncle of the current star Niall, in the right corner of defence.

Larry Stanley was an experienced 28-year-old, and his expertise helped Kildare enormously in their win over Louth (6-7 to 1-5) and in the replay against Dublin (2-5 to 1-2, after drawing 0-6 to 1-3 the first day), then a Leinster final win over Wexford (2-8 to 1-5). As in 1919, Galway succumbed easily enough in the semi-final (having won out in 1925) by 2-5 to 0-1.

THE HALCYON ERA OF THE LILY-WHITES OF KILDARE 43

Now it was a re-creation of the 1903 final pairing against Kerry, and another epic that saw thirty special trains bringing 38,000 people to a crammed Croke Park. The first game ended in a thrilling draw, 0-6 for Kildare to 1-3 for Kerry, with Bill Gorman catching Con Brosnan's cross, side-stepping Goff and shooting the equaliser three minutes from time after a hectic Kerry rally. Kerry, as almost always, won the replay, 1-5 to 0-4, with a much-improved display of fielding.

The great promise of 1926 was to be fulfilled in 1927. Larry Stanley decided to concentrate on athletics, thereby missing Kildare's two all-Ireland wins of 1927 and 1928. Paddy Loughlin was in at full-forward, with his brother Joe at midfield. Kildare first beat Kilkenny 1-4 to 0-2, then Meath 1-6 to 1-2. Next followed victory over Dublin in the Leinster final, 0-5 to 0-2, then a good win over Monaghan, 1-7 to 0-2, and at last an all-Ireland win over Kerry, 0-5 to 0-3. Kerry led by 0-3 to 0-1 at half time, but there was no stopping Kildare in the second half as Mick Buckley led the Lily-Whites to their third all-Ireland victory before a crowd of 37,000. Kildare, who faced wind and sun in the second half, were too fit for Kerry, who blamed a three-month American tour for this reverse.

This was Kildare's winning team in 1927, remarkable in that the same team won in 1928 (except that 'Darkie' Ryan came on as a substitute in 1928):

Martin Walshe

Mick Buckley (*captain*)   Matt Goff   Gus Fitzpatrick
Frank Malone   Jack Higgins   Jack Hayes

Bill 'Squires' Gannon   Joe Loughlin

Joe Curtis   Paddy Martin   Paul Doyle
Bill Mangan   Paddy Loughlin   Tom Keogh

Kildare became the first county to win two in a row with the same team, until Dublin performed a like feat in 1976 and 1977. Gus Fitzpatrick was the star of the day.

In 1928 Kerry lost out to Tipperary, and Cork came through in Munster. The news that Larry Stanley, George Magan and Joe Lynam were not declaring for their native Kildare was not the ideal start for retaining the crown. A hard win over Laois (0-4 to 1-0) was followed by an easy win over Longford, 3-6 to 0-2; and in the Leinster final Kildare beat Dublin in a very heated encounter, 0-10 to 1-6. Kildare led 0-9 to nil at the start of the second half, and a point by Joe Curtis with ten minutes to go saved the champions.

In the semi-final, Kildare easily beat Cork by 3-7 to 0-2, with two goals from Bill Mangan and one from Paddy Martin. Before an attendance of 25,000, Cavan were overcome in the final by 2-6 to 2-5 in a close game, in which the full-forward Paddy Loughlin was accused by Cavan of throwing the ball into the net for a vital goal. But these are the incidents from finals still talked about years later.

Kildare's star now tended to wane with the coming of Kerry's all-powerful four-in-a-row team and the retirement of the great Joe McDonald as trainer after the 1928 all-Ireland final win, largely because his great work was unappreciated at official level. Kildare kept on winning in Leinster, losing out to Kerry in the 1929 final by 1-5 to 0-5 before a record crowd of 44,000. Paul Doyle was now playing the best football of his long career, his scoring feats being talked about throughout the country. Larry Stanley was back again in the lily-white jersey in 1930; but Monaghan halted their gallop surprisingly in the semi-final with a score of 1-6 to 1-4.

1931 was to become known as the year of Paul Doyle. Meath were now Kildare's big opponents in Leinster, and for the third year in a row they brought Kildare to a replay. This time Kildare won again after trailing 0-5 to 0-1 at half time. Paul Doyle, who missed the drawn game, starred in the replay success of 1-5 to 0-5, scoring 1-3. He scored 1-5 in the Leinster final win over Westmeath, and 0-3 in the semi-final win over Cavan. But Kerry once again proved Kildare's masters in the final, winning by 1-11 to 0-8, Kerry's only goal coming near the end.

This was the end of the wonderful rivalry with Kerry, to be resurrected once again in 1998.

In 1932 Kildare were defeated by Wexford, for whom Martin O'Neill, later a senior Leinster official, was still starring. Dublin then took over in Leinster; but the Lily-Whites won out in Leinster again in 1935 and reached the all-Ireland final after defeating Mayo in Croke Park by 2-6 to 0-7. Jack Higgins was still to the good, but Cavan won the final by 3-6 to 2-5, thereby avenging the 1928 loss to Kildare.

This was the end of a glorious era. After this came the famine years, with a lone Leinster title in 1956, before Mick O'Dwyer came up from Kerry in the nineties and gave a new beginning to Kildare football. But those men of the twenties created a wonderful tradition and are spoken of with awe to this day. Kildare in 1998 came close to re-creating the old magic; but that's another story.

11

THE BIRTH OF THE SOLO RUN

There are very few skills that are absolutely peculiar to Gaelic football. Fielding or fetching or catching the ball is an essential one and one of the game's most thrilling facets, but it is shared with many other ball sports; the same applies to kicking and passing. Our own legitimate skill of picking the ball is peculiar to us, but placing the boot under the ball and chipping it off the ground to the hand when at full speed is a dying art. The only real Gaelic football skill that is absolutely peculiar to the game is the solo run or toe-to-hand.

Some players overuse the solo run, and it is so popular now that some recent committees charged with the task of suggesting changes to the rules have sought to modify its use.

The evolving game of Gaelic football was not prepared when a young County Mayo footballer-cum-athlete named Seán Lavan, in a game against Dublin in Croke Park, set off for goal at speed, playing the ball from toe to hand and then shooting a point, which was disallowed by the referee. The year was 1921, and Gaelic football had seen its first solo run.

Séamus O'Malley, later to captain Mayo in its first all-Ireland success in 1936, was a student in St Patrick's College, Drumcondra, training to be a national teacher, and he was present in Croke Park on that historic occasion.

> I first saw Seán Lavan play for Mayo v. Dublin in Croke Park and clearly remember him getting the ball around midfield and soloing to within twenty yards of the Dublin goal, and scoring a point. It was the first solo run I ever saw, and to the best of my knowledge the first exhibition of the skill in a Gaelic football game. As time went on it came to be accepted and used by players across the land. Take Kildare for instance, then at the

height of their football powers: I never saw Larry Stanley use the gambit, but one of their star forwards, Joe Curtis, mastered it and used it gainfully.

Who was Seán Lavan, the man widely acknowledged now as the inventor of the solo run? He was born in Kiltimagh in 1898 and trained as a national teacher in De La Salle College, Waterford, where he played for the De La Salle Emmets in 1917–18 (when one of his team-mates was Rody Nealon, father of Donie Nealon, secretary of the Munster Council). Seán Lavan was a top-class footballer for Kiltimagh and Mayo in the years 1918–24, then concentrated on athletics, becoming one of Ireland's top sprinters; he won no fewer than fifteen Irish titles in the years 1923–8 and represented Ireland in the Olympic Games of 1924 and 1928, captaining the Irish team in Amsterdam in 1928. After teaching for some years near Swinford, where he also attained fame as a handballer, Seán left teaching and entered UCD in 1922 to study medicine. While at university, as well as becoming one of Ireland's best-known athletes he also played Gaelic football in the Sigerson Cup in 1923 (on a team captained by Séamus Gardiner, later to be president of the GAA, and including the legendary Kerry trainer and coach Éamonn O'Sullivan). Seán won a Sigerson Cup medal in 1928–9, when he had as team-mates the famous Kerry stars Frank Sheehy, Joe Sullivan, and Éamonn Fitzgerald (another Olympic athlete). After qualifying as a doctor in 1927, Seán went on to study surgery and made a name for himself as a surgeon in later life. He came back to Gaelic football too and played for Dublin before returning to his native County Mayo as well as visiting the United States on Mayo's first touring side of 1932.

The late John D. Hickey, the well-known GAA correspondent of the *Irish Independent* in the era 1950–80, when writing on Mayo's football exploits told of his first visit to Dublin to visit an older brother in the early twenties and of going to Croke Park on the Sunday 'to see the great sprinter Seán Lavan playing football.'

> It was a club game and UCD were one of the sides in action. At that time Seán Lavan was one of my sports idols. I was as fascinated by his exhibition as his fluency with which he executed the completely new tactic of the solo run. The protestations to the referee of the game that a 'culchie from Mayo is making his own rules' convinced me that day may well have been the first occasion that the great Mayo athlete revolutionised

Gaelic football. At the end of the game I scampered on to the pitch and touched Seán Lavan's jersey.

People may disagree about the occasion on which Seán introduced the solo run; but there is no disputing that Seán Lavan introduced what is now so much part and parcel of the game.

Seán died in 1973, and Kiltimagh honoured the man by erecting a plaque in 1996 to commemorate him in his native place.

The legacy of the solo run bequeathed by Seán Lavan gave the game its most distinctive skill. Since the twenties the solo run has been perfected, and one of its greatest exponents today is Michael Donnellan of Galway, whose searing runs in the all-Ireland final of 1998 captured the imagination of all. Every youngster, as far back as I remember, loves to master the solo run, and I remember getting a tremendous kick out of mastering it myself. As a forward it is a wonderful thrill to set off for goal and to round off the movement with a score.

One of Michael Donnellan's greatest accomplishments is his ability to accelerate away from pursuers while on a solo. John Egan of Kerry was a wonderful exponent too: the way he could shield the ball while getting past defenders was his great forte. Pat Spillane and Mikey Sheehy, Tony McTague and Matt Connor of Offaly, Bernard Flynn of Meath, Michael Finneran of Roscommon and Gerry O'Reilly, the Wicklow half-back, used the solo run to great effect. Like John Egan of Kerry, Peter Solon of Mayo was very strong on the ball and very hard to stop.

Iggy Jones of Tyrone was another toe-to-hand wizard, and a run he made in the 1956 semi-final against Galway is often remembered. Packy McGarty of Leitrim, Mickey Kearins of Sligo, Martin McHugh of Donegal, Kevin Beahan of Louth, Frankie Byrne of Meath and my own team-mate Frankie Stockwell could all solo with style. In the Gael-Linn film *Peil*, Frank Stockwell demonstrated the skill superbly.

In all my years watching football games, two solo runs stand out now as I write these reminiscences. One was a wonder goal in the 1970 all-Ireland final scored by Din Joe Crowley of Kerry after a wonderful solo run. The other was on that dreadfully wet day of the 1993 Ulster final in Clones, when Anthony Tohill of Derry soloed through from midfield with power and determination—a solo run captured for posterity in the *Irish Independent* the following day and one that helped Derry on the road to its first all-Ireland. I can't remember whether it even led to a score, but victory and determination were etched on his face. You could see the rain coming down in buckets, but nothing was going to stop him. Din Joe Crowley and Anthony Tohill were not by any means the greatest stylists of the skill, but champions in their own right—the stuff of dreams.

12

SAM MAGUIRE

Proud to have hailed you friend
Long years ago!
Amid the fogs and fumes of London town
An empire's mart—
Astride the sluggish Thames
Building on plundered clans
Her dead renown!

Far from your heath-clad hills
And sheltered vales,
Where star-lit whispering rivers softly croon
To your brave heart—
The exile's song of songs.
Bringing you morns in May
And nights in June!

Strong in your deathless faith
Oh heart of gold!
Your kindly, generous smile
Gave strength to all
Who grasped your hand
In that great brotherhood:
Waiting throughout the years for Éire's call.

Sleeping in Irish earth,
Your exile o'er,
While she you loved enshrines
Within her soul
Her faithful dead:
Her dearest, bravest best—
Who wrought 'neath alien skies.

(Peadar Kearney)

On the fourth Sunday of September, football fans from all over Ireland and many from abroad converge on Dublin for the all-Ireland football final, the greatest annual sporting event in the country. For many it is an event not to be missed. The majority come from the counties involved, keen to cheer on their county in an almost tribal way to win the all-Ireland championship and to gain possession of the Sam Maguire Cup.

The atmosphere at the game is electrifying; the greensward of Croke Park looks its best, and the stands and Hill 16 are alive with colour. When the referee sounds the final whistle, supporters of the winning county give vent to their feelings as the winning captain raises the Sam Maguire Cup aloft. But how many people in Croke Park, or among the millions watching the game on television or on the internet, know anything about Sam Maguire, the man whose name is perpetuated by the cup?

About four miles north of Dunmanway, County Cork, on the right bank of the Bandon River, is the townland of Mallabracka, a place of wild beauty, where the Maguires lived for over two hundred years. They were respected members of a farming community, all tenants like themselves of the Shouldham estate. John and Jane Maguire reared six other children on their substantial farm; they were good and hard-working farmers, and the young Maguires were reared in an atmosphere of sharing with less-well-off friends. Industry and generosity went hand in hand.

Sam attended the Model School in Dunmanway and later the national school in Ardfield, where the schoolmaster, Mr Madden, had a reputation for preparing his pupils for the British civil service. Sam was successful and obtained a job in the Central Sorting Office in London, where he joined many past pupils of Ardfield school.

The period 1890–1900 was one of great national revival in Ireland—the era of the Land War, the founding of the Gaelic League, and the infancy of the GAA. The events developing at this time had a lasting effect on the young Sam Maguire in his formative years. Among his colleagues in the Post Office in London were Peadar·Kearney, author of the words of 'The Soldier's Song'; Liam McCarthy, whose name is perpetuated by the all-Ireland senior hurling cup; Pádraig Ó Conaire, the writer commemorated by the statue in Eyre Square, Galway; and Michael Collins, hero of the War of Independence, who, like Sam, hailed from west Cork and was to become one of Sam's closest friends.

When Sam came to London he immediately established links with the Gaelic League and the GAA, becoming a member of the

Hibernians Football Club. Tall, broad-shouldered, and slim, he soon became a top midfielder and played for London in three all-Ireland finals (1900, 1901, and 1903), captaining the team on the second two occasions but failing to win an all-Ireland medal. His playing career lasted till 1908, but he had already become involved in the administrative side of the GAA, being elected president of the London County Board in 1907; he attended many Congresses as a delegate from London, later becoming a trustee of Croke Park. Altogether, Sam's love and work for the GAA in London knew no bounds, and his service in those formative years stamp him as a man apart.

Great as was Sam's role in the GAA, it takes second place to the part he played in the War of Independence. It was he who recruited Michael Collins into the republican movement in 1909, and Collins might be said to have served his apprenticeship to his older fellow-countryman. Eventually Sam reached the position of Chief Intelligence Officer of the IRA in England; by then Collins was directing intelligence in Ireland, and Sam travelled regularly to Dublin for consultations with him.

He returned to Dublin in 1922 and worked in the GPO but became disillusioned following the death of Collins in the Civil War in 1922. He was eventually dismissed from the civil service—a sad ending to a career of selflessness and patriotism. Dispirited and in failing health, he returned to the obscurity and isolation of the old home he always loved in Mallabracka, where he died in 1927 at the age of forty-nine. He is buried in the Church of Ireland cemetery in Dunmanway. I attended the GAA centenary celebration of Sam Maguire in Dunmanway and Mallabracka in October 1984, when a memorial was unveiled near his birthplace. The cross over his grave bears the following inscription:

> Erected to the memory of Samuel Maguire, who died 6 February 1927, by the people of Dunmanway and his numerous friends throughout Ireland and England in recognition of his love for his country. Ar dheis Dé go raibh a anam.

Soon after Sam's death a group of his friends who felt that his name should be perpetuated met in Dublin; among its members were Dr Patrick McCartan, Dr Mark Ryan, Jerome Hurley, Tommy Moore, Jim Kirwan, Dan McAuliffe, and Mick Maloney—old comrades all. The Sam Maguire Cup was commissioned and was made by Hopkins and Hopkins of Dublin to the design of the Ardagh Chalice. It was made of silver, stood 16 inches high without the base, and was 17 inches in diameter. On completion it was presented to the GAA, which allocated it to the all-Ireland senior football championship. Bill 'Squires' Gannon captained Kildare to victory over Cavan in the all-Ireland final of 1928 to become the first recipient of the Sam Maguire Cup.

This first cup became the worse for wear over the years, and it was replaced with a trophy of similar design in 1988 made by the Kilkenny goldsmith and silversmith Desmond Byrne to the same specifications and dimensions. The old cup is kept in the New Museum in Croke Park. The first recipient of the new 'Sam' was Joe Cassells of Meath in 1988, when Meath defeated Cork in a replayed final.

In the early years of the all-Ireland senior football competition the Sam Maguire Cup did not mean as much as it came to mean later; it is now the most sought-after possession. It means even more when won by a county for the first time, or by any county after a long absence. When a team wins the all-Ireland, the cup is brought everywhere in that county: to schools, hospitals, factories, and to events and gatherings of that county's exiles everywhere. It has been lost and found more than once. Only six people have had the honour of being presented with the Sam Maguire Cup twice: Joe Barrett (Kerry), Jimmy Murray (Roscommon), John Joe O'Reilly (Cavan), Seán Flanagan (Mayo), Enda Colleran (Galway), and Tony Hanahoe (Dublin).

13

CAVAN'S ROYAL BLUE STRIKES GOLD IN THE THIRTIES

The breakthrough for Cavan football came in the thirties; but long before that, its royal blue had become a threat to the champions of the time.

From the earliest days, Cavan were a developing football power within Ulster, and from 1915 onwards Ulster titles fell to them regularly, while defeats in all-Ireland semi-finals were much closer affairs, with the odd controversial score deciding results against the men of Bréifne. A case in point was the 1925 loss to Kerry in Tralee in the all-Ireland semi-final by 1-7 to 2-3. Cavan players protested that Kerry's winning point, signalled by the Kerry umpire, the legendary Dick Fitzgerald, had gone wide of the post. An objection by Cavan and a counter-objection by Kerry saw both teams thrown out in a year of bizarre developments. But it had been very close.

A one-point loss to Kerry at the same stage in the 1923 all-Ireland semi-final in Croke Park (with the score Kerry 1-3, Cavan 1-2) also had undertones of hard luck and disputed scores. Eventually Cavan reached an all-Ireland final in 1928, before losing to Kildare again by a single point, 2-6 to 2-5, Paul Doyle scoring Kildare's winning point from a free late in the game. Would the breakthrough ever come?

The thirties started ominously enough with what became known in Ulster as the 'Carrickmacross affair'. Cavan v. Monaghan rivalry was very keen at this time, with Monaghan defeating Cavan in an Ulster final replay at Carrickmacross in 1929. Afterwards Cavan felt that the venue wasn't suitable for an Ulster final, and complained also about the treatment meted out to their star player, Jim Smith, by the large Monaghan crowd . Ten thousand had packed Carrickmacross for the replay, which Monaghan won by 1-10 to 0-7, with star players in Peter Lambe, Tom Shevlin, Paddy Kilroy, Billy Mason, and the wonder forward Christy Fisher, who scored 0-5 of Monaghan's total.

In 1930 the same teams qualified for the Ulster final, fixed once again for Carrickmacross. This caused a furore with Cavan, who opted to play anywhere except Carrickmacross and suggested such alternative venues as Dundalk, Drogheda, Navan, and Dublin. The Ulster Council wouldn't budge. Cavan voted not to travel, and the Ulster Council prevailed on a token Cavan team to travel. Monaghan won by 4-3 to 1-5. This almost caused a split within the Cavan team and a war between the Cavan County Board and the Ulster Council. Central to this was a personality clash between Séamus Gilheaney, chairman of the county board, and B. C. Fay, also of County Cavan, secretary of the Ulster Council.

Worse was to follow with the suspension of Cavan for refusing to field a junior team for that year's Ulster final after Séamus Gilheaney had earlier received a vote of confidence at the Cavan County Board. Eventually wiser heads prevailed, and Cavan were back in the fold of Ulster football. Success often comes after a battle when all looks blue.

The first good omen was a first appearance in the national football league final and yet another one-point loss to Kerry, 1-3 to 1-2. Then followed a win in the Ulster senior final over Armagh by 0-8 to 2-1, and a semi-final loss to Kildare, 0-10 to 1-5. The Ulster title was the first of a record seven in a row in the province, which beat Antrim's six in a row (1908–13).

In 1932, after an easy win over Monaghan, Cavan lost to Mayo in Croke Park through a late goal by Paddy Moclair. Mayo, also an emerging force, had been through many harrowing years on their way to the top.

The year of glory for Cavan was to be 1933. Neither Donegal nor Derry participated in the Ulster senior football championship that year, and Cavan's path to glory began with a win over Armagh (1-8 to 0-2) and a very easy 6-13 to 1-2 win over Tyrone. Cavan were through to meet their old rivals Kerry in the semi-final in their own Breffni Park. The date was 17 August 1933, a date that has gone into Cavan folklore. The Kerry team, who had arrived by train the day before, received a rapturous welcome in Cavan.

The big day dawned wet, and a record crowd of 17,000 turned up to see Cavan do battle against the mighty four-in-a-row champions. Scores were scarce, and Kerry led 0-2 to 0-1 at half time. Then luck favoured Cavan for a change, with two Kerry shots coming back off the upright and the goalkeeper, Willie Young, in excellent form. Then Kerry pulled away to lead by 0-4 to 0-1. Now Cavan came back, with M. J. Magee starting the rally with a point, followed by another from

Dónal Morgan; but Jackie Ryan of Kerry replied with a point. Now Cavan seemed to sense the breakthrough. Jack Smallhorne pointed, and M. J. Magee levelled the scoring from a free.

Excitement ran high, and in the dying moments the right-corner-forward, Vincie McGovern, rose high above the Kerry defence to punch the winning goal from a long centre and to earn his place in Cavan football immortality. Kerry fought like lions to hold on to their crown, but the final score remained Cavan 1-5, Kerry 0-5. Breffni Park went beautifully mad. It was Ulster's greatest football day. Kerry were mortal after all.

Cavan were into another all-Ireland final, this time against Galway, another emerging force in football, who had beaten Dublin in the other semi-final at the new Cusack Park in Mullingar. A record crowd of 45,000 thronged Croke Park for the first Connacht v. Ulster all-Ireland final. Willie Young, Patsy Lynch, Hughie Reilly, Packie Devlin and the captain, Jim Smith, had all played in the 1928 final. An army of supporters travelled from Cavan to Dublin; eight hundred travelled by train from Killeshandra.

A downpour of rain on the Sunday morning made conditions difficult. Play was even until a goal direct from a fifty from Jim Smith in the twenty-third minute decided the outcome. Another goal by M. J. Magee left it 2-3 to 0-2 at half time. Though Galway fought back with a goal and a disallowed one (Mick Donnellan's pass to Brendan Nestor was judged a foul throw), Cavan went on to win by 2-5 to 1-4. Jim Smith, the captain from Killinkere (who played for Cavan from 1920 to 1937, winning thirteen Ulster senior football championship medals), was chaired shoulder high to receive the Sam Maguire Cup from the president of the GAA, Seán McCarthy. Smith is rightly acclaimed as one of the best players ever to come out of Ulster. Bonfires blazed at every County Cavan crossroads that night, and the team returned to a heroic welcome on Monday after a banquet in the Shelbourne Hotel the previous night.

This was the victorious Cavan team:

Willie Young

Willie Connolly   Patsy Lynch   Mick Dinneny

Terry Coyle   Jim Smith (*captain*)   Packie Phair

Hughie O'Reilly   Tom O'Reilly (Cornafean)

Dónal Morgan   Packie Devlin   Jack Smallhorne

Vincie McGovern   Louis Blessing   M. J. Magee

Substitutes: Tom Crowe, Paddy McNamee, Paddy Brady, Tom O'Reilly
(Mullahoran), Jack Rahill.

Jim Smith was the acknowledged star of the day. There is a photograph of the march before the game, with Mick Donnellan, the Galway captain, carrying a youngster as a mascot on his right shoulder, while lanky Jim Smith leads another young Cavan hopeful on his right-hand side. Innocent times! Years after the match, I discussed it with Galway's star forward, Brendan Nestor. He recalled an incident from the second half when Patsy Lynch was injured seriously in a collision with a Galway opponent. 'Before Patsy was carried off we knelt around him and prayed for his safety.' Thankfully, Patsy recovered after a stay in the Mater Hospital. Innocent times, and caring times too.

1934 saw Cavan travel to the United States, where they lost to New York in a two-game series (the first game ended 1-7 each, the second saw New York win, 1-6 to 0-7). 1934 was the golden jubilee year of the GAA, and this American tour was the first official one since Maurice Davin led the 'American invasion' of 1888. The Irish party sailed from Galway and remained in America for over a month.

Cavan retained the Ulster title, easily beating Armagh by 3-8 to 0-2 in the final. Cavan now qualified to meet Galway in Parkmore, Tuam, in the semi-final, a repeat of the 1933 final and a much-anticipated encounter that attracted a massive crowd to Tuam on 12 August 1934. Special trains came from Galway, Clifden, Dublin, Knockcroghery, Sligo, and Westport, and nine hundred people packed into the train from Cavan.

Despite a great deal of planning, the pitch couldn't cope with the massive influx of 25,000 people, and from an early stage there was chaos. The game began at 4:13 p.m. and ended at 6:12. There were numerous stoppages during both halves as a result of encroachments. During a long-drawn-out half time, with Galway leading 1-5 to 0-5, a meeting of officials decided to continue the game.

Worse was to follow in the second half. The playing space at times was little over half the regulation width. The ball often rebounded off spectators. Cavan—without Jim Smith, who didn't appear—failed to convert a late penalty through M. J. Magee. Galway won in the end, 1-8 to 0-8, amid scenes of jubilation. Cavan felt hard done by and objected. The Central Council rejected the complaint and awarded the game to Galway.

With hindsight it's clear that the game should have been abandoned and replayed at a more suitable venue. It was Parkmore's last semi-final, and to this day Cavan feel aggrieved at losing. Many tales are still told of the 1934 semi-final in Tuam. The Cavan train could not take its full load on the gradient to Milltown afterwards and had to make two journeys. The first batch spent the time in Keane's pub, the 'Blue Pig', and local people tell of many squabbles between themselves and the downhearted Cavan fans in a packed bar.

1935 was to be another glory year for Cavan. Though poor in the semi-final against Tipperary (Kerry withdrew from the championship that year in protest over the internment of prisoners in the Curragh), Cavan won by 1-7 to 0-8 with a last-minute goal by the captain, Hughie Reilly. Cavan's luck was turning. A record crowd of 50,000 saw Cavan defeat Kildare in the final by 3-6 to 2-5. It was the end of the great Lily-White era, and the winning captain, who had a star game, was rightly acclaimed. This was Cavan's greatest football day. There were great celebrations in Cavan on the Monday as the all-Ireland champions arrived home by train.

The team differed slightly from that of 1933. Jim Smith was at full-back, Terry Dolan right-half-back, Big Tom O'Reilly at number 6, and Tom O'Reilly (Mullahoran) at midfield instead of Big Tom. There was only one change in attack: Pat Boylan in the right corner instead of Vincie McGovern.

Cavan were on top of the football tree once more, and in 1936 the team set off again for America, where this time they won a two-game series with New York (the first game by 1-7 to 0-5 before 40,000 at Yankee Stadium, the second a draw, 2-3 each). Later in the year Laois shocked them in the semi-final, winning deservedly by 2-6 to 1-5. The golden era of the thirties was not over yet.

1937 saw Cavan come out of Ulster for the seventh successive time, and in the semi-final at Cusack Park, Mullingar, they dethroned the 1936 all-Ireland champions, Mayo, by 2-5 to 1-7. Again there were stoppages because of overcrowding: a huge attendance of 26,000 overtaxed the venue. Mayo were leading by five points with just a few minutes to go. First there was a goal by the sharpshooter Magee, followed by a last-second goal from Blessing, which sealed Mayo's fate. The score was Cavan 2-5, Mayo 1-7.

At home in County Cavan, M. J. Magee and Louis Blessing were heroes of the day. All was set for the final against Kerry in Croke Park, where the Cusack Stand was being constructed, and a record crowd of 60,000 packed the ground. (The official attendance was 52,325, but almost ten thousand more were let in free.) Space was so limited that a section of the crowd climbed onto the scoreboard, and the scoreboard-keeper had to abandon his job.

The game was an epic. John Joe Landers of Kerry scored two brilliant goals. Kerry led by 2-0 to 0-4 at half time. The final ten minutes go down as one of the most exciting of all finals. Big Tom O'Reilly starred at centre-half-back, alongside his younger brother, John Joe, and started the move that led to a smashing goal by Packie Devlin, which saw Cavan lead for the first time with five minutes to go. Kerry equalised through Gearóid Fitzgerald, and Seán Brosnan edged them ahead, only to be negatived by a point by M. J. Magee off a free with three minutes to go.

Then came one of the most controversial scores of any all-Ireland final. A free by Vincent White was collared by Packie Boylan, who put it over the bar for the winner. But the referee, M. Hennessy of Dublin, deemed it a foul throw and awarded Kerry a free out. The match commentator, Father Hamilton of Clare, misinterpreted the result and told all Ireland that Cavan had won. No scoreboard was in operation; there was utter confusion; but the score was Kerry 2-5, Cavan 1-8. Cavan felt they were robbed.

As often happens, the replay was an anti-climax. The interest was huge, and another big crowd of 51,000 attended, with Hennessy again refereeing. It was a dour game, full of incidents, frequent fouls, and many stoppages for injuries; at one point seven Cavan players were down injured. Kerry won, 4-4 to 1-7. There was bad blood between the counties afterwards—so much so that Kerry refused to travel to America with Cavan in 1939, Laois stepping in to take their place. It was Cavan's third American visit in four years.

Cavan's supremacy in the game seeped through to the younger players in the county, and this resulted in two successive all-Ireland minor titles, in 1937 and 1938, when youngsters such as Barney Cully, T. P. O'Reilly, Patsy Clarke, J. D. Benson, Bill Doonan, P. P. Galligan and Simon Deignan showed signs of future greatness. There would be other great days ahead for Cavan; but the men of the thirties lit the torch and sowed the first seeds of Ulster football greatness.

14

MAYO-GALWAY RIVALRY DOMINATES THE THIRTIES

The nineteen-thirties were a marvellous time for Gaelic football in Connacht, for Mayo and Galway particularly. The cold statistics alone tell the story. Galway and Mayo met in all Connacht finals from 1933 to 1940, inclusive—nine in all, including one draw in 1936, with honours going four times to each.

During the thirties, three all-Irelands came to the west, Galway winning two (1934 and 1938), Mayo winning the county's first in 1936. In that period too Mayo became known as the 'League specialists', winning six in a row from 1933/4 to 1938/9, then withdrawing for a year when Galway won the title and returning again to win the 1940/41 League title—making it eight League titles in a row for the west.

The Railway Cup interprovincial series at the time emphasised the depth of Mayo and Galway dominance. Connacht footballers won the Railway Cup four times in the thirties: 1934, 1936, 1937, and 1938. In 1934, for instance, when Mick Donnellan led Connacht to its first Railway Cup success, eight Mayomen were complemented by seven Galwaymen in the line-out; in 1937 there were ten Mayomen to Galway's five.

It was a wonderful time for football in the west, especially from 1933 to 1940. The Connacht final was usually played in the old St Comán's Park in Roscommon and attracted huge attendances from all over Ireland. That was the era of the 'meat teas', and the ordinary houses at the venue became guest-houses for the day to feed hungry souls, many of whom travelled by bicycle to the venue. I was six when I was brought to my first Connacht final in 1939. All I remember is being disappointed at Mayo winning so easily, and I clearly remember a Mayo supporter rolling out a barrel in the Mayo colours and the crowd singing 'Roll Out the Barrel'. Many years afterwards, when I played in a Connacht final at the same venue in 1958, I felt proud to play on such hallowed ground, made famous for us all through tales handed down of feats unrivalled by men like Purty Kelly, Jimmy McGauran, Paddy Moclair, Bobby Beggs, Dinny Sullivan, Gerald Courell, and Brendan Nestor, to name just a few of the immortals from that period who have passed on, with the exception of Séamus O'Malley, who is still alive and well.

Séamus O'Malley, who captained Mayo in their first all-Ireland senior success in 1936, was happy to talk about that glorious time. A sprightly 96-year-old who plays the odd round of golf, he was thrilled to see his grandson Niall Finnegan carry on the football tradition with Galway in 1998.

> It was a great place to live and a wonderful time to be young and be part of such an intense rivalry between Mayo and Galway. Our teams dominated Gaelic football in Ireland in that period, and they came in droves from the other three provinces to see our Connacht finals. Despite the keen rivalry, behind it all we were great friends, and this is something that has always existed between Mayo and Galway. After I retired I kept up that friendship with my Mayo and Galway colleagues. It makes me sad to think of them all now, as they are all gone to Heaven. Of all that Mayo team of the period, I'd place Henry Kenny at number 1. He had a great spring for the ball in the air, had both feet, was intelligent, and his all-round football ability was unbeatable. Dinny Sullivan of Galway was a marvellous back. He had wonderful positional sense, and I never saw any forward block his kick. I was as lucky as a black cat to captain that 1936 team, and actually came out of retirement to lead the side.

A young lad from that time named Jimmy Murray from Knockcroghery was inspired by the excitement of it all, seeing every one of those finals in the west from 1933 to 1940. The same Jimmy was to lead Roscommon to all-Ireland success in 1943 and 1944. Jimmy, eighty-three years of age at the time of writing, saw his first Connacht final in 1933 in Castlerea.

> I remember Mick Donnellan led Galway to Connacht final victory in 1933 in Castlerea, and a year later Galway triumphed again at the same venue, where the venue was overtaxed by a huge attendance, and I clearly remember Galway wore green

jerseys in the 1934 Connacht final. Later they went on to win the 1934 all-Ireland final in the maroon and white we have long come to associate with the county. It was great to be a teenager at this time, and I can still place that Galway team of 1934 and the Mayo team of 1936 in their positions. We were all football daft, and the excitement of Connacht final day gave us youngsters a wonderful feeling. Hearing the band play, seeing these heroes march out onto the field, I was dying to do the same thing for my own county.

We had a shop at home in Knockcroghery, grocery-hardware-cum-bar, and my father suggested I should go and serve my time with Naughton's in Galway. That gave me ideas of playing alongside Bobby Beggs for his Galway city club, Wolfe Tones, but the opportunity didn't materialise, and I served my time as what we called a shop-boy then in Molloy's of Roscommon town. After Castlerea was unable to contain the crowds in 1934, the Connacht final venue switched to St Comán's Park, Roscommon. For Connacht finals in that venue Galway always used my uncle's hotel, called Murray's, as their HQ, and as a helper in the bar I was privileged to meet all the great Galway players of the period. Afterwards I'd be so proud to tell my pals I met Dinny Sullivan, John Dunne, Brendan Nestor and Mick Connaire in the flesh.

Of all those Connacht finals the one I enjoyed most was the 1934 one. Henry Kenny was such a clean player; you could put a ten-year-old playing on him. He was an absolute gentleman and a fine cut of a man. Great pair of hands, and quite the longest kicker of a ball I have ever seen.

Another Mayo player of the period of the same sporting disposition was Gerald Courell. He could score points from all angles, was often a marked man and, like Henry, a man of striking appearance, with distinctive wavy ginger hair. But Brendan Nestor of Galway was my hero. I modelled myself on Brendan and was so impressed with his body swerve, which often left defenders groping for him. Another charismatic character was Galway's Mick Connaire. His was a household name everywhere. A big strong man, he contested every ball and captured the imagination of all with his flamboyance and courage. He often called to our place in Knockcroghery, and even his entrance created ripples of excitement in the bar.

Let's take the championship first. Galway began that glorious period best, winning the 1933 and 1934 Connacht titles, then falling to Cavan in the 1933 final. After defeating Cavan in the 1934 all-Ireland semi-final at Parkmore, Tuam—a highly controversial game because of severe overcrowding—they qualified to meet Dublin, victors over Kerry in Tralee in the other semi-final. Up to the late thirties many all-Ireland semi-finals were played in the provinces; but from 1939 onwards, with the odd exception, all semi-finals were played in Croke Park.

Galway wore their now distinctive maroon-and-white jersey with the badge for the first time in the 1934 final. That was a significant year in the history of the GAA, being the fiftieth anniversary of its foundation. A national newspaper strike during the summer months didn't help matters, but, as always, the provincial papers played their part in preserving GAA history for immortality. In April 1934 both the *Irish Press* and *Irish Independent* produced wonderful supplements to commemorate the occasion.

Collective training was very much in vogue for the major games at this time. For the 1934 final Dublin trained in the Wicklow Mountains, while Galway stayed and trained in Tuam under the stern eyes of the 1925 star Tom Molloy.

In the final itself, watched by 36,000 people, Galway led at half time by 2-4 to 1-2, thanks to two great goals from Mick Ferriter. But Dublin made a great second-half comeback, after which Martin Kelly scored Galway's third goal. Galway held on to win by 3-5 to 1-9, the last time they beat Dublin in a senior football championship game.

This was Galway's winning team:

Michael 'Cussaun' Brennan

Hugo Carey   Mick Connaire   Dinny O'Sullivan

Tommy Hughes   Tadhg McCarthy   Frank Fox

John Dunne   Mick Higgins (*captain*)

Dermot Mitchell   Martin Kelly   Ralph Griffin

Mick Ferriter   P. J. McDonnell   Brendan Nestor

Later that year Galway went on a highly successful American trip, very much the norm then. All that team are now dead and gone. I interviewed the right-full-back Hugo Carey in 1994 in his home in Longford. He remembered 1934 well. He talked about Tom Molloy's strenuous training methods.

We stayed in Canavan's Hotel in Tuam. He used to bring us out the country for miles and miles, over stone walls and fields, up one side of Cnoc Meá and down the other side; then over to Corrofin and back to Tuam—well over ten miles. He always did it himself too. No wonder we were fit! We played our football in St Jarlath's College.

This was the first time the Sam Maguire Cup was lifted across the Shannon in triumph. Mayo were to take over in a big way for the next few years, winning three Connacht titles in a row, the 1936 final in a replay. That was to be Mayo's golden year, the crowning glory being their first all-Ireland win of 1936 in the middle of a wondrous League run of successes.

Mayo's quest for all-Ireland glory in 1935 was halted by Kildare in Croke Park in the semi-final by 2-6 to 0-7. But the nucleus of a fine side was emerging, with that wonderful midfield partnership of Henry Kenny and Patsy Flannelly together for the first time. The drawn Connacht final of 1936 between Galway and Mayo ended in a welter of excitement. Mayo led Galway by three points in the dying minutes, when Brendan Nestor punched the ball to the Mayo net for the equaliser. While the goal umpires hesitated, Brendan snatched the green flag and waved it aloft, whereupon the pitch in Roscommon was invaded by excited supporters. After some consultation the goal was awarded, the pitch was cleared, and soon afterwards the final whistle sounded. Mayo won the replay by 2-7 to 1-4 (the drawn game ended with Mayo 2-4, Galway 1-7).

Then followed Mayo's first victory over Kerry in a senior football championship game: the 1936 all-Ireland semi-final in Roscommon, won by Mayo, 1-5 to 0-6, to qualify to meet Laois in the final. Whatever happened to Laois, whether it was stage fright, staleness, or just a bad day, Mayo ran them ragged in a very one-sided final to win by 4-11 to 0-5, with Josie Munnelly scoring 2-3 and the ace full-forward Paddy Moclair getting 0-5. Mayo took over from the start with a point by Moclair and a goal by Paddy Munnelly and led at half time by 2-5 to 0-2. They continued to dominate and ran out easy victors. The Sam Maguire Cup was on its way to County Mayo for the first time, to add to the three successive national football league titles.

This was the Mayo team:

Tom Burke

Jim 'Tot' McGowan	Paddy Quinn	'Purty' Kelly
Tommy 'Danno' Regan	Séamus O'Malley	George Ormsby
	(captain)	

Patsy Flannelly		Henry Kenny
Jackie Carney	Tommy Grier	Peter Laffey
Josie Munnelly	Paddy Moclair	Paddy Munnelly.

There were big celebrations in Dublin afterwards, and Séamus O'Malley told me that he remembers driving home through the night and arriving in his native Claremorris with the dawn. It was fair day in Claremorris, and as he lifted the Sam Maguire Cup from the car there was little or no interest from the farmers gathered to sell their stock. Séamus himself didn't bother going to bed but taught a day's school in the normal way. Contrast the innocence of 1936 with the hype that attends the homecoming of the Sam Maguire Cup in these times!

The great League run continued for Mayo in 1937, and also a third successive Connacht title. But then Cavan proved to be Mayo's conquerors in an over-packed Cusack Park, Mullingar, in the semi-final, when it seemed as if Mayo were skating to success. Without Paddy Quinn and Purty Kelly, they still led by five points with five minutes to go, when the crowd surged onto the playing area. When play resumed, Cavan scored a goal. Another break ensued, and the pitch was once again cleared. Cavan now had the initiative and squeezed ahead to win by 2-5 to 1-7. The year that was to be one of Galway's greatest was 1938. It was a wonderful time for Connacht football.

I grew up in awe of the Galway team of 1938; we heard so much about them in our house that they were larger than life. I grew to know many of them subsequently, and now with the wheel turned full circle I cherish the fact that I walked in the guard of honour at so many of their funerals: John Dunne, Dinny Sullivan, Brendan Nestor, Bobby Beggs, Charlie Connolly, Mick Raftery, Ned Mulholland, Jimmy McGauran—what wonderful names!

In the first round, Galway beat Sligo in Tuam by 3-11 to 2-3, with Mickey Mannion of Corrofin scintillating. Galway defeated Mayo in the Connacht final by 0-8 to 0-5 before 17,000 people. The report by 'Green Flag' in the *Irish Press* began: 'It was a wonderful struggle right from the start with Mayo setting the pace and leading by 0-4 to 0-2 at half time.'

Galway's second-half display was one of sheer football power, which saw them win deservedly. In the all-Ireland semi-final at Mullingar (with the first commentary broadcast by Mícheál O'Hehir) Galway beat Monaghan 2-10 to 2-3 to qualify to meet Kerry in the final. The few people who are still alive and lucky enough to have seen the drawn 1938 final all avow that it was the greatest exhibition ever of the code. Conditions were perfect, on a day of sweltering heat. In the end of a see-saw epic the score read Galway 3-3, Kerry 2-6.

'Green Flag' on the Tuesday after the game wrote:

> The meeting of Galway and Kerry was a triumph for those methods which delighted football fans in the days when Kerry and Kildare ruled the roost at the start of the century ... It is a long time since we saw such a whirlwind of grand football with never a movement spoilt by over indulgence in hand passing ... Brendan Nestor's artistry made him the man of the hour.

'Recorder' in the *Irish Independent* reported the record attendance of 68,950. The day of huge crowds at finals had arrived. Another column in the *Irish Independent,* written by 'NN', really does justice to the occasion. The writer described the last five minutes—

> the greatest minutes of the greatest final ever played in Croke Park. It came as a climax to an hour brimful of soul-stirring thrills and throbs in a match which was Gaelic football at its best and cleanest. Over on Hill 16, 20,000 spectators swayed like rolling waves. No stoppages had stayed the furious course of the hectic struggle and as it rose to a crescendo of excitement with score for score, Kerry scored it seemed the winning goal. Three minutes later Galway equalised. The scene was unforgettable. I doubt if any sports event in the world ever so faithfully mirrored a nation as did yesterday's all-Ireland final.

Every player on the field was a hero in the drawn game, and Galway were lucky when the referee, T. Culhane, blew the full-time whistle just before a kick by J. J. Landers sailed over the bar. Lucky for Galway the score didn't count!

There was great excitement leading up to the replay. Kerry dropped the full-back Joe Keohane. The replay didn't live up to the standard of the drawn game, and Galway, with Mick Connaire and Bobby Beggs excelling, won in the end by 2-4 to 0-7. The ending of the game was full of drama, with the Galway followers rushing onto the field thinking the game was over, with two minutes still to go and Galway 2-4 to 0-6 ahead. It took fifteen minutes for Kerry to re-emerge. Only three of the original players, a number of substitutes and others returned to finish the last two minutes. In fact Seán Brosnan scored a Kerry point from a free to end the scoring. Kerry had been beaten for the first time in a replayed all-Ireland final.

The following was the Galway team in the replay:

Jimmy McGauran

Mick Raftery   Mick Connaire   Dinny O'Sullivan

Frank Cunniffe   Bobby Beggs   Charlie Connolly

John Dunne (*captain*)   John Burke

Jackie Flavin   Ralph Griffin   Mick Higgins

Ned Mulholland   Martin Kelly   Brendan Nestor

Substitutes: Mick Ryder and Pat McDonagh.

In the drawn game, Mick Higgins played at centre-half-forward, with Ralph Griffin on his left.

Jimmy McGauran, the goalkeeper, remembers the training regimen in Ballinasloe under Tom Molloy.

> We stayed in what was the old workhouse, where Dick Kenny looked after us well, and we really enjoyed it. Mass at 8 a.m., then a three or four-mile walk. Breakfast (a big fry). Cross-country then for a few hours. Home to lunch and a shower. After a rest there was football practice for about two hours, followed then by a game. After tea another three or four-mile walk. You could then have a pint or two in one of the local pubs, but the whole town was watching you. Word would be fast getting to the workhouse if you stepped out of line.

Tom Molloy's methods didn't change much.

While this historical record concentrates mainly on championships, we cannot ignore Mayo's wonderful record-breaking run of six national football league titles in a row and seven in eight years—a truly remarkable achievement. Gerald Courell captained Mayo in the first three years of the series, while Paddy Moclair took over at the helm for the next three years. In that six-year run of success Mayo lost five times in forty-four games.

This was the amazing victory run:

1933/4	Beat Meath 2-4 to 1-5	Drew with Cavan 1-6 to 1-6
	Beat Galway 2-8 to 1-3	Drew with Dublin 2-3 to 1-6
	Beat Louth 4-3 to 1-3	Beat Dublin 2-4 to 1-5
1934/5	Beat Dublin 2-5 to 1-7	Beat Galway 1-8 to 1-3
	Beat Louth 5-3 to 1-4	Beat Tipperary 6-8 to 2-5
	Beat Laois 4-6 to 3-6	Beat Fermanagh 5-8 to 0-2
	Lost to Kildare, 2-5 to 4-9	
1935/6	Beat Kildare 3-6 to 0-6	Beat Tipperary 1-14 to 1-0
	Beat Louth 2-5 to 0-2	Beat Cavan 5-2 to 0-3
	Beat Laois 2-6 to 0-3	Lost to Dublin 0-6 to 2-5
	Beat Galway 1-8 to 1-3	Lost to Meath 0-5 to 2-2
1936/7	Beat Tipperary 4-7 to 1-1	Beat Offaly 5-4 to 1-5
	Beat Clare 2-7 to 0-5	Beat Galway 7-0 to 2-4
	Beat Laois 3-4 to 0-2	Beat Meath 5-4 to 1-8
	Beat Kerry 2-10 to 2-1	
1937/8	Beat Longford 1-9 to 1-7	Lost to Kerry 0-4 to 3-7
	Beat Clare 8-13 to 1-3	Beat Offaly 2-11 to 3-1
	Beat Laois 3-4 to 0-2	Beat Kerry 2-8 to 0-7
	Beat Galway 4-3 to 1-6	Beat Wexford 3-9 to 1-3
1938/9	Beat Kerry 3-3 to 1-3	Beat Wexford 3-7 to 0-4
	Beat Galway 4-3 to 0-5	Beat Meath 5-9 to 0-6
	Beat Kerry 1-6 to 0-6	Lost to Galway 0-6 to 0-7
	Beat Laois 0-8 to 0-7	

Their likes will never be seen again.

15

ANOTHER KERRY THREE-IN-A-ROW, 1939–41

After the drama of the 1938 draw and replay, Galway and Kerry toured America together, with great success. On their return they had contrasting fortunes, with the national football league specialists Mayo dethroning Galway in Connacht and Kerry winning their sole Munster senior football championship game against Tipperary by 2-11 to 0-4, qualifying to meet Mayo in the semi-final on 13 August in Croke Park.

This proved to be a dour, closely contested affair, resulting in a low-scoring 0-4 draw. Mayo were embittered because of a refereeing decision that denied what they believed was a legitimately won close-in free near the end. But despite their protestations, Kerry won the replay in Croke Park handily enough, 3-8 to 1-4.

Meath were their opponents in the final, after defeating Cavan in the semi-final. It was Meath's first Leinster senior football success since 1895. Now they were after their first all-Ireland, Kerry their thirteenth crown.

Kerry, of course, were hot favourites, but the doughty men of Meath put it up to them, watched by an attendance of 47,000. Kerry, wearing the Dingle jersey (to avoid a clash of colours) started off with gusto, but a wonderful goal for Meath by Mattie Gilsenan levelled the game at half time: 1-2 apiece. After half time Kerry raced ahead again and led 2-4 to 1-2 after eleven minutes; but Meath, as so often later, fought back for Jim Clarke to goal, to leave it 2-4 to 2-2. Dan Spring put Kerry three points ahead, but Tony Donnelly pulled one back for Meath, and that's the way it ended: 2-5 to 2-3. It was a close one for Kerry; Meath's day would come before the next decade was over.

In 1940 the provincial champions were Kerry (Munster), Galway

(Connacht), Cavan (Ulster), and Meath again in Leinster. The two semi-finals were played on the same day in Croke Park before 33,000 spectators, with Kerry edging out Cavan by 3-4 to 0-8 and Galway beating Meath by 3-8 to 2-5.

The repeat of the 1938 final was eagerly awaited, and the final turned out to be a cliff-hanger. Galway led at half time through a fine goal by Joe Duggan; and as the game entered the closing stages it seemed as if it must end in another draw, with a score of 0-6 to Galway's 1-3. But you never have Kerry beaten. Paddy Kennedy drove a long ball into the Galway half; Charlie O'Sullivan raced onto it, held it safely, turned, and shot it over the bar with the left foot from forty yards. His name has often been mentioned in County Galway as the villain of the piece; but it has gone into Kerry folklore. It's a sweet way to win; a sore way to lose.

Kerry, trained by the former star Con Brosnan, had won title number 14. Their captain, Dan Spring, got a rousing reception when he brought the Sam Maguire Cup to his native Tralee. Kerry were now level with Dublin in the all-Ireland roll of honour, with fourteen titles apiece.

The year 1941 was to see Kerry win another three-in-a-row and forge ahead of Dublin. The four provincial champions were Kerry, Cavan, Dublin, and Galway. Kerry were lucky to draw 0-4 each with Dublin in Croke Park but won the replay easily in Tralee by 1-9 to 0-3. Galway beat Cavan by 1-12 to 1-4, and we had a repeat of the 1940 final. But, unlike the previous year, when 61,000 attended, wartime restrictions cut down on train services; there was no 'ghost train' from Kerry at all. Still, a crowd of 46,000 was present on 7 September, many having cycled from their home counties. There was no need for a late point by Charlie O'Sullivan this time: Kerry won by 1-8 to 0-7. But it was closer than the final result showed. With the teams level at half time, 0-4 each, Galway shot into the lead with a point from Big Pat McDonagh and went two up when John 'Tull' Dunne pointed. Kerry's goal from the Dingle man Tom 'Gega' O'Connor, who grabbed possession after a free by his fellow-townsman Paddy Bawn Brosnan, really decided the issue; and though Galway never yielded, Kerry went on to win their fifteenth crown. Galway pummelled the Kerry goal nearing the end, but what might have been a penalty was adjudged to be an ordinary free in. There are always might-have-beens in finals; but in general the luck and the decisions tend to balance out.

This was the Kerry line-out:

Danno Keeffe

Billy Myers   Joe Keohane   Tadhg Healy

Bill Dillon   Bill Casey   Eddie Walsh

Seán Brosnan   Paddy Kennedy

Johnny Walsh   Tom 'Gega' O'Connor   Paddy Bawn Brosnan

Jimmy O'Gorman   Murt Kelly   Charlie O'Sullivan

Substitutes: M. Lyne for Johnny Walsh, Tim Landers for Billy Myers.

The three-in-a-row had been achieved. Many years afterwards I grew to know Johnny Walsh, Murt Kelly, Joe Keohane, Paddy Kennedy, and Paddy Bawn Brosnan. I knew most of the Galway team well; they were all lovely men who were not in any way affected by the adulation bestowed on them and the place they held in the esteem of so many. Paddy Bawn Brosnan became a folk hero, playing on and on for Kerry, finishing up as a full-back. When he died, in July 1995, he received a funeral in his native Dingle fit for a king. And as his body was laid to rest in the Dingle he loved, another Kerry footballer of a later vintage, Gary McMahon, paid tribute to the legendary fisherman-cum-publican-cum-footballer. Jimmy Murray of Roscommon, who attended the funeral of his old opponent, told me you could hear a pin drop as the master of the ballad in his sean-nós style sang:

His fishing boat at Dingle Pier stands silent in the dawn;
No more will it be skippered by the peerless Paddy Bawn.
At the end of all we'll kick football
                          when we meet on God's green lawn,
And the man who'll lead us round the field
                          will be the peerless Paddy Bawn.

16

ROSCOMMON COMES LIKE A
BOLT IN PRIMROSE AND BLUE

September 1939 is associated throughout the world with the
outbreak of the Second World War; but for Roscommon people
everywhere it recalls also the month and the year in which this
wonderfully keen football county won its first all-Ireland title. That
was the county minor football team, which, captained by Liam
Gilmartin, defeated Monaghan in the final.

It was to be the start of a glorious six years of achievement, when
no fewer than five all-Ireland titles were won: minor (1939 and 1941),
junior (1940), and senior (1943 and 1944). To say that Roscommon
footballers dominated the game during the stringent war years is an
understatement.

Roscommon contested well in the early years in Connacht,
winning provincial senior football titles in 1905, 1912, and 1914,
losing in a final to Mayo in 1931 and falling into the doldrums during
the Mayo-Galway supremacy of the thirties, when these two counties
between them won three all-Ireland senior titles and eight successive
national football league titles. In fact Roscommon were granted junior
status in 1939, their senior team being deemed not strong enough to
contest the Connacht senior football championship—a situation that
applied also to other weaker counties at the time.

All this was to change in 1939 with the minor all-Ireland win and
the regraded juniors going all the way to the all-Ireland final before
losing to Dublin by 2-6 to 1-6, having beaten en route Leitrim, Mayo,
and Limerick (a team that included the Mackey brothers, Mick and
John, of hurling fame). The factors that undoubtedly assisted the
upsurge included the election of Dan O'Rourke TD, principal of
Tarmon National School outside Castlerea, as chairman of
Roscommon County Board in 1935, the election of J. J. Fahey as

county secretary in 1938, and the arrival in 1937 of the Christian Brothers to establish Roscommon Christian Brothers' School, taking over from the De La Salle Brothers (who had themselves established a solid GAA tradition). Brother Kennedy, a Kerryman, became the prime motivator in steering a wonderful group of lads to Connacht colleges football and hurling successes, many of them to become the backbone of Roscommon's golden five all-Ireland wins. Young lads like Bill Carlos, Phelim Murray, Liam Gilmartin, Brendan Lynch and Gerry Dolan were to become household names throughout the country.

Dan O'Rourke, who later became chairman of the Connacht Council and president of the GAA, was an inspirational figure and took a hands-on approach to the task of training the teams. Those were the days of collective training, and in 1939 and again in 1940, as the Roscommon teams progressed, they stayed in a hall near Dan's house called the Garage, which was used as a dance hall and concert hall at the time, being fed in the nearby school by some of the local people.

Colm Hannelly, a well-known GAA aficionado and statistician, was a pupil in Tarmon National School at the time.

> It was a wonderful time for us youngsters, and I remember Dan, whom I revered, sending me on messages into Castlerea, for glucose mostly (no steroids heard of then!). And Phil Gannon, who worked in Hayes's chemist shop and later became secretary of the Roscommon Board, used to supply all needs.

In 1940 Roscommon were regraded as junior again, and this time the juniors, captained by Hugh Gibbons, went one better, winning the all-Ireland junior title, defeating Westmeath in the final by 2-9 to 0-5. These two successive all-Ireland wins excited much interest, and great was the welcome for the triumphant returning teams. Many of the stars of the 1939 and 1940 junior teams, cutting their football teeth, were to sparkle later with the seniors—men like Jimmy Murray, J. P. 'Doc' Callaghan, Owensie Hoare, Willie Heavey, Frank Glynn, Dónal Keenan, Pat McManus (who later played for Galway), Kevin Winston, Éamonn Boland, Liam Gilmartin, Larry Cummins, and Hugh Gibbons. It was time to challenge the might of Galway and Mayo at senior level.

And so the momentum continued, with a second minor all-Ireland in 1941. In the final at Longford, Roscommon beat the 1940 champions, Louth, by 3-6 to 0-7 to become the first holders of the Tom Markham Cup, presented that year. The team was captained by

Bill Carlos, and with him were Brian O'Rourke (son of Dan), Gerry Dolan, Tim Lynch, and Brendan Lynch—other names to feature prominently later. All these teams were trained by the Galway hero of 1925, Tom Molloy of Corrofin, a strict disciplinarian who also brought Galway's masseur, Toddy Ryan of Tuam, to rub weary muscles into shape.

The training of teams was still continuing in Tarmon; but in 1941, in a close Connacht senior football final at St Comán's Park, Roscommon, before 15,000 people, the experience of Galway proved too much, with the score 0-8 to 1-4. In 1942, at Duggan Park, Ballinasloe, Galway continued the supremacy in that year's Connacht final, this time winning by 2-6 to 3-2. It was getting closer, and Roscommon's day wasn't far away.

First Leitrim were beaten in Carrick-on-Shannon by 2-12 to 1-3. Galway beat Mayo and so met Roscommon in the 1943 Connacht final (at Roscommon) for the third successive year. It was a thundering game. Frankie Kinlough shot a great goal early on to start Roscommon, and the Galway flag was lowered with a score of 2-6 to 0-8. It was Roscommon's first Connacht senior title since 1914. The Roscommon players were chaired off the field in triumph. The Sam Maguire now beckoned.

In the all-Ireland semi-final, Louth succumbed in a high-scoring game by 3-10 to 3-6. Frankie Kinlough scored two goals, and this new Roscommon team became the big talking-point of Ireland. Roscommon had reached their first all-Ireland senior final, and for the first time the team wore the primrose-and-blue trim, replacing the old jersey of blue with a yellow band.

This was wartime, a time of scant resources. People travelled to games by all types of conveyance: trains, hackney cars, bicycles, traps. Many also cycled the distance to Dublin.

A record crowd of 63,000 came to see this new team battle with the Ulster kingpins, Cavan. Mícheál O'Hehir was king of the air waves, and every wireless set in County Roscommon brought his voice to packed houses as the fair-haired captain, Jimmy Murray from Knockcroghery, led his team around Croke Park.

Jimmy's description of his feelings then has gone into GAA folklore.

> When I led Roscommon out it was a dream come true for me, and the whole thing struck me as awesome. The grass looked so green as I ran onto the field, and I felt so much alone that I glanced back to see if the rest of the lads were there at all. I'll

never forget the crescendo of cheering; and most of the crowd had never seen the Roscommon colours till then. Then the march around, and the thoughts started to swim in my head. One moment I'd love to be up in the stand looking on. A terrible weight lay on your shoulders. You're carrying the honour for your family, your village, your county. I remember passing by Mícheál O'Hehir's box and thinking of my native village, Knockcroghery, and thinking to myself, 'What are they doing at home just now?' I could imagine all the neighbours around the old radio in the kitchen. My mother would be upstairs praying we'd win. My father would be down with the neighbours, hoping (he travelled to the final in 1944).

Big Tom O'Reilly was captain of the Cavan men, who led Roscommon a merry dance in the first half and had an interval lead of 1-4 to 0-3. Jimmy Murray continues the story:

We were down and out, but I remember both John Dunne and Brendan Nestor of Galway, men I always respected as footballers, came to visit us, and their genuine encouragement did us a power of good. We went on to draw the game, 1-6 all, and won the replay two weeks later by 2-7 to 2-2.

Once again Frankie Kinlough struck for an early goal, and this was followed by another Roscommon goal from Jack McQuillan after Jimmy Murray's shot came back off the Cavan goalkeeper, Benson. Joe Stafford responded with a goal for Cavan. Two points by Phelim Murray, followed by a goal for Cavan by Packie Boylan, left the half-time score 2-2 to 2-0, in Roscommon's favour.

But Roscommon took over in the second half, and the free-taking specialist Dónal Keenan (later to become president of the GAA) put them four points clear. Tempers became frayed more than once before the end of the game, which Roscommon won well in the end by 2-7 to 2-2. The Sam Maguire Cup was on its way to Roscommon for the first time.

The receptions accorded the new and unheralded champions on the train journey home the following day were hectic. From Athlone to Roscommon, crowds gathered along the railway line with bonfires blazing. The first real welcome was in Athlone, as always; then a torchlight parade and an address of welcome in Jimmy and Phelim Murray's own Knockcroghery. The reception in Roscommon was the best of all. The team was paraded from the station to the Square, led

by the Knockcroghery Band. Many more receptions were to follow.
The winning team was:

Frank Glynn

Larry Cummins   J. P. Callaghan   Bill Jackson

Brendan Lynch   Bill Carlos   Owensie Hoare

Éamonn Boland   Liam Gilmartin

Phelim Murray   Jimmy Murray (*captain*)   Dónal Keenan

Derry McDermott   Jack McQuillan   Frankie Kinlough

Bill Heavey, injured in the drawn game, was replaced by Owensie
Hoare for the replay. The great work of Dan O'Rourke, J. J. Fahey and
Roscommon Christian Brothers' School had borne fruit, as had all
those collective training sessions in Tarmon and later in Roscommon.
War or no war, the west was truly awake.

I was a mere ten-year-old, an impressionable youngster living in
Dunmore, County Galway, on the Roscommon border, and remember
the great surge of pride at Roscommon's win. We listened in to
Mícheál O'Hehir, who painted glorious pictures of that wonderful
half-back line of Brendan Lynch, big Bill Carlos, and Owensie Hoare.
His voice always seemed to rise in pitch at the mention of Carlos—
'the lion with the velvet paws,' as he was once called—the towering
midfielders Éamonn Boland and Liam Gilmartin, as good a
partnership as ever played in Croke Park, and wee Jimmy Murray—
or Jamesie, as he was called at home—with his wavy fair hair, who
soloed his way in leading his attack as a great captain. Roscommon
football would never look back.

After the all-Ireland win of 1943, Roscommon's star dimmed
somewhat with successive losses in challenge games to Kerry, Louth
and Galway and a draw with Longford. Had it been a flash in the pan?
Just before the championship they lost again to Westmeath in a
tournament game. Worse still, Larry Cummins broke a leg, and
Frankie Kinlough was injured, and when Roscommon faced Sligo at
Boyle to defend all their titles they had to field without Cummins,
Kinlough, or Jimmy Murray, injured in a club game; they were lucky
to draw 1-5 to 0-8 for Sligo. But two weeks later at the same venue,
before a massive attendance, Roscommon, with Murray and Kinlough
back, survived a tough struggle to win by 0-13 to 1-6. Sligo
dominated the first half, but when John Joe Nerney replaced the still
injured Kinlough the course of the game changed. Nerney's all-go
action and Boland's supremacy at midfield won the day.

I saw Roscommon defeat Mayo in the Connacht final in Tuam, 2-11 to 1-6. With hundreds of others I cycled the nine miles to Parkmore (no need for locks on bicycles then); and I still remember seeing Phelim Murray pointing two fifties and getting close to such radio heroes as Carlos, Lynch, Kinlough, Murray, and Keenan.

Cavan fell in the semi-final by 5-8 to 1-3. It was even enough in the first half, 2-3 to 1-3, but a rout in the second. All was now ready for a tilt with Kerry, conquerors of Carlow (yes, Carlow) in the other semi-final.

Because of the severe wartime restrictions on paper, the newspapers carried scant coverage. Still, a record crowd of 79,000 crammed Croke Park; thousands more were locked outside as the gates closed an hour before the game. The railway wall, tops of stands, the roofs of nearby houses, even the tops of nearby telegraph poles, were all used as vantage points. 'Safety' was a word never mentioned then.

Roscommon led by 1-4 to 1-2 at half time, Kinlough again the goal-scorer. Then Kerry lorded it and led by two points with ten minutes to go. Now Roscommon showed their mettle, and Dónal Keenan's two points equalised the score. Kinlough—that man again—put Roscommon in front, and Keenan's accurate boot put over the final score for Roscommon's second all-Ireland in a row, 1-9 to 2-4. It was Roscommon's finest football hour. Jimmy Murray with the Sam Maguire Cup was chaired around Croke Park. Kerry, as always, were gracious losers.

This time the journey home was by car, with huge receptions in Athlone, Kiltoom, Knockcroghery, Ballymurray, and Roscommon. The future looked bright for the primrose and blue.

The winning Roscommon team was:

	Owensie Hoare	
Bill Jackson	J. P. Callaghan	Jack Casserly
Brendan Lynch	Bill Carlos	Phelim Murray
Éamonn Boland		Liam Gilmartin
Frankie Kinlough	Jimmy Murray (*captain*)	Dónal Keenan
Hugh Gibbons	Jack McQuillan	John Joe Nerney
	Substitute: D McDermott.	

The all-Ireland champions suffered a surprise defeat to Mayo in the first round of the 1945 Connacht senior football championship at

Sligo, losing by 2-8 to 1-6; but they were back again in 1946 in all their glory—almost, first beating Galway, 0-7 to 0-4. Phelim Murray was now at midfield with Éamonn Boland. Jimmy's younger brother was a most versatile player, serving Roscommon well in many positions. Gone at a tender age was the 1939 minor captain, Liam Gilmartin, struck down with a serious illness—a terrible blow this— from which he thankfully recovered many years later.

Training, as was usual now, was in the capable hands of an army man, Sergeant McMahon, at the Infirmary in Roscommon. In the Connacht final at Ballinasloe, on a very wet day, Roscommon beat Mayo by 1-4 to 0-6 after getting a hotly disputed goal (when Jimmy Murray went in and waved the green flag himself!). There followed an objection, and a counter-objection, and a repeat fixture at St Comán's Park, a game won easily by Roscommon by 1-9 to 1-2, with J. J. Fallon, Bill Carlos and Jimmy Murray scintillating. In the semi-final Roscommon defeated Laois of all the Delaneys and the 'boy wonder' Tommy Murphy by 3-5 to 2-6, qualifying to meet Kerry in the final— a repeat of 1944.

This is often referred to as 'the one that got away,' in County Roscommon anyhow. Roscommon were leading by 1-7 to 0-4 with five minutes to go, and spectators were drifting away—just as happened in Roscommon in 1998, when Roscommon themselves seemed beaten by Sligo. But two late goals by Kerry made it level, and Roscommon had lost the initiative. Jimmy Murray had to leave the field in the second half after a very heavy tackle, but he returned to the fray in his own courageous way later on—to no avail.

In the replay, Kerry upheld their great record in replays, winning by 2-8 to 0-10. In 1947, the year of the Polo Grounds all-Ireland, Roscommon won out in Connacht again but lost to Cavan in a well-contested semi-final by 2-4 to 0-6.

That was really the end of Roscommon's golden era of football; but this team left a glorious legacy and to this day is revered not alone in County Roscommon but throughout Ireland.

Jimmy Murray's grocery and bar in Knockcroghery is a great calling-place, festooned with GAA photographs old and new. You are always assured of a royal welcome, especially if Jimmy himself is around. I once asked him which game he remembered best.

The 1943 final win, and that first Connacht final win over Galway in 1943 also. It was our first in twenty-nine years, and not one of the team had been born in 1914. Besides, I admired those Galway players so much: Beggs, Nestor, Dunne, the Sullivans, Mulholland, and Connolly.

Colm Hannelly, a native of Tarmon, still a Roscommon fan, recalls the era.

It was a wonderful time to be a youngster growing up in the county. They were all heroes: Brendan Lynch, my all-time favourite, not forgetting our own Tarmon lads, Boland, Carlos, Callaghan, Jackson, Glynn, and Cummins. If we only had club all-Irelands then!

Interest in Gaelic football in County Roscommon has been keen ever since, but there was no senior title, despite a national football league win and all-Irelands at minor and under-21 level. Yes, there were two unsuccessful senior final appearances, in 1962 and 1980, and four great Connacht senior football titles in a row (1977–80), but no senior all-Ireland.

Roscommon football is highly respected, and you can always depend on the team to give of its best. Like Kerry, Roscommon can never be written off. In the years since the golden era of the forties, men like Gerry O'Malley, Dermot Earley, Tony McManus, Michael Finneran, Ronan Creaven and Harry Keegan became household names. O'Malley is regarded as one of the most wholehearted players of any era. And the county won't rest till the Sam Maguire comes to Roscommon again.

17

THE 1947 FINAL AND CAVAN'S RENEWED DOMINANCE

After the great Cavan spell of the thirties their dominance in Ulster continued, and the team won seven Ulster titles in a row, 1939–45; but the best was still to come. A new generation of footballers in royal blue had come along to take the place of big Jim Smith, Patsy Lynch, Mick Dinneny, Hughie O'Reilly, Jack Smallhorne, and M. J. Magee.

Cavan's rebirth began in 1947, a historic year in which the all-Ireland senior football final was played outside Ireland for the first and only time. The all-Ireland final of 1947 in the Polo Grounds, New York, will go down in history as the most talked-of final ever.

I remember the winter of 1947 as the harshest ever. It was in the early aftermath of the Second World War, and times were hard, though becoming more normal. Emigration to America had died off during the war but had begun again. In the United States, and in New York particularly, interest in Gaelic games had dimmed and died in places; what had been a steady stream of American tours by the top hurling and football teams had ceased. It was also the centenary year of the Great Famine, a most appropriate year in which to involve Irish emigrants in America in some magnanimous way. It was against this background that the idea of playing the 1947 all-Ireland senior football final in New York was born. Though this proposition, the brainwave of John Kerry O'Donnell in New York, received scant attention at first, it was suggested to Canon Hamilton of Clare, then chairman of the Munster Council, and he supported it from the beginning. The idea took root, and support slowly gathered momentum; and late in 1946 the saga of the all-Ireland football final in New York began.

The proposal was carried at the Clare GAA convention in January

1947 and was mentioned again later at the Munster convention. Finally it was presented at the 1947 Congress and supported by the eloquence of Canon Hamilton, a respected figure in the GAA, whose appeal to the delegates' emotions carried the day. Pádraig Ó Caoimh, the general secretary, was to look into the feasibility of it all; and despite many obstacles with regard to transport, venue, marketing, and press coverage, the excitement of this novel proposal gripped the imagination of the Irish people and then of their many exiled relatives across the Atlantic. After the venues available were considered, the Polo Grounds—home of a baseball team, the New York Giants—were decided on as coming closest to requirements. The question of transport caused even more worries; but as the year went on and the championship continued, it all fell into shape.

The all-Ireland senior football campaign of 1947 now took on an extra dimension. Crowds at games swelled, and every footballer in the country hoped he would be lucky enough to play for a county that would get to play in the final.

The early rounds of the championship saw Sligo, powered by Frank White, score a surprise win over Galway in St Comán's Park, Roscommon—their first victory over Galway in seventeen years of the championship. Up north, Monaghan held Cavan to a draw in their own Breffni Park: Cavan 0-9, Monaghan 1-6, the equalising score coming from Eugene McDonald of Monaghan. In the replay at Clones, Cavan won a close contest, 1-11 to 1-9.

Huge crowds saw Laois defeat Kildare and Offaly. On 2 July a record crowd of 42,000 saw Meath defeat Laois in the Leinster final by 3-7 to 1-7, while in Ballina on the same day Roscommon defeated Sligo (in the only Connacht final between these two counties) by 2-12 to 1-8. In a third provincial final played on the same day, that of Ulster, 33,000 fans in Clones saw Cavan defeat Antrim by 3-4 to 1-6 in a downpour. A week later in Cork, Kerry defeated Cork by 3-8 to 2-6; again the rain bucketed down. It was, as always, a hotly contested encounter, with Kerry ahead at the break by 2-5 to 1-5. They continued to press and with ten minutes to go led by a comfortable five points. But Cork fought back and forced a penalty, to be taken by the free-taker Jim Aherne, after a break in the game while an injured Kerry player required treatment. But to gasps of astonishment from Cork's large following, Jim's penalty kick was exceptionally weak, and the Kerry goalkeeper, Dan O'Keeffe, had no trouble in clearing it. With that kick, Cork's hopes of going to New York died.

Years later Éamonn Young, who played at midfield for Cork that day, told the story of the penalty in *A Lifetime of Gaelic Sport*.

We forced a penalty—a penalty that could mean a trip to New York for us. The ball was placed and 'Danno' Keeffe, Kerry's great goalkeeper got ready. But someone—I think it was Bill Casey—was down injured and we had to wait a few minutes. Lazily, and with innocence stamped all over his honest face, Joe Keohane ambled out from the Kerry goal-mouth, stood near the placed ball and chatted in easy amiable terms with our Jim Aherne, who was waiting to take the shot. Now Jim had a kick like a young horse, and in spite of 'Danno' Keeffe it looked as if he was going to score. The referee blew the whistle and we got ready. Just picture the scene ... 'Danno' poised in the goal ... half a dozen Corkmen waiting tensely to charge behind the penalty ... silence all over the ground. Jim ran up and kicked ... And the ball trickled harmlessly up to 'Danno' who cleared downfield with a mighty kick. Shortly afterwards it was all over.

Years later, when good wine mellowed us all, big Joe admitted his guilt. When Jim Aherne kicked the penalty, the ball was two inches down in clinging mud! While Joe Keohane chatted to Jim Aherne, he quietly stood on the ball, and his huge frame did the rest. 'Sure I could hear the Statue of Liberty calling Youngy!' The late Joe Keohane was a wonderful full-back, later a Kerry selector. Éamonn Young, a great Cork footballer who, like Joe Keohane, served in the army, became an outstanding trainer, raconteur, and writer.

In the all-Ireland semi-finals Cavan defeated Roscommon by 2-4 to 0-6, the main difference being Cavan's two goals from Peter Donohoe and Tony Tighe, the star of the game. It was a close affair, with a Roscommon goal by Jack McQuillan disallowed. A week later, on 10 August, Kerry beat Meath by 1-11 to 0-5 before a massive attendance of 66,000. It was not a great game, but there were brilliant displays from Eddie Dowling and Tom 'Gega' O'Connor of Kerry. 'Bruddy' O'Donnell, a lovely man, whom I later got to know when he worked for a time in Galway, got Kerry's only goal.

The huge crowds at the semi-finals—60,000 attended the first one—reflected the marvellous interest generated. The people knew this was their chance to see the two finalists in their last game before the New York final. Earlier in the year the finalists, Kerry and Cavan, had clashed in a game at Mitcham Stadium in London, Cavan winning the engagement. Next stop Broadway.

The date chosen for the historic event was Sunday 14 September. The Polo Grounds had previously staged many exhibitions of Gaelic games between touring Irish sides and New York; indeed Galway played Kerry there in 1939, the last tour by Irish teams before 1947. Much of the summer had been spent by the GAA authorities organising the trip, deciding on travel arrangements, the size of the parties, mode of travel, and all ancillary arrangements. Martin O'Neill of Wexford, the Leinster GAA secretary, was chosen as referee. A group of twenty-five, including players and officials from both counties, embarked on the *Mauritania* at Cóbh on Tuesday 2 September and arrived in a hot and humid New York the following Monday. The remainder of the Irish party travelled by plane from Shannon and arrived in New York twenty-nine hours later, on the day after the liner disembarked, after a refuelling stop at Gander. Planes were much slower then! It was a first flight for all those travelling, and the party included three journalists: Mitchel Cogley (*Irish Independent*), Anna Kelly (*Irish Press*), and the 27-year-old Mícheál O'Hehir, who was to provide the commentary on the game and bring the story live to every Irish household lucky enough to have a wireless set. It was an onerous task for O'Hehir, but that particular ball could not fall into safer hands.

There was a huge welcome, which included a tickertape parade down Broadway and a reception by the Mayor, Bill O'Dwyer of Mayo. A heat wave had gripped New York, so the training of both teams before the great event was pretty light.

The two teams were brought to see the stadium on the Friday before the game. The ground was as hard as a rock. As Batt Garvey, one of the Kerry team, commented,

> Very little grass. It's ridiculous to play a game of Gaelic football on it. It was rock solid, like concrete.

And the mound used by the baseball pitcher was allowed to remain in place, despite many entreaties by GAA officials.

Everything was now in readiness for the big day. Irish exiles were beginning to converge on the Polo Grounds from all parts of the United States. An attendance of 35,000, while good, did not stretch the capacity of the stadium and was less than expected when the idea had been mooted. Because of extended formalities, the game, fixed for 3:30 p.m. (New York time) did not start till 3:38. We can picture the scene back home in Ireland, especially in Counties Cavan and Kerry; and believe me, it was similar all over the country. I was a youngster of fourteen huddled with all the other boarders of St Jarlath's College, Tuam, in a corner of our huge study hall beside an old crackling wireless set, waiting in expectation at 8:30 p.m. (Irish time) for

Mícheál O'Hehir to set the scene, as only he could. His great glory was that he could make it all so real.

When Martin O'Neill threw in that ball a hush descended on Ireland as O'Hehir's commentary brought the story back home. We cheered every score: Batt Garvey running riot for Kerry, soloing through and goaling; Eddie Dowling catching the ball out of the clouds, he too soloing through and goaling. Kerry were all over Cavan and led 2-4 to 0-2 after fifteen minutes.

But Cavan were not beaten. Mick Higgins and Tony Tighe went to midfield, and Kerry's superiority was halted. Cavan's wonderful passing in attack baffled Kerry, leading to frees that the ace free-taker Peter Donohoe converted. We thought we heard the thud when Eddie Dowling fell on his back on the concrete-like ground and had to be stretchered off. Then, just before half time, Cavan hit Kerry with two rapid goals from Joe Stafford and Mick Higgins, to leave Cavan leading at the break by 2-5 to 2-4. What a turnaround, and what a great first half! Scores make our Gaelic games the great spectacles they are. In St Jarlath's College we all breathed a sigh of relief.

Kerry suffered many injuries in the second half, and though they fought the hard fight so typical of their county, Cavan for the most part kept ahead and in the end, with a late flurry of three points, won deservedly by 2-11 to 2-7. Thousands of Cavan exiles rushed onto the park to chair their heroes off the field. Back home in County Cavan the whole population went wild, and bonfires blazed on all the Cavan hills.

The two teams sat down to a celebratory dinner in the Commodore Hotel. It was to be some time before Cavan could embrace their heroes on home soil. The newspapers both at home and in New York wrote extensively on the game. The *New York Times* writer Arthur Daley dubbed Peter Donohoe, whose eight points, mostly from frees, contributed handsomely to Cavan's success, the 'Babe Ruth of Gaelic football,' a wonderful comparison to a legend of baseball, America's national sport. All the Cavan heroes were lauded to the skies, with special mention of the wonderful half-back line of P. J. Duke, John Joe O'Reilly, and Simon Deignan.

After much celebration, the Irish party sailed out of New York on the *Queen Mary* on Wednesday 24 September, arriving in Southampton on Thursday 2 October. Between receptions in England and Dún Laoghaire, being paraded through O'Connell Street by the Artane Boys' Band, and more receptions in the Mansion House and Áras an Uachtaráin, the team didn't get to their own town of Cavan till the early hours of Monday morning, 6 October, arriving in their old bull-nosed bus, with all their luggage on the roof-rack, preceded by fifteen bands. It was Cavan's most historic night.

Every one of us remembers the all-Ireland final of 1947 and where we were on the night. It was a famous first, never to be repeated. I'll never forget Mícheál O'Hehir pleading for extra time to finish the commentary, and his request falling on friendly ears. It was one of his finest moments. Just as so many other stars were immortalised by him before and afterwards, the names of Garvey, Dowling, Donohoe, Higgins, Tighe, Duke and O'Reilly went into the pantheon.

Just what O'Hehir meant to Irish life in those days was brought home to me recently by an interview John B. Keane gave to Radio Kerry. Talking of youthful influences, he said:

> I used to go often with my Uncle Jackeen Keane to games in his pony and trap. But Jackeen had the most priceless possession in that street from the thirties onwards. He had the most modern radio. Through that radio came the magic of Croke Park via Mícheál O'Hehir. We'd sit around there, the house packed from top to bottom, up the stairs, out the hallway, down the side of the street—not a sound to be heard only O'Hehir. Kerry and Galway. Jackeen broke the wireless three times in temper at O'Hehir. He always blamed O'Hehir—not the referee. And the excitement was enormous.

This was the winning Cavan team:

	Vincent Gannon	
Bill Doonan	Brian O'Reilly	Paddy Smith
John Wilson	John Joe O'Reilly (*captain*)	Simon Deignan
	P. J. Duke	Phil Brady
Tony Tighe	Mick Higgins	Columba McDyer
Joe Stafford	Peter Donohoe	T. P. O'Reilly

Cavan went on to record their first national football league victory in 1947/8, defeating Cork in the replayed final (the first game having ended in a draw, Cavan 2-11, Cork 3-8) by 5-9 to 2-8 in October 1948 after the all-Ireland final of that year. 1948 was to be another great Cavan year. Beating Antrim easily in the Ulster final, 2-12 to 2-4, they defeated Louth in the semi-final, aided by a gale, 1-14 to 4-2, having led at half time by 1-10 to 0-1. The team selection differed little from 1947. J. D. Benson replaced Vincent Gannon in goal, P. J.

Duke took over from John Wilson at number 5, Victor Sherlock partnered Phil Brady at midfield, and the left wing of attack was J. J. Cassidy (12) and Edwin Carolan (15). Owen Roe McGovern replaced John Joe O'Reilly during the game.

The Cavan team, with two consecutive all-Irelands, had now established themselves as the county's greatest team ever, a team of quality led at centre-half-back by a wonderful footballer and leader, John Joe O'Reilly, considered by many to be the greatest ever in the position. The half-back line of Duke, O'Reilly and Deignan was the team's anchor. At midfield the partnership of the durable Phil Brady and the stylish high-catching Victor Sherlock was hard to beat. In the forwards, Mick Higgins had been recognised as one of the greatest centre-half-forwards ever, with Tony Tighe a flier on the wing.

After Meath's defeat of Cavan in 1949, Cavan got quick revenge in the 1950 national football league home final, defeating their near neighbours by 2-8 to 1-6. They took the field that day wearing black armbands, and two minutes' silence was observed in memory of their late and great right-half-back P. J. Duke, who died on 1 May in St Vincent's Hospital, Dublin, after a short illness. At twenty-five he was in his prime and is reputed to be one of the greatest players ever to represent UCD. The photograph of his funeral through O'Connell Street flanked by his team-mates, led by the captain, John Joe O'Reilly, still hangs in many a County Cavan home.

This morning early, as the birds were singing,
And Mass bells ringing in fervent tone,
To his great promise, the Lord took from us
Our fearless champion from sweet Stradone.

New stars may rise in the years before us,
But none like him will they then bethrone,
The boy from Bréifne, the pride of Ulster,
God rest you, PJ, in sweet Stradone.

Subsequently, Cavan lost the 1950 national football league final proper to New York, who came to Croke Park to win their first League title with men like Bill Carlos, Pat McAndrew, Pat Ryan, and Tom Gallagher. But Cavan weren't finished yet, though they lost the 1950 and 1951 Ulster finals to Armagh and Antrim, respectively. They came back with a bang in 1952, though none too impressively early on. But they improved as they advanced, and in defeating Monaghan in the 1952 Ulster final, with some new faces, they looked like an all-Ireland side, winning by 1-8 to 0-8.

I saw them beat Cork in an entertaining all-Ireland semi-final with an amazing comeback in which they snatched victory in the last few seconds. J. J. Cassidy got the vital late points to see them win by 0-10 to 2-3; but the star of the day was Mick Higgins, in one of his greatest hours.

Meath qualified to meet Cavan in the final, continuing a wonderful rivalry of the time, heightened in no small way on this occasion when three members of the same family played in the final—the amazing Maguires: Des, Liam, and Brendan. Des and Liam lined out for their native Cavan, while Brendan lined out for Meath, where he was then living. Because of continuous rain, the minor final between Galway and Cavan was postponed, and the senior final ended in a draw, with Cavan lucky to survive with a late point by Edwin Carolan when Meath were sure the day was theirs. The score: Cavan 2-4, Meath 1-7. But Cavan, captained by Mick Higgins, duly won the replay by 0-9 to 0-5, thanks to their midfield dominance and fine place-kicking by Mick Higgins.

This was Cavan's winning team:

Séamus Morris

Jim McCabe	Phil Brady	Des Maguire
Paddy Carolan	Liam Maguire	Brian O'Reilly

Victor Sherlock   Tom Hardy

Séamus Hetherton	Mick Higgins (*captain*)	Edwin Carolan
J. J. Cassidy	Tony Tighe	Johnny Cusack

Substitute: Paul Fitzsimons for J. J. Cassidy.

This was Cavan's fifth all-Ireland title and their third in six years. The football flame still burns strongly in the county, though its fortunes have tended to dim with the rise of such teams as Tyrone, Derry, Down, Armagh, Donegal, and Monaghan. Six Ulster senior crowns were won between 1954 and 1969, when such stars as Jim McDonnell, Tom Maguire and that brilliant forward Charlie Gallagher were in the van.

Scarcely had the cheers died down after the all-Ireland success in 1952 than the county was rocked once again when Cavan's most celebrated player, Commandant John Joe O'Reilly, died on 21 November in the Curragh Military Hospital. His funeral to County Cavan—on the same route as P. J. Duke's in 1950, the same route on which he had twice brought the Sam Maguire Cup—was huge and tear-jerking. A lament was written that is sung to this day; on the

Monday after Cavan beat Derry in 1997 it was sung in Cavan before thousands with greater gusto than ever before.

> God rest you, John Joe Reilly, 'neath each cold November air,
> As the grey dust falls so quickly round the plains of old Kildare.
> God rest and keep you, John Joe; may your memory last in fame
> Throughout each hill in Ulster and your own loved Cornafean.
>
> We bless and keep you in our prayers;
>   may he count you with his own
> While Ulster mourns your passing, from Ards to Inishowen.
> God rest and keep you, John Joe, and we pray for you today
> When Cavan lost their bravest man on a cold November day.

Cavan didn't win an Ulster crown again until 1997, with a wonderful success over Derry in Clones. I was present that day to witness the emotional scenes as the captain, Stephen King, lifted the Anglo-Celt Cup in what seemed like a first success. Later on in Croke Park before a huge attendance, memories of the 1947 New York final were recalled when Cavan, after an early flourish, fell to Kerry's experience and the football brilliance of Maurice Fitzgerald. Though they lost in the end by 1-17 to 1-10, they brought colour and excitement back to Croke Park and a huge following that had waited patiently since 1969.

18

MEATH'S TRADITION REWARDED AT LAST

There was always a great football tradition in County Meath, but it took some time for the county team to win an all-Ireland senior crown. They won their first Leinster title in 1895 but lost the all-Ireland final by a point to Tipperary. They didn't win in Leinster again until 1939, and again they lost out in the all-Ireland, this time to Kerry, by 2-5 to 2-3. They made more regular appearances on the all-Ireland stage after this; but 1949 was to be a special year.

There was nothing exceptional about the start of the 1949 campaign. First there was a win over Kildare by 0-11 to 1-5, followed by a 0-14 to 4-0 win over Wexford—a rare score that in any year. Then followed the wonderful three-game saga against Louth in the Leinster semi-final. The two teams drew, 1-5 all, the first day, Paddy Meegan equalising for Meath in the dying seconds. In the replay, on 10 July, Louth scored 2-1 in a late rally to equalise: Louth 3-6, Meath 2-9; and then a fortnight later Paddy Connell's late point from midfield decided the issue Meath's way by 2-5 to 1-7.

This particular series of games captured the imagination of the public, and over 100,000 people attended all three contests. Meath's Leinster final win was a complete anti-climax, Westmeath being easily beaten by 4-5 to 0-6. In the all-Ireland semi-final Meath had a good win over Mayo by 3-10 to 1-10, with Paddy O'Brien, full-back *par excellence,* starring. This gentleman-footballer, popularly known in County Meath as 'Hands' O'Brien because of his great fielding ability, was selected at full-back on the 'team of the century' and will always be numbered among the greats in this position.

Meath qualified to meet their near neighbours and old rivals Cavan in the final. There is nothing quite like the meeting of adjacent counties for generating interest in every townland; this county rivalry

Kerry Football Team (1903-1904), All-Ireland and Railway Shield Champions.

Dick Fitzgerald.

Kerry's first All-Ireland winning team. The Kingdom has dominated inter-county football, winning the championship at least once in every decade of the twentieth century. **Front**: J. Buckley, D. Kissane. **Front Row** (*from left*): W. Lynch, R. Fitzgerald, F. O'Sullivan, T. O'Gorman (Captain), P. Dillon, J.T. Fitzgerald, A. Stack. **Second Row**: John O'Gorman, J.P. O'Sullivan, James O'Gorman, J. Myers, C. Healy, R. Kirwan, M. McCarthy, E. O'Sullivan (President, County Board), T.F. O'Sullivan (Hon. Sec., County Board). **Back Row**: E. O'Neill, D. Breen, D. Curran, D. McCarthy, M. Murray.

Ballina Stephenites v Dublin Keatings

An early photograph of the Ballina Stephenites and the Dublin Keatings, taken before their match.

The Dublin Keatings team of 1909.

St Enda's College junior football team of 1911.

The great Wexford four-in-a-row team of 1915–18, captained by Seán O'Kennedy.

Michael Hogan, the Tipperary corner-back murdered in Croke Park on Bloody Sunday.

The great Kildare team which won the championship in 1927 and 1928. This is the 1928 side which won the Sam Maguire Cup when first presented to winning captain Bill 'Squires' Gannon.

The Kerry team of 1929 frustrated Kildare's hope of a three-in-a-row while setting up the first leg of their own first four-in-a-row. Here it is captained by Joe Barrett of Austin Stacks, Tralee.

Joe Barrett of Kerry and Jack Higgins of Kildare before the All-Ireland final of 1929.

Henry Kenny of Mayo, one of the finest players of his era, in action in the 1930s.

UCG's 1933 Sigerson Cup winning team, captained by Mick Higgins holding ball and cup.

The parade before the All-Ireland final of 1937 featuring Cavan and Kerry. The old Cusack Stand is under construction in the background.

Jimmy Murray, Roscommon's victorious captain in 1943 and 1944.

The Cork team of 1945 arrives at Glanmire station, with the Sam Maguire Cup being held by their captain Tadhg Crowley.

Action from the historic meeting of Cavan and Kerry in the 1947 All-Ireland final, played in the Polo Grounds in New York.

Mayo, 1951 All-Ireland champions. Players only are named. **Front Row** (*from left*): W. Casey, S. Wynne, M. Flanagan, E. Mongey, S. Mulderrig, P. Quinn, P. Carney, S. Flanagan (Captain), P. Prendergast, J. Curran, J. Staunton. **Back Row:** P. Jordan, M. Loftus, J. Forde, J. Gilvarry, T. Langan, P. Irwin, J. McAndrew, H. Dixon, L. Hastings, M. Mulderrig.

The throw-in for the drawn final of 1952, Cavan v. Meath. Cavan won the replay to take their last championship to date.

Action from the 1953 final, Kerry v. Armagh. (G.A DUNCAN)

One of the great All-Ireland occasions: the 1955 clash between Kerry and Dublin. It established one of the modern game's keenest rivalries. (CONNOLLY COLLECTION/SPORTSFILE)

Des Foley, one of Dublin's finest footballers. (CONNOLLY COLLECTION/SPORTSFILE)

The great Mick O'Connell leads Kerry in the parade before the 1959 final, in which the Kingdom beat Galway.

The captains of the 1960 finalists, Kevin Mussen of Down (left) and Paudie
Sheehy of Kerry, flank the referee, John Dowling of Offaly, before the match.
Down made history by taking the Sam Maguire Cup across the border for the first
time. (CONNOLLY COLLECTION/SPORTSFILE)

Down retained their title in 1961 under the leadership of Paddy Doherty. **Front Row** (*from left*): J. Carey, B. Morgan, S. O'Neill, P. Doherty, G. Lavery, E. McKay, P. O'Hagan. **Back Row**: J. McCartan, A. Hadden, J. Lennon, L. Murphy, P.J. McElroy, J. Smith, D. McCartan, P. Rice.

Seán O'Neill of Down, a truly wonderful footballer.

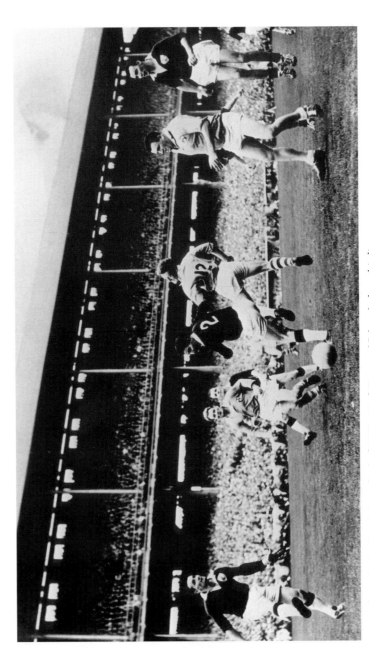

Action from the Dublin-Galway final of 1963. Noel Tierney (Galway) clears his lines.

is the soul of the GAA and the envy of every other sports organisation in Ireland. And when one of the counties is after its first title against the champions of the previous two years, nothing could be better.

I remember this time well. It was the era of collective training; and though the media coverage couldn't be compared to today's, there was huge publicity in the national dailies, and reporters and photographers visited the training camps of the rival teams to present stories of Meath's trainer, Father Paddy Tully, chatting to his squad in Gibbstown and pictures of Mick Higgins and John Joe O'Reilly training away in County Cavan.

They were innocent times. Teams whiled away training hours going on long walks or playing cards, pitch-and-toss and the other simple pastimes of the time. Alcoholic drink was almost taboo. Marvellous camaraderie was generated. As one who tasted the experience in my early years with Galway, I can say it was a wonderful time, with much innocent fun, plenty of good food, and as near as you could get to professional training. The 'training-camp specials' in the daily papers were read far and wide, and we got to know the Brian Smyths, the Christo Hands, the Tony Tighes, and the Big Tom O'Reillys. Mícheál O'Hehir's radio commentaries were a help too.

There was no team manager in those days; Father Tully was the team trainer and performed the functions of the modern equivalent, without half the fuss. His back-room team included Billy Eggleston of Navan; Joe Loughran, a former star from Kilmessan; Paul Russell, the former Kerry star, then living in Oldcastle; Mattie Gilsenan, who captained the Meath team in 1939; Ted Meade of Castletown; and one of Meath's best-known officials over the years, Jack Fitzgerald of Kilcloon. Father Tully was chairman of the county board as well as team trainer, while Billy Eggleston served as county secretary. It is significant too that three of the selection committee were former stars. Paul Russell's inclusion was a master stroke, for he could speak from experience of all-Ireland finals, having played in six and having won ten Munster senior football championship medals. The other star selectors, Joe Loughran and Mattie Gilsenan, are numbered with Tony Donnelly in any galaxy of Meath football heroes.

Attendance records were broken by a crowd of 79,000 the day Meath went to their first all-Ireland win, defeating Cavan deservedly by 1-10 to 1-6. They led from the second minute and never looked like losing. The foundations of success were laid at midfield, where Paddy Connell and the recalled Jim Kearney ruled. Paddy Connell fielded at will, and his long, raking kicks kept the forwards well supplied, with Brian Smyth, the-schemer-in-chief, scoring four invaluable points, ably helped by the ever-stylish Frankie Byrne and the youthful Matty McDonnell. Bill Halpenny was a strong full-forward, and there were two wonderful corner men in the elusive Paddy Meegan and one of Meath's most celebrated personalities, Peter 'the Man in the Cap' McDermott. Mick O'Brien starred at corner-back; and Paddy Dixon of Ballivor was the king-pin of a great defence.

This was Meath's winning team:

Kevin Smyth

Mick O'Brien	Paddy O'Brien	Kevin McConnell
Séamus Heery	Paddy Dixon	Christo Hand

Paddy Connell   Jim Kearney

Frankie Byrne	Brian Smyth (*captain*)	Matty McDonnell
Paddy Meegan	Bill Halpenny	Peter McDermott

Substitute: Pat Carolan for Frankie Byrne

Bringing home the Sam Maguire Cup on the Monday night is still talked about in County Meath, with the first stop at Clonee and the grand finale in Navan. The procession to the platform was led by the Navan Boys' Band and members of the De La Salle juvenile team. No reception in Navan ever bettered this.

Meath continued to stay high on the football ladder, winning the national football league in New York in 1951 after a successful American trip in the company of the Galway hurlers and losing two all-Irelands in a row in 1951 and 1952. Mayo beat Meath in 1951 by 2-8 to 0-9, and their rivals in the 1949 final, Cavan, were victorious in a replay in 1952 by 0-9 to 0-5 (having drawn on the first day, Cavan 2-4 to Meath's 1-7). Louth too were important rivals at this time, winning in Leinster in 1950 and 1953; but Meath were back again in 1954 for title number 2, once again trained by the county chairman, Father Paddy Tully.

Peter McDermott was now county secretary, having retired from inter-county football in 1953 after helping Navan O'Mahonys to win the Meath county senior football title. But as Meath progressed through Leinster in 1954, the Man in the Cap took down the boots again for a last hurrah. Not alone that but Peter took over captaincy at the age of thirty-six.

With wins over Wicklow, Kildare, and Longford, Meath defeated Offaly in the Leinster final by 4-7 to 2-10, with Paddy O'Brien returning to top form and Kerry-born Tom Moriarity scoring two of the four goals. In a closely contested semi-final, with Tom O'Brien in dazzling form before breaking his collar-bone, a goal by Brian Smyth swung the game against Cavan, 1-5 to 0-7.

Kerry, champions in 1953, were raging favourites for the final, but in a poor game Meath won well by 1-13 to 1-7, with young Michael Grace of Kells giving a brilliant display at right-half-forward. It was my first all-Ireland final, and I was enthralled by the atmosphere, the cheering of the crowd, the march-round, the Artane Boys' Band, and that wonderful sensation of singing 'Amhrán na bhFiann' when you know you're Irish and feel the pride.

Kerry led at half time by 1-5 to 0-7; but there was only one team in it in the second half. That wonderful warrior from Tralee, John Dowling, led the Kerrymen. Meath's full-back line of Mick O'Brien, Paddy O'Brien and Kevin McConnell was excellent—one of the greatest full-back lines of all time. Once again Paddy Connell rose to the occasion at midfield. Patsy McGearty, an old college opponent of mine, manned the goal safely.

Peter McDermott's victory speech after the game was unforgettable in its graciousness to the defeated Kerry team. 'Beating Kerry in a final is as good as winning two finals.' That was the message. Paddy Meegan had returned from his honeymoon and scored five precious points in his unobtrusive way. The rival teams were feted together in the Gresham Hotel after the game. Later that night in the Mansion House, Frank Sheehy, chairman of the Kerry County Board, at a céilí run by Conradh na Gaeilge, presented the set of all-Ireland medals to Peter McDermott, Meath's captain, before a crowd of 750. Later again that night the Meath party were guests of the Royal Meath Association at a function in the Portmarnock Hotel.

Meath's 1954 team contained eight of the 1949 team.

Patsy McGearty

Mick O'Brien	Paddy O'Brien	Kevin McConnell
Kevin Lenehan	Jimmy Reilly	Ned Durnin
Paddy Connell		Tom O'Brien
Michael Grace	Brian Smyth	Matty McDonnell
Paddy Meegan	Tom Moriarity	Peter McDermott (*captain*)

Simon Deignan of Cavan refereed. Meath didn't come out of Leinster again until 1964, when they won with a completely new panel but with Father Paddy Tully still the trainer and Peter McDermott very much in the wings.

It was unfortunate for Meath's new team of the sixties that just as they were about to blossom, Galway's greatest football machine was about to fire on all cylinders. Meath certainly ran Galway close in the 1964 semi-final, but they were comprehensively beaten by them in the all-Ireland final of 1966 by 1-10 to 0-7. This was unexpected, as Meath had pulverised Down in the 1966 semi-final by 2-16 to 1-9 in an unbeatable performance highlighted by a magnificent left-half-back attacking performance by Pat Reynolds. Just as Jim McDonnell of Cavan did eleven years earlier against Kerry, Reynolds reminded us of all the great exponents of the position: Seán Quinn of Armagh, Martin Newell of Galway, Christo Hand of Meath, Eddie Walsh and Teddy O'Connor of Kerry. After the defeat by Galway in 1966, Pat 'Red' Collier, their dynamic wing-half-back and popular hero, vowed to the welcoming party in the Square in Navan on the Monday night after the final that Meath would be back as champions in the same square a year on. And they were.

First Meath beat Louth by 2-9 to 0-3, with Noel Curran excelling: he scored 2-5. Then Westmeath fell 0-12 to 0-6, with Mattie Kerrigan and Tony Brennan scoring 0-4 each. In the Leinster final Offaly were beaten 0-8 to 0-6 after a close struggle. In the all-Ireland semi-final Mayo fell by 3-14 to 1-14 when Bertie Cunningham (a strong and reliable centre-half-back in the mould of Paddy Dixon), Terry Kearns, Ollie Shanley (a dainty forward) and Mick Mellett excelled.

Cork were Meath's opponents in the final, and they raced into a lead of 0-4 to nil after twenty minutes. Eventually Paddy Mulvaney pointed, to leave it a rather ominous 0-4 to 0-1 after a 'first half of bits and pieces,' as John D. Hickey of the *Irish Independent* aptly called it. But what a second half we got! The last quarter was 'contested in a frenzy of excitement.' Terry Kearns on the forty had a blinder and scored a telling 1-2; but John D. Hickey's men of the match were the entire half-back line of Pat 'Red' Collier, Bertie Cunningham, and Pat Reynolds, as well as Ollie Shanley, so successful in his third midfielder role. The score: Meath 1-9, Cork 0-9. Later that year Bertie Cunningham won the Footballer of the Year award. Pat Collier had kept his promise.

Meath's winning team was:

Seán McCormack

Mick White   Jack Quinn   Peter Darby (*captain*)

Pat Collier   Bertie Cunningham   Pat Reynolds

Peter Moore   Terry Kearns

Tony Brennan	Matt Kerrigan	Mick Mellett
Paddy Mulvaney	Noel Curran	Ollie Shanley

Noel Curran is of course the father of Dublin's present-day star Paul. Jack Quinn at full-back is a folk hero in County Meath and lived up to the Paddy O'Brien tradition.

Finally, and most remarkably, fifteen clubs were represented on the winning team of 1967: Kilmainhamwood, Rathkenny, Kilbride, Trim, St Patrick's, Ballivor, Walterstown, Ballinabrackey, St Vincent's, Enfield, Summerhill, Martinstown, Skryne, Dunshaughlin, and Duleek.

19

SEÁN FLANAGAN AND MAYO'S TWO TITLE WINS, 1950 AND 1951

Mayo's two title wins in 1950 and 1951 followed a barren enough period for most of the forties, during which Galway first and Roscommon especially stole the limelight. But even after the darkest night there sometimes comes a bright dawn. That dawn happened in the shape of a courageous draw with the all-Ireland champions, Kerry, in a tournament game in Tralee in which Mayo had to call on one of their drivers to play and also pressed the county secretary, Finn Mongey, into service as a substitute.

The Dublin-based players on the team later wrote a letter to the county board, which appeared in the local papers, demanding a new approach to training and team selection. The results began to show in 1948 after a wonderful two-game Mayo v. Galway Connacht final series from which Mayo eventually emerged as champions on the score 2-10 to 2-7 after extra time in the replay. I have seen almost sixty Connacht finals, and I still regard these epics as the best I've seen. In these super games there were many wonderful duels, but the ones of Seán Purcell against Pádhraic Carney, Tom Langan against Tom Sullivan and Frank Stockwell against Peter Quinn have stood the test of time.

Subsequently Mayo pulverised Kerry in the semi-final by 0-13 to 0-3, holding them scoreless in the second half when the mighty Pat McAndrew from Bangor, a giant of a man, had a stormer.

All-Ireland day dawned wet and windy. Before 75,000 spectators, with many more locked out, Mayo fell to Cavan on the score 4-5 to 4-4 in a strange game that finished controversially. Cavan led a half time by 3-2 to nil. Mayo fought bravely in the second half, aided by a penalty goal from Pádhraic Carney—the first penalty goal scored in an all-Ireland final. Peter Donohoe from a free had put Cavan in front, 4-5 to 4-4, in the dying minutes, and after hitting the post with another free, Mayo were back, earning a close-in free that Mick Higgins blocked to save the day.

In County Mayo to this day there are two grievances about this game. It is felt that Mick Higgins was too near the free-taker, Pádhraic Carney, when the free was taken, and that it should have been re-taken. (Cavan people, including Mick Higgins, have always felt that the rule about being fourteen yards away was not transgressed.) Mayo people also felt that they were short-changed in time by the referee, J. Flaherty of Offaly. It was a hard pill to swallow; but Mayo were still on the up, and better days lay ahead.

Mayo lost out to Meath in the 1949 semi-final with a strange team, having three recognised forwards in their half-back line; but 1950 saw them ready for glory. The Connacht title was won with style on a wet day in Tuam Stadium against Roscommon on the score 1-7 to 0-4. I'll never forget that score, for I operated the scoreboard in Tuam that day.

Mayo easily defeated Armagh in the all-Ireland semi-final by 3-9 to 0-6. Collective training was still in vogue, and the former stars Gerald Courell and Jackie Carney had the Mayo team in great shape after a very methodical yet relaxing routine in Ballina. Tom Langan scored two great goals from centred frees by Pádhraic Carney to kill off Armagh.

Mayo went on to defeat Louth in the final by 2-5 to 1-6 after being outplayed for three-quarters of the game. Louth led by 1-4 to 1-3 at half time and then moved into a 1-6 to 1-4 lead, Mayo obviously feeling the effects of Billy Kenny's early retirement after eleven minutes with a compound fracture of his right leg. Éamonn Mongey played the game of his life and inspired Mayo when prospects looked bleak, ably helped by Seán Flanagan in one of his greatest hours, Mick Flanagan, Joe Gilvarry, and Peter Solon. Tom Langan had moved to the forty, and he played a huge part in Mick Flanagan's winning goal, blocking a clearance by Seán Boyle and flashing the ball to the speedster Mick Flanagan, who soloed through to ram the ball past the Louth goalkeeper, Seán Thornton. It had been so near for Louth! Mick Mulderrig added a final point; and Mayo had won title number 2.

This was Mayo's team:

Billie Durkan

John Forde   Paddy Prendergast   Seán Flanagan (*captain*)

Peter Quinn   Henry Dixon   John McAndrew

Pádhraic Carney   Éamonn Mongey

Mick Flanagan   Billy Kenny   Joe Gilvarry

Mick Mulderrig   Tom Langan   Peter Solon

Substitutes: Seán Wynne for Billie Durkan, Mick Caulfield for Billy Kenny, and Seán Mulderrig for Mick Caulfield.

There are few counties in which Gaelic football is taken as seriously as in County Mayo. Enthusiasm in the county now reached fever pitch. In the west the team was well-nigh unbeatable. It had its stars: Paddy Prendergast, a high-catching full-back, sporting and mobile; Henry Dixon, strong as a horse at centre-half-back; Seán Flanagan, astute captain and wonderful reader of the game; Pádhraic Carney, star of stars, great college player and brilliant free-taker, perpetual motion his hallmark; and Tom Langan, one of the greatest of all full-forwards. There is and always will be only one Langan.

Mayo came out of Connacht as champions again in 1951, defeating Galway crushingly by 4-13 to 2-3 in Tuam Stadium. I was a substitute on the Galway team that day, a mere nineteen-year-old hopeful, and I firmly believed Galway would never beat Mayo again as we walked away from the stadium with Mayo fans delirious. You'd never have believed then that Mayo would not defeat Galway in a senior football championship game at the same venue till 1997, forty-six years later.

But Kerry nearly upset the apple-cart in the semi-final. Mayo were four points down nearing the end, and there wasn't much hope left. But a deft flick of a wet ball to the roof of the net by the peerless Langan after he had switched to full-forward on the hitherto unbeatable Paddy Bawn Brosnan, followed by a long-distance point by Paddy Irwin, saved the day for Mayo, leaving the score 1-5 apiece at the end. It had been close!

The replay was sunny and summery. We queued for hours to get decent sideline seats for my first all-Ireland semi-final, and a wonderful attendance of 53,000 enjoyed a great game, with Mick Flanagan, the hero, scoring two great goals and Mayo deservedly winning by 2-4 to 1-5. As in the drawn game, the duels between Pádhraic Carney and Jackie Lyne were memorable; but no-one excelled in quite the same way in which Paddy Bawn Brosnan dominated the drawn game.

Mayo were now into the final against Meath, to whom they owed one after the semi-final defeat of 1949. A football fever swept County Mayo and the west, and hopes were high that the double would be achieved. And it was achieved, quite emphatically, by 2-8 to 0-9 before 78,000 spectators, with Pádhraic Carney monarch of all he surveyed in attack and Father Peter Quinn, playing his last game before going on missionary work abroad, dynamic in defence. Mayo led at half time by 2-3 to 0-8 and really lorded it all over the field in the second half. The double had been achieved, and Mayo eyes were smiling.

This was Mayo's team:

Seán Wynne

John Forde	Paddy Prendergast	Seán Flanagan (captain)
Joe Staunton	Henry Dixon	Father Peter Quinn

Éamonn Mongey   John McAndrew

Paddy Irwin	Pádhraic Carney	Seán Mulderrig
Mick Flanagan	Tom Langan	Joe Gilvarry

Substitute: Liam Hastings for Henry Dixon.

I have always had a great grá for Mayo. They are Galway's oldest and greatest rivals; and there is something unique about a Galway v. Mayo senior football championship game. Galway love to beat Mayo, and vice versa, but the rivalry has also bred deep respect. This is never better exemplified than at the funeral of some of the former Mayo and Galway stars, where former opponents pay their respects and swap reminiscences, as happened recently in Claremorris at the funerals of Joe Duggan of Galway and Henry Dixon of Mayo.

Éamonn Mongey, a great midfielder of the fifties, a writer of quality and articulate after-dinner speaker, tells a good story against himself. Some time after his playing days were over he was asked to give a pair of the boots he used to wear for a fund-raising sale in aid of the mentally handicapped. The boots were bought by Tom and Anne Killoran of Tobercurry, whose bar and restaurant in the town are famed far and wide for all the artefacts hanging from its roof, reflecting life as it was some fifty or more years ago: ploughs and harrows, pots and pans—you name it; and among them all Mongey's boots. If you call you'll see them, and you'll wonder how players could run in them at all. Éamonn tells the story:

A few years ago, after heart surgery, my wife and I journeyed west for a holiday during my convalescence, and we decided to visit Killoran's and see the old boots again. On entering we ordered coffee and enquired of the man at the bar about the boots and who owned them, etc. He told us they belonged to a fellow named Mongey who won all-Irelands with Mayo about fifty years before. He then added: 'You know, the same Mongey looked old when he was playing and often wore a cap to hide his baldness, and I do believe the so-and-so is still alive.' Now what could I say but laugh?

This story, told at a gathering of Mayo people resident in Galway in May 1997, on the eve of Mayo's first victory over Galway since 1951, brought the house down. There also were other members of the Mayo team from the halcyon days, Joe Staunton and Pádhraic Carney. All three had starred on that famous day in 1951.

20

ST VINCENT'S AND THE WONDERFUL DUBLINERS OF THE FIFTIES

I n this history of Gaelic football there have been chapters heralding the emergence of wonderful county teams, the details of different winning sequences, the birth of new football powers that captured the imagination of the country; but it is doubtful whether anything touched the sporting nerve of Ireland quite so much as the emergence of the native Dublin team of the nineteen-fifties, backboned by the great St Vincent's club, possibly the greatest Gaelic football club team ever.

It was a marvellous time to be playing and following the game; and though Dublin footballers captured only one all-Ireland in that decade, the wearers of the sky blue were the talk of the nation. I'm privileged to have known them all and to have played against them on many occasions.

Last year the first St Vincent's team to win the Dublin senior football championship, that of 1949, was honoured in a golden jubilee celebration. That success was the beginning of a marvellous club sequence that saw them win thirteen Dublin senior football titles in fifteen years. As Tony Hanahoe, another St Vincent's hero of a later age, said on the night, 'Their likes won't be seen again.' That St Vincent's club team, wrote Tom Humphries in the *Irish Times,* 'created a standard and a rule [Dublin players for Dublin teams] which profoundly influenced the GAA in Dublin city.'

Just picture the scene when Dublin won their first national football league title in 1953, defeating the all-Ireland champions, Cavan, by 4-6 to 0-9 with a team of fifteen Dublin players, all products of the primary school leagues. Many of them shared the same classrooms in primary and secondary school, fourteen of them from St Vincent's club (together with the goalkeeper, Tony O'Grady of Air Corps). On that famous day Dublin wore the St Vincent's club jersey—white with a blue band— and Mícheál O'Hehir had the entire country on its toes as he regaled us with Dublin's (that is, St Vincent's) style of play, which led the all-Ireland champions a merry dance; and the newspapers next day raved about them. At that point it seemed that Dublin might be on the threshold of a run of all-Ireland successes; but it was a decade of keen competition, and Meath, Kerry, Galway and Louth won all-Ireland titles before Dublin eventually climbed the all-Ireland mountain in 1958.

For all of us who lived through that post-war time the names of those young Dubliners from the fifties come tripping off the tongue: the Freaneys (Ollie and Cyril), Kevin Heffernan, Mick Mangan, Danno Mahony, Jimmy Lavin, Mick Moylan, Marcus Wilson, bespectacled Nicky Maher, Jim Crowley and his midfield partner of many a battle, Maurice Whelan, Dessie Ferguson, Jock Haughey, Tony Young, Tim Mahony, Cathal O'Leary, Norman Allen, Bernie Atkins—all Vincent's men, later to be supplemented and complemented by Dubliners from other clubs.

About this time, while I was a clerical student in St Patrick's College, Maynooth, I remember the stir in the place when word spread that Mossie Whelan was one of the workmen helping to renovate the old St Mary's building in the college. We quickly identified him as one of the men putting a new roof on the building. He was blissfully unaware that his every movement was monitored by many of the student body. Years afterwards, in the company of Jim Crowley, I told him of our adulation and how much he helped to put sparkle into an otherwise mundane, often dreary life.

Dublin, after great League campaigns, had some sensational early exits from the Leinster senior football championship in the early fifties. In fact they lost in close games to Meath in three successive years, 1951–3, all these games at provincial venues. Then Offaly, a rising force, beat them in 1954.

But 1955 saw a new Dublin force on the march. The men from the capital came storming through the League, completely mastering the all-Ireland champions, Meath, in the final by 2-12 to 1-3. The Vincent's-powered forward line, with Ollie Freaney as spearhead and Kevin Heffernan as a roving full-forward, played precision football, and I remember travelling to that final from Enniskillen, where I was working, with the former Monaghan footballer Father Tom Marren. We couldn't see anybody to beat them in the championship later. And so it proved—almost.

Dublin came flying through Leinster and once again demolished Meath, this time by 5-12 to 0-7, before a record crowd of almost 50,000 (43,000 had watched the 1955 national football league final). Kevin Heffernan, described by Pádhraic Puirséal of the *Irish Press* as 'the Scarlet Pimpernel of Gaelic football,' had one of his greatest games on no less an opponent than the doyen of full-backs, Paddy O'Brien, then nearing the end of an illustrious career. It was forward play at its best. Eleven St Vincent's players were on the winning team that brought to the Liffey its first Leinster football senior title since 1942. The native-Dubliner policy was bearing fruit. They looked invincible that warm July day in 1955. It was a glorious summer, and I was enthralled with Dublin's play from my seat in the upper deck of the old Cusack Stand.

But the first weakness surfaced in the all-Ireland semi-final against an ageing Mayo team when Dublin were held to a draw, 0-7 to 1-4 for Mayo. Mayo's temporary halting of the Dublin surge was due to a first-class midfield display by John Nallen and by Paddy Prendergast's curbing of the threat of the roving Kevin Heffernan. Prendergast was much more mobile than Paddy O'Brien and followed Kevin all over the place, with success.

On the previous Sunday, Cavan, another ageing side, had drawn with Kerry, 1-13 to 2-10, in a game that featured a wonderful individual display of wing-back football from Jim McDonnell. Left-half-back is a position that has produced wonderful players over the years; but it's doubtful whether any all-Ireland semi-final witnessed as spirited a display as that given by the blond County Cavan teacher that day.

The replay of both games was fixed for Sunday 11 September in Croke Park, and on this historic occasion Kerry easily defeated Cavan; but Dublin had to show true grit to win by 1-8 to 1-7. The prospect of a Kerry v. Dublin final captured the imagination of the land.

I'll never forget the build-up to that final. The native-Dublin policy took the capital by storm, especially north Dublin, where St Vincent's had their base. Kerry trained quietly under Dr Éamonn O'Sullivan and in their own self-effacing way built up the challenge as an insurmountable one. At full-back they selected Ned Roche, a deceptively ponderous-looking player who, it was freely forecast, would be destroyed by Kevin Heffernan's roving tactics. That was not how it turned out.

Hype and media attention around all-Ireland finals really started in 1955. We had no television then, and Mícheál O'Hehir was king of the air waves; his contribution to the popularity of Gaelic games is at last getting the credit it deserves. The press was sacred then, and the views of John D. Hickey in the *Irish Independent*, Pádhraic Puirséal and Mick Dunne in the *Irish Press*, Pato (Paddy Mehigan) in the *Irish Times* and Seán Óg Ó Ceallacháin in the *Evening Press* were read with fervour, both before and after games. I remember savouring the atmosphere in the capital city as a group of us walked up and down O'Connell Street on the eve of the final, meeting friends and discussing the pros and cons with supporters we had never met before. Then a white horse ridden by a supporter dressed in the Dublin colours led thousands of Dublin supporters in a parade through O'Connell Street, something totally unexpected and absolutely fitting; for it was a salute to the arrival on the all-Ireland scene of the native Dubliner. All who were privileged to be there remember with nostalgia that night of innocent fun.

What all-Ireland day, 1955, meant to the native Dubliners can only be expressed by one of themselves. In the history of St Vincent's Club this extract says it all:

> All-Ireland final day 1955 is remembered as one of the most colourful and emotion filled days in all-Ireland history. It was the day that for the first time Hill 16 became the undisputed property of Dublin supporters. To have stood on the Hill that day, is to boast of a singular honour and to lay claim to have been part of one of Ireland's great sporting occasions. For the thousands who crossed Ballybough Bridge and made their way to the terraced slopes, the thrill of at last seeing the sky blue of an all-Dublin team take the field in an all-Ireland final transcended all previous experiences.

But, as happened so often in the past—whether it was Wexford or Kildare, Cavan or Mayo, Galway or Louth—Kerry were too seasoned and too wily when the big day came.

It was my second all-Ireland football final, and with Peter Tierney I sat beside Jim Crowley's wife, Mary O'Leary (sister of Cathal), and her sister Sheila. The excitement was incredible as a record attendance of 87,000 (two entrances were forced open, which means an actual attendance of perhaps 90,000) roared for the march-round, that wonderful ritual unique to Gaelic games, reflecting the great contrast of colours. Kerry was led by John Dowling of Tralee, while Denis Mahony of St Vincent's led out the men in sky blue. The crowds on Hill 16 and the canal end swayed to and fro. In those days the wall at the railway end was seated end to end. Sometimes supporters climbed onto the roofs of the stands; yet there were few, if any, accidents.

Kerry won in the end by 0-12 to 1-6. Ned Roche didn't follow Kevin Heffernan all over the place but manned the full-back position with credit, while the corner-backs, Jerome O'Shea and Micksie Palmer, played a stormer of a game. John Cronin was a tower of strength at centre-half-back.

Kerry were well on top as the game drew to a close, leading 0-12 to 0-6. But just when everybody ruled Dublin out, Ollie Freaney scored a goal from a 21-yard free. Dublin now threw everything at Kerry in what John D. Hickey described as 'a glorious finish that compensated for a struggle that did not come up to expectations.' He selected Micksie Palmer and Seán Murphy as his Kerry stars and Jim Crowley as Dublin's number 1. For my part I remember it as a game in which Kerry's great skill and experience were too much for a raw and inexperienced Dublin team, who would benefit enormously from the contest. The wisdom of 'the old dog for the hard road' was never better exemplified. I have been present at every all-Ireland final save two since then, and I look back on this as one of the great all-Ireland final occasions.

Nothing surpasses the feeling when your own county triumphs, but that's a passionate thing: you're better able to assess the mood, the emotion and the historic nature of events when your own county is not involved.

Dublin's football machine was to achieve its ambition in 1958. And they did it with style. Now under the captaincy of Kevin Heffernan, they first won the national football league, defeating Kildare in the final. My own Galway team had a battle royal with them in the semi-final, only to lose to a pointed free by Ollie Freaney with the last kick of the game—a cruel way to lose a semi-final, but a lovely way to win it.

Derry, having come out of Ulster for the first time, surprised Kerry in the semi-final when two goals on a slippery pitch from the cultured half-forward Seán O'Connell won the day for the Derry men. It was the first time the public really saw the great Jim McKeever in action. For a lightly built man he was one of the most graceful fielders of a ball ever to play in Croke Park. Like Seán Purcell of Galway—the greatest player I have ever seen—the man had style.

While the arrival of Derry as an all-Ireland team commanded attention, this final didn't quite capture the imagination in the way the 1955 one did. The native Dubliner wasn't a wonder any more. Dublin had learnt from 1955 and had built a team on more solid lines. Paddy O'Flaherty in goal was agile and fearless. The full-back line of Lar

Foley, Marcus Wilson and Joe Timmons took no prisoners. The half-back line of Cathal O'Leary, Jim Crowley and Johnny Boyle had an attacking flair; and the new midfield of John Timmons and Seán 'Yank' Murray was full of football. The forwards were now well known. Was their day of fulfilment at hand?

All neutrals were for the underdogs, Derry, who now threatened to be the first team to bring the Sam Maguire Cup across the border. But bravely though they fought, they bowed the knee to a superior force and lost in the end by 1-12 to 1-9. But not without giving Dublin a rare fright. Dublin led by 0-8 to 0-4 at half time, aided by the wind; but with Jim McKeever in majestic form, Derry levelled the score after just ten minutes of the second half. Now Dublin played a master-stroke in bringing the versatile Lar Foley to midfield and bringing on Maurice Whelan in defence. When Paddy Farnan goaled, Dublin's forward machine went into overdrive, and they won deservedly, though not quite as convincingly as the score suggested (Dublin's second goal came in lost time). The native Dubliner was at last king of the Gaelic football world.

The following Sunday, Dublin defeated New York to win the St Brendan's Cup to complete the grand slam. This was their winning team:

Paddy O'Flaherty

Lar Foley   Marcus Wilson   Joe Timmons

Cathal O'Leary   Jim Crowley   Johnny Boyle

Seán Murray   John Timmons

Pádhraic 'Jock' Haughey   Ollie Freaney   Dessie Ferguson

Paddy Farnan   Johnny Joyce   Kevin Heffernan (*captain*)

Substitutes: Maurice Whelan for Seán Murray, Paddy Downey for John Timmons.

21

GALWAY'S GLORIOUS YEARS

The early fifties were a pretty barren period for Galway football. The emergence of Roscommon in the early forties and the re-emergence of Mayo in the late forties and early fifties saw Galway striving at their coat-tails. It's difficult to be objective when you're involved in it all yourself, but it was a great time to be there, when you could see a resurgence in the maroon-and-white in the distance. No matter how low the standard drops, there is a deep interest in the game in north and west Galway, though it has fallen considerably of late in the Ballinasloe area.

It had been very close in the epic 1948 Connacht final draw and replay against Mayo; but the first real sign of a Galway return came with a wonderful first all-Ireland minor title in 1952. My younger brother Brian was captain of that team, which included Gerry Kirwan, later to win a senior title in 1956. An older brother, the late Father Paddy Mahon, had been elected chairman of the Galway Football Board early in 1952 and remained in that position for almost twenty years. If ever there was a man with a greater passion for Gaelic football or love of Galway, I haven't met him. Seán Purcell, Galway's greatest player ever, described him in an interview in the *Irish Press* in 1957:

> A young man, Fr. Paddy brought enthusiasm to the Board. Ever hopeful, he never lost faith and his confidence was infectious.

The secretary of the board was the former star and 1938 all-Ireland captain John 'Tull' Dunne, a tireless worker for Galway football all his life. A man often described as 'the soul of Galway football', he is remembered as an institution whose catchphrases in pre-game pep talks, such as 'Make every post a winning-post,' are often recalled.

The first real sign of life came in 1954 when the national football league champions of the month before, Mayo, were defeated by

Galway in Tuam by 2-3 to 1-5. We had a team of no-hopers, it seemed; nobody gave us a chance. It was my first senior football championship game against Mayo. Seán Purcell at full-back gave a majestic display, and we were all chaired off the field in triumph afterwards. Never since have I seen a Galway following quite so happy, except perhaps after the all-Ireland win over Kildare in 1998. The cheering in Tuam Stadium that day lasted for ten minutes after the game. Three years earlier Mayo had overwhelmed Galway at the same venue. Afterwards, Galway won their first Connacht final against Sligo, also in Tuam, in a close one, and failed to the all-Ireland champions, Kerry, in Croke Park in the semi-final by 2-6 to 1-6.

It was my first game in Croke Park, the first of six semi-finals played there. It's a great experience to represent your county at that stage. You're extremely nervous, with feet of putty, and the roar of the crowd is awesome. But you gradually get used to it; most players are affected, so you know you're not alone. But all in all it's a great feeling, and once the baptism is over you crave a return.

We pummelled Kerry at the end of that game after Seán Purcell switched from full-back to midfield. My own opposite number that day was the late Paudie Sheehy, as sporting an opponent as one could hope to meet and a most accomplished and stylish player. Our team learnt from the experience, and when we came surging out of Connacht again in 1956 there was a more confident air about Galway's approach. We had appointed two county team managers, John Dunne and Brendan Nestor. In a selection poll for captain voted on by the panel, Jack Mangan was chosen, with myself as vice-captain. Billy O'Neill, an army officer based in Galway and left-half-forward on the team, was chosen as trainer. He ran the guts out of us around Kenny Park, Athenry, and we raced out of the west with easy wins over Mayo in Castlebar by 5-13 to 2-5, Roscommon in Tuam by 1-9 to 0-2, and Sligo in their own Markievicz Park by 3-12 to 1-5. An all-Ireland title beckoned.

Tyrone had won in Ulster for the first time, and a wave of northern euphoria swept behind the team on the road to Croke Park. Jackie Teggart, my immediate opponent in the semi-final, was the star of the 1956 Ulster final, alongside such players as Thady Turbett, the Devlins (Jim and Eddie), Jody O'Neill, the captain, Iggy Jones, Paddy Corey, Frankie Donnelly, and John Joe O'Hagan. A huge crowd of 54,000 attended Croke Park for a dour struggle, which Galway just managed to win, by 0-8 to 0-6. At one point in the second half Iggy Jones, in an amazing solo run, knifed through Galway's defence; but a superlative save from the goalkeeper, Jack Mangan, saved Galway's bacon.

Now it was all go for the final against Cork, which was delayed until 7 October because of a polio outbreak in that county.

It was a wonderful time in County Galway. The training sessions in Tuam Stadium had huge attendances of followers, eagerly looking for tickets for the game. It became difficult to sleep at night. Would the big day ever come?

We stayed in the Grand Hotel, Malahide, where the Leitrim minors, who were playing Dublin in the minor final, also stayed. It was a long night; sleep was hard to come by. The morning wait was even longer; but before we knew it we were on our way to Croke Park, with Father Paddy playing the accordion at the front of the bus and all of us singing. The final flourish was an emotional rendering of 'The West's Awake'. We entered the dressing-room under the old Cusack Stand—a dreary place before games: the smell of wintergreen; the sound of football studs on boards; John Dunne giving the pep-talk: 'Fifteen men from Galway were always as good as ...' Then the eerie feeling as the fresh air from the tunnel hits your face, followed by an absolute crescendo of noise. After the photo call you are in the march-round, and you silently meditate. This is the hour.

Time has not erased the memory of the marvellous displays of Seán Purcell, Frank Stockwell, and Jack Mangan—all from Bishop Street, Tuam—who had grown up together and gone to school together and knew each other inside out. This was the day Frank Stockwell scored 2-5 from play (he had another goal disallowed), many of the scores a direct result of passes from Seán Purcell. Some time later this pair were labelled the 'Terrible Twins'. The partnership was never better than in this final. I have always regarded Seán Purcell as the greatest player I've seen. What a joy it was for me to play directly behind him all those years! He could play anywhere. He had balance, style, versatility—everything. This was his greatest day.

Frank Stockwell was years before his time. He had style in abundance and marvellous appeal, and his ball control was unique. It was an epic game, which we won eventually by 2-13 to 3-7 after surviving a wonderful Cork rally in which 'Toots' Kelleher scored two marvellous goals. Galway led at half time by 2-6 to 0-6, but there were times when we were hanging on, especially with six minutes to go, when Eric Ryan cut the deficit to the minimum. But then Purcell and Stockwell sealed our success with late points.

Afterwards there was pandemonium. We were all carried shoulder high off the field towards the Hogan Stand, where Jack Mangan, our captain, spoke eloquently. This was the team:

Jack Mangan (*captain*)

Seán Keeley	Gerry Daly	Tom 'Pook' Dillon
Jack Kissane	Jack Mahon	Mick Greally
Frank Evers	Mattie McDonagh	
Jackie Coyle	Seán Purcell	Billy O'Neill
Joe Young	Frank Stockwell	Gerry Kirwan

Substitute: Aidan Swords for Joe Young.

We relished the papers next morning, especially John D. Hickey's introduction.

> Greybeards may tell tall stories of the 'days when men were men' but never I feel certain, was there an all-Ireland Senior Football Final so completely and, let me add, so distressingly satisfying as the 1956 decider yesterday at Croke Park where Galway defeated Cork 2-13 to 3-7. This game had just everything.

So it wasn't all a dream!

The nucleus of that team went on to win five Connacht titles in a row and a wonderful national football league triumph over Kerry in 1957, and reached the 1959 final after an easy enough win over Down, only to fall to Kerry. The score was level going into the final quarter, 0-7 to 1-4, but, inspired by Seán Murphy, Tom Long, and Mick Dwyer, Kerry dominated the final stages, to win decisively by 3-7 to 1-4. Seán Murphy's display at right-half-back goes down as one of the finest defensive displays ever seen in a final. A great footballer chose an all-Ireland final to show his talents at their best, as Seán Purcell did in 1956.

New players were now emerging in Galway; the 1956 team gradually rode into the sunset. Galway's greatest era was dawning.

The friendship of that 1956 bunch, built on service together in many a battle, lives on; defeats had to be faced and lived with too. We had a fine midfield partnership of Frank Evers and Mattie McDonagh, and Tom 'Pook' Dillon was a great piece of stuff and in many ways a father figure. Big Mattie, the baby of our squad, became the father figure of the next team to capture the headlines, which came racing out of Connacht in 1963. It was built largely on the brilliant minor all-Ireland champion team of 1960, six of whom—Johnny Geraghty, Noel Tierney, Enda Colleran, Séamus Leydon, Christy Tyrrell, and Seán Cleary—were involved in the three-in-a-row achievement of 1964-6, while Pat Donnellan, John Keenan and Cyril Dunne had played on the team that won the Connacht minor title in 1959.

In the 1963 semi-final Galway came from behind against the all-Ireland champions, Kerry, in a whirlwind finish that saw Séamus Leydon score three winning points after the effervescent Pat Donnellan appeared out of nowhere to grab a goal and drag Galway back into the game. For once Kerry suffered an experience they so often inflicted on others: defeat meted out to them as victory approached. The score: Galway 1-7, Kerry 0-8.

The final against Dublin was a different story. In a clean, sporting contest before an attendance of 88,000, Dublin's experience won the day, 1-9 to 0-10. Galway led at half time by 0-6 to 0-4; but Dublin, inspired by Des Foley, Mickey Whelan, Paddy Downey, and John Timmons, took over and, despite a really gallant effort late in the game by Galway's captain, Mick Garrett, held on to win.

The experience gained by Galway's young lions was to stand to them in the future. After a good national football league campaign ended in a surprise defeat at Offaly's hands in Tullamore, Galway almost came a cropper to Sligo in their first senior football championship game of 1964 at Markievicz Park, Sligo, winning by 2-12 to 1-12. Sligo led 1-9 to 0-3 at half time, inspired by the doyen of forwards, Mickey Kearins; but the old deliverer Mattie McDonagh saved Galway blushes with a vital late goal when their stars were Noel Tierney and Cyril Dunne. Mayo were easily beaten, 2-12 to 1-5, in the Connacht final, thus allowing this emerging team to tot up Connacht title number 2.

Meath proved difficult in the semi-final, and Galway were considered lucky to have won by 1-8 to 0-9, with Noel Tierney impeccable at full-back and Mattie McDonagh getting another important goal. Frank Stockwell had now joined Galway's managerial team and added a youthful touch as well as engendering an easy and comfortable relationship between management and panel. 'Stocky', as we called him, was always a healer and never fuelled divisions. That three-in-a-row's 'happy family' atmosphere wasn't accidental, and the chairman of the Football Board, Father Paddy Mahon, helped in the general environment and smooth-running policy of the time.

Kerry were Galway's opponents in the final and were humbled, 0-15 to 0-10. Galway were on top at all times, led at half time by 0-7 to 0-3, and coasted to a great win, with Johnny Geraghty, Cyril Dunne, John Donnellan and Seán Meade excelling.

This was the day Mick Donnellan, John's father, died in the Hogan Stand while watching his eldest son lead Galway to victory. Mick himself had played for Galway and won an all-Ireland medal in 1925. It fell to my own brother, Father Paddy, to inform John of his father's death after John's acceptance speech on the Hogan Stand. Another former Galway all-Ireland hero, Mick Higgins, our winning captain in 1934, died on the same day while watching the game on television in his home in Galway. The joy of victory was tinged with sadness as we saw the Sam Maguire Cup come into my native Dunmore on the Monday after the game in the car behind the hearse carrying Mick Donnellan's body home on his final journey. It was a tearful time as we watched the hero of our young lives, a figure who brought so much excitement to a country town, coming home for good.

This was the 1964 final team:

Johnny Geraghty

Enda Colleran   Noel Tierney   Bosco McDermott

John Donnellan (*captain*)   Seán Meade   Martin Newell

Mick Reynolds   Mick Garrett

Cyril Dunne   Mattie McDonagh   Séamus Leydon

Christy Tyrrell   Seán Cleary   John Keenan

Title number 1 had been achieved.

Galway's winning sequence continued apace before huge crowds, culminating in a national football league (home) final win over Kerry (again) by 1-7 to 0-8, Galway's goal coming near the end from the fleet-footed Séamus Leydon, which came from a pass from Mattie McDonagh following a very doubtful pick-up by the Ballygar man.

Kerry were now more or less frustrated by Galway's dominance. A few years ago Mattie McDonagh was playing golf in Ballybunnion with his three-in-a-row colleagues Pat and John Donnellan and Bosco McDermott. As they approached their golf balls on the fairway three other golfers approached on a parallel fairway. Mattie, on his way to his ball near the rough, found a stray ball and pocketed it. He moved on, and as he was about to play his own ball he distinctly heard one of the golfers on the other fairway say: 'You picked it foul.' Mattie, thinking he had pocketed one of the others' ball, immediately retreated to the place where he found it and was about to drop it back when the same voice reassured him: 'I'm not talking of that ball at all—I'm referring to the ball you picked foul in 1965.' They don't forget in Kerry!

The Connacht Council had wisely fixed Galway with a straight entry into the 1965 Connacht final because of their national football league exertions, which saw them win the title on aggregate scores in New York after an exciting two-game series with the exiles. Sligo reached the Connacht final, and a leaden-footed Galway team had great trouble in winning by 1-12 to 2-6, being best served by John Donnellan, big Mattie, John Keenan, and Christy Tyrrell. The highlight of the day was the first-half aerial duels of Mickey Durkan against Noel Tierney. We don't see this kind of combat any more.

. Down were beaten 0-10 to 0-7 in a semi-final game in which their poor shooting contributed to their defeat; but Galway, after surviving a third-quarter onslaught, took over in the end. Enda Colleran, now captain, really inspired the team against Down.

The final against Kerry was almost an exact repeat of the 1964 one. No goals again; Galway's combination was still too much for Kerry. The score: 0-12 to 0-9. The game was not as sporting as previous clashes of the counties; perhaps these teams were meeting too often. Only punched passes were in vogue at this time, and Galway had mastered the art of point-scoring with the fist from close range. Martin Newell was tremendous at left-half-back; it was his greatest hour. Speedy and intelligent and one of the most sporting of men, Newell had, and still has, a wonderful sense of humour. The only change from the 1964 team was Pat Donnellan for Mick Reynolds at midfield.

And so the winning sequence continued until Longford won their first national football league title, defeating Galway in the final by 0-9 to 0-8. I listened to that game on radio, being a patient in Galway Regional Hospital after a hernia operation. Mícheál O'Hehir in his generous way sent me good wishes on the air, and later that night John Donnellan arrived in my room with a first-hand account of the game. After the initial shock, everybody was delighted for Longford, whose first taste of football glory this was. Names like Barden, Hanniffy, Flynn, Murray, Gillen, Donlon, Burns and Gearty are remembered with great pride in the football-loving county of Longford, where St Mel's College has consistently produced footballers of quality and teams of repute. Nurseries like St Mel's and St Jarlath's College, Tuam, St Colman's College, Newry, St Brendan's, Killarney and St Patrick's College, Maghera, are invaluable in their own areas.

Would Galway now go on to three in a row? It always gets that little bit harder. The first win was over Roscommon, 1-11 to 0-6, in Castlebar, with the newcomers Tom Brennan and Liam Sammon in action and Michael Moore in goal for the injured Johnny Geraghty. John Keenan's goal from a penalty on a very wet day was decisive. The Connacht final win over Mayo in Castlebar is still remembered as a classic. It was a repeat of all that was great between these rivals in the thirties, with Galway winning by 0-12 to 1-8 in a dramatic finish. First a glorious point from a sideline kick by Cyril Dunne from the right corner, and a punched point by Liam Sammon for the winner after a long drive downfield by John Donnellan. The kick-out after that score signalled the end of the game. Mayo players and supporters were crestfallen; their chances of lowering Galway were coming soon. Another newcomer, Jimmy Duggan, straight out of St Jarlath's College, was an impressive addition to Galway's team. It was one of those magical occasions still remembered in the west when bygone days are recalled. Cork had beaten Kerry in Munster; so new opponents in the semi-final added variety and excitement.

Cork proved to be difficult opponents before losing by 1-11 to 1-9, largely through Johnny Geraghty's brilliance in goal and Cyril Dunne's power-scoring of 1-7 in attack. Now the maroon-and-white were in their fourth successive all-Ireland final, this time against Meath. Mayo defeated Dublin in the minor final, and it was the first time I heard the chant of 'Mayo! Mayo! Mayo!' Galway fans took the cue and launched the 'Galway! Galway! Galway!' chant for the senior final.

Galway really turned on the style in the first half and led Meath 1-6 to 0-1 at half time, the goal coming from the old reliable Mattie McDonagh, from a centre by Cyril Dunne. Though Meath rallied somewhat, the score of 1-10 to 0-7 didn't do justice to Galway's superiority. Galway's stars were Noel Tierney and Pat Donnellan, with the newcomers Coleen McDonagh and Jimmy Duggan fitting in perfectly. Duggan showed no nerves at all, and there was no prouder man there than his father, Joe, who had the unenviable record of having played on losing Galway teams in three successive all-Ireland finals, 1940–42. Justice was done at last. John Donnellan, who had lost his place to Coleen McDonagh, came on to a rousing cheer near the end. The only changes from the 1965 team were Coleen McDonagh at right-half-back for John Donnellan, Jimmy Duggan at midfield for Mick Garrett, and Liam Sammon on at right-corner-forward instead of Christy Tyrrell.

Nineteen players in all took part in the three winning finals, and Mattie McDonagh became the first Connacht man to win four all-Ireland senior football championship medals—a record he still holds—as well as the only Connacht man to win ten Connacht senior football championship medals.

Little did we think that day that this marked the end of Galway's greatest era. Mayo came along a year later in Pearse Stadium, Salthill, to beat Galway decisively after a trip by Galway to New York also ended in defeat on aggregate scores to the home side in the 1966/7 national football league final. Many of the three-in-a-row stars retired, or were retired, prematurely. Some Galway folk almost took winning for granted. They couldn't wait to see a new team emerge. It was thirty-two years before the Sam Maguire Cup came over the Shannon again.

22

LOUTH'S ALL-IRELAND SUCCESS, 1957

There has always been a thriving Gaelic football tradition in County Louth. We have seen how Louth's early all-Ireland victories of 1910 and 1912 and their epic Croke Memorial Football Tournament games with Kerry in 1913 (draw and replay) attracted huge attendances and paved the way for the GAA's purchase of Croke Park. There followed a drought; but the flame never died. It sparked again in the thirties, when Louth lost three Leinster finals in four years (1934–7), losing out to Dublin in a second replay in 1934.

That resurgence was maintained and heightened in the forties and got a huge injection with Louth's first two all-Ireland minor titles, in 1936 and 1940, when the team also won three Leinster minor titles in succession: 1940–42. Louth football was on the move again; the tradition established in the first decade of the twentieth century by men like Jack Carvin and Jim Smith was being passed on.

These minor successes helped pave the way for Louth's first Leinster senior title since 1912, that of 1943—a lapse of thirty-one years. On their way to the Leinster final they defeated Meath, Dublin (the all-Ireland champions), then Offaly, and won the final easily against Laois by 3-16 to 2-4. Jim Thornton and Gerry Devine shone at midfield, and the star forward Peter Corr had a personal tally of 1-8.

In the all-Ireland semi-final, before 18,000 spectators, Louth fell to Roscommon by 3-10 to 3-6 in an absorbing game. At full-back was the great Eddie Boyle, one of Louth's greatest players ever, while the forwards included the clerical students Kevin Connolly (a champion sprinter), Mickey Hardy, and Larry Carr, all in attack, with the lethal Peter Corr.

The next Leinster title came in 1948. Louth accounted for Dublin,

Longford and Meath before coming from behind to defeat Wexford in the final by 2-10 to 2-5, with Kevin Connolly outstanding at midfield, Paddy Markey a star at centre-half-back, Seán Boyle on his right also outstanding, and a strong forward line fronted by Mickey Hardy, Frankie Fagan, and Jim Quigley. In the semi-final on a windy day, Louth, after winning the toss, elected to play against the wind and were behind 1-10 to 0-1 at half-time. But they had a magnificent recovery in the second half, in which Mick Hardy scored two goals. Inspired by the brilliance of Seán Boyle at right-half-back, Cavan held on to win by 1-14 to 4-2 and went on to win the all-Ireland. A Louth all-Ireland win was getting closer.

At this time a marvellous rivalry developed, or rather reached its zenith, between the neighbours Meath and Louth. It began in 1948 when Louth beat Meath in the Leinster semi-final by 2-6 to 2-5. Then there were the three epic games in 1949, again in the semi-final (1-5 to 1-5, 3-6 to 2-9, and 2-5 to 1-7, the third game in Meath's favour), before Meath went on to their first all-Ireland title. They drew again in the Leinster final of 1950, 1-3 each, before Louth won the replay, with Nicky Roe pointing a last-minute free for the winner: 3-5 to Meath's 0-13.

The replay was a thriller, the lead changing hands all the time. Tom Conlon of Stabannon Parnells captained the side at full-back. Seán Thornton was in goal, while Hubert Reynolds lined out at full-forward.

After a lapse of thirty-eight years Louth qualified for the all-Ireland final, defeating Kerry by 1-7 to 0-8, but fell to Mayo in a closely contested final by 2-5 to 1-6. Louth's best were Tom Conlon, Seán Boyle and Paddy Markey in defence, while Nicky Roe was outstanding in attack. Louth were getting closer.

At this time the *Irish Independent* 'sports star of the week' was introduced; and the first nominee to get the coveted honour was the goalkeeper Seán Thornton. In 1950 also the first Ireland team to play the Combined Universities in an annual challenge game was selected, and Louth were represented at right-corner-back by Jack Bell.

In 1951 there was a repeat of the Louth v. Meath close rivalry, again in the Leinster semi-final. It was another draw, 0-6 apiece; and in the replay Meath edged ahead, 0-7 to 0-6. Meath later fell to Mayo in the all-Ireland final.

These Meath v. Louth games attracted huge interest, somewhat akin to that in the present rivalries of Kildare v. Meath, Dublin v. Meath, Galway v. Mayo, and Kildare v. Dublin; and for the Leinster semi-final replay there was a record attendance of 44,000 in Croke

Park. In 1951 also Louth again won the Leinster minor football crown with a team that included Kevin Beahan from Ardee, a lovely ball-player, typical of Louth's flashing forward play. Louth later fell to Roscommon on the score 2-5 to 1-3. The year 1952 saw a continuation of the Louth v. Meath saga, this time in the Leinster final, when a crowd of 44,000 saw Meath win by 1-6 to 0-8. They later fell to Cavan in a replayed all-Ireland final. But their big day was coming.

In 1953 Louth won the Leinster crown again, beating Wexford in the final, 1-7 to 0-7; and this win was preceded by the minors defeating Kildare for the minor crown by 1-6 to 0-6. The minor team had Seán Óg Flood in goal and Patsy Coleman of Ardee at right-half-back.

I have a much-thumbed first edition of Raymond Smith's book *The Football Immortals,* published in 1968. I was at the launch of the book in Dublin and cherish the autographs of the many immortals present, including the late Larry Stanley (Kildare), Paddy McDonnell (Dublin), Bobby Beggs (Galway and Dublin), Seán Flanagan (Mayo), and Pat Markey and Kevin Beahan (Louth).

A wonderful attendance of 64,000 thronged Croke Park on 23 August 1953 to see both Louth teams in their vivid red colours take on the Clare minors and Kerry seniors. The minors fell limply to Clare by 1-10 to 0-3; but the senior semi-final, played in wet conditions, was a classic game. Kerry led 3-1 to 0-5 at half-time, a two-goal salvo in two minutes rocking Louth. The day is remembered also as the one on which an unnumbered substitute came on for Louth just before half time under the name 'Kevin McArdle', cloaking the identity of Father Kevin Connolly, one of Louth's stars in the late forties during his days as a clerical student. He gave a superlative performance. Operating at the top of the left, he ranged far and wide, using his speed and strength to great effect. It was one of the greatest virtuoso performances of Gaelic football ever seen in a semi-final. Unfortunately for Louth, the goal they needed in order to win the game never came. It certainly wasn't the fault of the Louth forward Jim McDonnell, who had a blinder.

A slender youngster, Dermot O'Brien of Ardee, had made it onto the Louth fifteen. Dermot, a wonderful entertainer on the traditional music scene who works in cabaret during the summer months, was later to captain Louth in 1957. He has often told this stroy from that 1953 semi-final.

I was young and light then, and the occasion was too big for me—facing the might of Kerry in your first semi-final. To be candid, I played poorly, and the wet conditions didn't help. During the second half I was moved into left-corner-forward to face Kerry's captain, Jas Murphy—a huge man. Whatever chance I had of improving my game vanished when he gripped my hand and said, 'How are you, poor créatúr?' Shortly after, I was replaced.

Still no all-Ireland for Louth. Would the wee county ever climb Gaelic football's highest mountain again?

It was 1957 before Louth next won a Leinster senior title—their eighth in all. The Galway team of which I was a member had won the 1956 all-Ireland, and I remember this Louth team well, having played against them in the national football league a number of times. Dermot O'Brien was now their captain. Tom Conlon at full-back was nearing the end of his days. Stephen White, another great servant, was still starring at left-half-back, one of the greatest wing-half-backs I have ever seen. After wins over Carlow, Wexford, and Kildare, Louth deservedly beat Dublin in the Leinster final by 2-9 to 1-7, with Jimmy McDonnell in great form in attack and Tom Conlon marshalling the defence well. Then followed a good win over Tyrone in the semi-final, by 0-13 to 0-7. Two Mayomen then working in County Louth, Dan O'Neill and Séamus O'Donnell, gained selection for Louth, and both played a prominent part in the march to the final.

I attended that final, sitting upstairs in the old Cusack Stand. I saw many a great game in those days from the Cusack Stand and developed a great grá for the place. Louth won the final, defeating Cork by 1-9 to 1-7. John D. Hickey in the *Irish Independent* wrote:

> No matter what the future may hold, and I sincerely hope that it contains legions of great games, I will always treasure the memory of the football fury we saw at Croke Park where Louth won their first Senior all-Ireland since 1912 in ideal if overcast conditions ... The football was breath-taking in its vigour and determination and made one pine that such a spine-tingling battle would not go on until night fall rather than end in a fleeting hour.

The games were still of sixty minutes' duration. Because of a clash in colours, the teams lined out in the colours of their provinces: Cork in blue and white, Louth in green and white. Cork led by 1-4 to 0-5 at half time, but two Louth switches on the resumption worked wonders. Séamus O'Donnell and Kevin Beahan swapped places, giving an all-Mayo midfield pairing, and Stephen White changed places with Peadar Smith at centre-half-back. Instantly Louth took on a new aspect, and they never looked back.

Séamus O'Donnell was a revelation at midfield, while Stephen White was majestic at centre half-back, as were the two corner-backs, Jim 'Red' Meehan and Ollie Reilly. Kevin Beahan also inspired after going to right-half-forward. Still, it was anyone's game until the twenty-fifth minute of the second half, when Seán Cunningham rose high to punch a centred free from Kevin Beahan to the Cork net. My abiding memory is of a defiant Jim Meehan clearing his lines in a late and frenzied Cork attack.

It was Louth's first all-Ireland success in forty-five years, and the celebrations began immediately. Dermot O'Brien remembers the homecoming clearly.

> There were over forty thousand delirious fans in the streets of Drogheda when we arrived with the Sam Maguire Cup. Bonfires blazed all along the route home. It was three in the morning when we got to my native Ardee. Nobody wanted to go to bed.

All-Ireland success had come to Louth at last.

This was Louth's winning team:

Seán Óg Flood

Ollie Reilly	Tom Conlon	Jim 'Red' Meehan
Patsy Coleman	Peadar Smith	Stephen White

Kevin Beahan   Dan O'Neill

Séamus O'Donnell	Dermot O'Brien (*captain*)	Frank Lynch
Seán Cunningham	Jimmy McDonnell	Jim Roe

In 1958 Louth travelled to America with the all-Ireland hurling champions, Kilkenny, where they both played New York in the Polo Grounds and in Gaelic Park on successive Sundays. Unfortunately Louth's star dimmed after this, and, after losing the 1958 Leinster final to Dublin and the 1960 final to Offaly, they have never reached a Leinster senior final since. But the interest in Gaelic football is still alive and well, and in the intervening years Louth has produced quality players, such as Benny Gaughran, the O'Hanlon brothers, Colin Kelly, Stephen Melia, and Stephen White's son, Stefan. In recent years there have been signs of a Louth come-back; let's hope it is sooner rather than later.

23

DOWN'S BREAKTHROUGH IN THE SIXTIES

T he emergence of Down as a football power was so unexpected it was unreal. It was, however, a developing trend, this increase in the standard of Gaelic football in the north. Antrim had always been a strong football force. Armagh made a spirited effort in 1953, before falling to Kerry in a superb all-Ireland final after missing a penalty. Next up were Tyrone in 1956 and 1957, who lost two closely contested semi-finals, to Galway and Louth. Then came Derry in 1958, with Jim McKeever in the van, before falling to Dublin in the final after defeating the might of Kerry in the semi-final. Now it was Down's turn.

The first year that Down came to the public's notice was 1958, when they reached their first Ulster senior football final before losing to Derry (who won their first Ulster senior title that day) by 1-11 to 2-4. It was an encouraging start. Behind the scenes, though, Down established a small senior football selection committee, consisting of Maurice Hayes (then acting county secretary, now a prominent writer and a director of Independent Newspapers) and two former Down players, Barney Carr and Brian Denvir. These three men of vision decided to plan for the long term and established a four to five-year programme aimed at leading Down to all-Ireland success. They were prepared to invest heavily in their senior panel and to treat them to the best standards, and as a result a trust developed between an enlightened management structure and a panel that grew in confidence and responded with an effort and commitment not hitherto associated with Down teams.

The management structure grew to a more imaginative level in 1959 with the appointment of one of the selection committee, Barney Carr, as team manager, together with Danny Flynn as team trainer and the former player Dr Martin Walsh as team doctor. Down's management, which set a precedent for many other counties, was now fully in place, and the results were quickly to be seen by all.

I had never seen Down play—didn't even know Down's county jersey—until I lined out against them in the London County Board's Whitsun Tournament final in May 1959. In the hotel we shared with our opponents there was great excitement and a buzz surrounding these County Down lads. Our Galway team was pretty experienced then, and I remember being introduced to James McCartan, a very young-looking Seán O'Neill, Paddy Doherty, and a baby-faced young man called Leo Murphy. Then, after we raced onto the pitch at Wembley Stadium together, you couldn't but be impressed with the brand of total football Down played.

On a scorching day, in a classic game of changing fortunes, Down defeated Galway by 3-9 to 4-4 before 32,000 spectators. It was one of the most breathtaking games in my football career, opposing directly Joe Lennon and Seán O'Neill. The sight of James McCartan soloing across Wembley's green turf out of defence is one I won't forget, nor some wonder scores from Paddy Doherty and Patsy O'Hagan. Down had arrived as a football force, never to be taken lightly again. It was the beginning of a great dream and a step in the planning of a far-seeing management. We were to meet again in 1959 and many times thereafter.

Down consolidated their London success with an enterprising draw with the all-Ireland champions, Dublin, in a friendly at Croke Park, another match of classic standard, Dublin's levelling goal coming at the end of a great game. Down had already set out with heaps of style and not a little flamboyance to win their first Ulster title, defeating Antrim in Newcastle (4-9 to 1-3), followed by a draw with Tyrone (1-6 apiece) in Casement Park, Belfast, then an easy replay win by 1-12 to 0-4 to set up an Ulster final with Cavan in Clones.

The clash of David and Goliath—Down, with no title, v. Cavan, with thirty-three—took place on Sunday 9 August 1959, a day of brilliant sunshine in a brilliant summer, before 30,000 mostly delirious Down supporters. The sun shone especially on Down's football all through. They led Cavan at half time by 1-10 to 0-2 and went on to win by 2-16 to 0-7. John D. Hickey in the *Irish Independent* described the Down forwards as 'an attack of rare splendour.'

In the west the Galway team came out with style, and the repeat of the London clash was eagerly awaited. Down had given a forewarning to Galway, and we trained like demons in Tuam Stadium to match the fleet-footed Downmen in speed especially. By now Down had all Ulster raving about their new style of total football. They started brilliantly; but the Galway team showed experience in weathering the early storm and winning convincingly in the end by 1-11 to 1-4. The young Down team, so full of hope, learnt a hard lesson. But it was to be our Galway team's last hurrah, and Down's big day was about to dawn.

The defeat by Galway, instead of halting Down's gallop just checked them momentarily from the ultimate objective of national titles in league and championship. First the league, which Down won with conviction, defeating Kerry in the semi-final by 2-10 to 2-8, with Seán O'Neill scintillating; then a defeat over Cavan in the final before a record crowd of 49,000 to win Down's-first national senior title.

But the big one had still to be won. After relatively easy wins over Antrim and Monaghan, Down were through to another Ulster final tilt with Cavan at Clones. They began devastatingly with an early goal by Paddy Doherty, followed in less than a minute by another from James McCartan. But Cavan rallied and, early in the second half, tied the game. A switch bringing the versatile Tony Hadden to midfield worked wonders, and Down went on to win a second successive title by 3-7 to 1-8.

Now it was the unknown Offaly team who had come through in Leinster to challenge the men of Down in the semi-final—the beginning of a football rivalry that has lasted to this day. Offaly proved to be opposition of rare quality and led Down by 2-4 to 0-3 at half time. A fortuitous late penalty earned by the Down dynamo James McCartan and goaled by Paddy Doherty saved Down's bacon. The score: Down 1-10, Offaly 2-7.

At this point the Down management team enlisted the coaching skill of the experienced Meathman Peter McDermott, and his familiarity with the big time and his simple and easy-going approach helped to cool nerves. Offaly were beaten in a close replay, 1-7 to 1-5. James McCartan was once again a rallying force: I can still picture him racing through the field with his peculiar running gait. He was inspiration, the man to lead, to rally the crowd—the soul of Down football. He had no fear.

Down were now in their first all-Ireland final, and who better to oppose them than the men of tradition, the all-Ireland champions, Kerry. Peter McDermott's experience as county secretary in Meath, all-Ireland final star, both player and captain, and former all-Ireland final referee was invaluable now. I'll never forget the colour of that All-Ireland, which I watched from the Hogan Stand as part of a record attendance of 88,000. They say a good team makes its own luck, and so it seemed in the eleventh minute of the second half when Down, after much pressure had forced three fifties in a row, saw a speculative lob by James McCartan from about forty yards slip through the hitherto safe hands of the Kerry goalkeeper, Johnny Culloty, and into the net. Kerry fell apart after this, and Paddy Doherty goaled yet another penalty, to see Down cruise home by 2-10 to 0-8.

Croke Park went mad in the most unbelievable and happy scenes I've seen in that hallowed arena; it was the first time I saw spectators gather pieces of the sod as souvenirs. Many tears were shed in emotional scenes as Kevin Mussen raised aloft the Sam Maguire Cup, soon to travel across the border for the first time. As Sighle Nic an Ultaigh, that wonderful Down supporter all through a long life, described it in her brilliant history of the GAA in County Down, *An Dún: The GAA Story: Ó Shíol go Bláth,* it was 'a victory for every man and woman who ever played a game or sat in a committee room or raised a shout for the glory of Down.' The Down flag was hoisted on top of one of the uprights at the railway goal. 'We have come at last to win an all-Ireland,' it seemed to say, 'and we intend to stay.'

John D. Hickey in the *Irish Independent* selected James McCartan as his star, 'an indestructible character … His utter determination to serve his county is infectious.' He gave sweet praise too to George Lavery in his most glorious hour.

The celebrations on the journey home to Newry are still talked about. Seán O'Neill, in a contribution to a fortieth anniversary edition of *Gaelic Sport* in 1998, wrote about what that first victory meant to Down.

> It was the result of a superhuman combined effort by players and management which forged bonds between those who were privileged to be part of it all which remain steadfast to this day. The achievements of this group were the beginning of a great Down tradition which has been carried on from that day to this and has been an inspiration to all Down senior football teams down the years. It will always be that way.

This was Down's winning team:

Éamonn McKay

George Lavery   Leo Murphy   Pat Rice

Kevin Mussen (*captain*)   Dan McCartan   Kevin O'Neill

Joe Lennon   Jarlath Carey

Seán O'Neill	James McCartan	Paddy Doherty
Tony Hadden	Patsy O'Hagan	Brian Morgan

Substitute: Kieran Denvir for Joe Lennon.

Down kept the impetus going in 1961, beating Fermanagh first by 0-12 to 0-7, then Derry by 2-12 to 1-10, and Armagh in the Ulster final in Casement Park—a close game before a record crowd—by 2-10 to 1-10. Kerry were beaten in the all-Ireland semi-final by 1-12 to 0-9; they would never be feared again. Pat Rice had a field day.

Offaly were through to the final to renew rivalry once again. The game was only six minutes old and Offaly led by 2-2 to 0-1, but by half time, through an incredible goal by James McCartan, Down led by 3-3 to 2-3. There had been five goals in one half. It ended in a crescendo of excitement, with Down holding on to win 3-6 to 2-8 before the greatest crowd ever to attend Croke Park or any Irish sports fixture—a massive 91,000. Paddy Doherty captained the team from left-half-forward, and that half-forward line of Seán O'Neill, James McCartan and Paddy Doherty is the best I have ever seen. The only changes from 1960 were John Smith for Kevin O'Neill at number 7 and P. J. McElroy for Patsy O'Hagan at full-forward.

It was a great decade for Down football. The Sam Maguire Cup came three times, the third occasion being 1968. There were three national football league titles, a St Brendan's Cup, and an east-to-west tour of the United States. The county contested twelve Ulster senior football championships in a row, from 1958 to 1969, winning seven, and won every senior all-Ireland final they reached.

1968 was another wonderful year for Down. First there was a national football league title, in which they defeated Galway in the semi-final, Kildare in the final. Some of the great ones of 1960 and 1961 were there to lend experience to younger men inspired by the feats of the early sixties. Joe Lennon was now captain, and there to help guide the youngsters were Seán O'Neill, now a top-class full-forward, Dan McCartan, and the evergreen Paddy Doherty. Wins over Derry (1-8 to 1-6), Donegal (2-4 to 0-8) and Cavan (0-16 to 1-8) in the Ulster final were followed by an all-Ireland semi-final win over Galway, 2-10 to 2-8, in which the corner-back Tom O'Hare gave a brilliant display.

In the final, Down defeated Kerry (yes, again) by 2-12 to 1-13, helped by a superb goal by Seán O'Neill that only he could score, showing marvellous reflexes to edge a rebound off the post over the Kerry line. With two minutes to go, Down led by six points, Kerry's consolation goal on the stroke of time giving a misleading impression of Down's dominance.

The winning Down team was:

Danny Kelly

Brendan Sloan   Dan McCartan   Tom O'Hare

Ray McConville   Willie Doyle   Joe Lennon (*captain*)

Jim Milligan   Colm McAlarney

Mickey Cole   Paddy Doherty   John Murphy

Peter Rooney   Seán O'Neill   John Purdy

Substitutes: Larry Powell for Joe Lennon; George Glynn for Larry Powell.

New players had come along to carry on the proud tradition, none better than the superlative midfielder Colm McAlarney, who was named RTE's 'man of the match'. Mícheál O'Hehir, who interviewed him after the presentation, asked what his thoughts were before the match when he knew his opponent was the legendary Mick O'Connell.

'I thought he was the greatest midfielder ever,' replied Colm.

'And in the light of your great game against him in the final,' asked Mícheál, 'what do you think of him now?'

It was a testing question for the mild-mannered Down man. Back came the reply: 'I still think he's the greatest midfielder ever.' In those days, star players knew how to win with dignity.

In 1968 Gerry Brown was team manager and Des Farrelly the trainer. The back-room team of officials consisted of Paddy O'Donoghue, T. P. Murphy, Gerry Brown, Des Farrelly, Dan Rooney, and George Lavery. In the early victories of the sixties the chairman of the Down County Board was the ever-loyal George Tinnelly. No man better deserved to be captain of the great ship on their greatest voyage.

I can't end this tribute to Down without saluting my favourite Downman of them all: Terry McCormack, a former star, who I met in the early sixties, when Down were in their heyday. I cherish the memories of pleasant days at games; his home in Warrenpoint was like our own, where football discussions could last for hours and from where he too travelled to a game Sunday after Sunday. The greatest and truest Down fan of all.

24

CORK'S YEARS OF FOOTBALL GLORY

No history of Gaelic football would be complete without a chapter devoted to Cork's football glory. It began in the early days of the GAA—in 1890, in fact with Cork (Midleton) defeating Wexford (Blues and Whites) by 2-4 to 0-1 on 26 June 1891. It was Cork's first all-Ireland senior football title; and Midleton is now very much a hurling town.

Cork's next all-Ireland success was in 1911, when Cork (Lees) defeated Antrim (Shauns) by 6-6 to 1-2 on 14 January 1912. That winning team was captained by Mick Mehigan (brother of Paddy), and the selection included Jerry Beckett and Jack Young (Dunmanway), whose sons Derry and Éamonn were members of the next Cork team to win the all-Ireland, in 1945.

In earlier times, Cork football always lived in the shadow of Kerry. Between 1909 and 1945 they never beat Kerry in a Munster final, and the two teams seldom met at that stage then; but their win in 1945 over Kerry by 1-11 to 1-6 was the start of an upward trend, which gained momentum until a time has now been reached when Cork football is up there alongside Kerry and well capable of beating them at any level. This breakthrough took time, and one name in particular, that of Billy Morgan, will for ever be associated with Cork's rise in standard.

The tradition of Gaelic football was rooted in west Cork: Clonakilty, Macroom, Dunmanway, Béarra, Skibbereen, Glengarriff. Around 1945 a fine bunch of players formed a team in Collins Barracks, and five of these army men—Éamonn Young, Mick Tubridy, 'Togher' Casey, Moll Driscoll, and Caleb Crone—were on the 1945 Cork team. These, together with the west Cork men, mostly from Clonakilty, together with the Cork city man Jack Lynch, later to become Taoiseach, made up the 1945 team.

In 1943 Cork had beaten Kerry (in a replay) for the first time in thirty-three years but fell to Cavan after beating Tipperary in the 1943 Munster final by a point. Cork fell to Tipperary in 1944, but they started 1945 by defeating Tipperary in a close contest by a single point, 1-7 to 1-6, after a disputed winning point from Jim Cronin, and then beat Kerry in the Munster final by 1-11 to 1-6.

Then followed a superb win over Galway in the all-Ireland semi-final by 2-12 to 2-8. I remember listening to Mícheál O'Hehir's broadcast of that game, which he described as a classic, and marvelling at the wonderful performance from the Galway midfielder Tom Sullivan, lauded afterwards in the *Tuam Herald* (under a headline 'Sullivan versus Cork') for his individual performance. But I recall too the brilliance of Weeshie Murphy, Tadhg Crowley, Éamonn Young, Fachtna O'Donovan, and Moll Driscoll in goal.

Cavan won the other semi-final, defeating Wexford by 1-4 to 0-5 before 45,000 spectators. Cavan were fancied to win the final; but having to field without the injured Mick Higgins was a severe handicap. Cork led at half time by 1-4 to 0-5 (Mick Tubridy got the goal). Cavan pressed hard in the second half, but Jack Lynch's change to midfield helped restore parity—in fact he started the move that led eventually to Derry Beckett's winning goal, a vital score in Cork's win by 2-5 to 0-7, which ended a 34-year drought.

This was Cork's winning team:

Moll Driscoll

Dave Magnier   Weeshie Murphy   Caleb Crone

Paddy Cronin   Tadhg Crowley (*captain*)   Din O'Connor

Fachtna O'Donovan   Éamonn Young

Ned 'Togher' Casey   Humphrey O'Neill   Mick Tubridy

Jack Lynch   Jim Cronin   Derry Beckett

Substitute: Jim Ahern for Togher Casey.

That 1945 team is still highly regarded in County Cork, with Weeshie Murphy, Tadhg Crowley and Éamonn Young the characters and star footballers. Weeshie later became a senior GAA official in County Cork and in Munster. Tadhg was the mainspring behind Clonakilty's successful years in Cork football, when between 1939 and 1952 the club won seven Cork senior football championships after losing six county finals in seven years immediately beforehand. Tadhg was a stalwart figure on every one of those triumphs and later became a leading referee. Éamonn Young, or 'Youngy', later became one of the great characters of the GAA—county trainer, writer, raconteur; he is one of my favourite people.

Jack Lynch, better known as a hurler, had the unique record of winning six all-Ireland senior medals in a row with Cork (senior hurling 1942–4, senior football 1945, and senior hurling 1946). He never claimed to be as good a footballer as he was a hurler, but, as in hurling, he was a great competitor and served the 1945 team nobly.

Éamonn Young was the trainer of the Cork team that lost successive all-Ireland finals to Galway and Louth in the fifties, a fine team that was very unlucky not to win the Sam Maguire Cup. At the time he wrote some wonderful material for the long-defunct *Gaelic Weekly,* a little paper that went on sale every Friday and for almost twenty years was a must for many GAA fans. That team included a great half-back line of Paddy Harrington, Denis Bernard, and Mick Gould, a strong midfield partnership of Eric Ryan and Seán Moore, fine forwards in Niall Fitzgerald, Nealie Duggan, and Toots Kelleher, and two wonderful backs in Paddy Driscoll and Dan Murray. Twice in the sixties Cork also got out of Munster but in 1967 fell at the last hurdle against Meath. But better times were coming.

In the seventies Cork really began to bite at Kerry's dominance in Munster. Their first defeat of Kerry in a Munster final in that decade was a devastating 0-25 to 0-14 in the Cork Athletic Grounds in 1971, when Denis Coughlan, who came on as a substitute, inspired Cork by scoring 0-10 in all (eight from frees). Cork fell subsequently to Offaly in the semi-final by 1-16 to 1-11; but the learning process had begun.

I attended my first Munster senior football final in 1972 in Killarney on one of the hottest days I remember. Kerry deservedly beat Cork by 2-21 to 2-15. Senior championship games were now of eighty minutes' duration, rather than sixty—hence the high scoring. The atmosphere at the game was marvellous, with great banter between rival fans. Holidaying at the time in Drimoleague, I marvelled at the way Cork fans proudly waved their flags from the windows of their cars as they drove home through County Kerry, defeated but unbowed.

Mick O'Connell, though nearing the end of his days, was still a shining star, ably helped by the younger and very versatile John O'Keeffe; but the star of the day was Cork's right-half-back, Kevin Jer O'Sullivan, who gave an exhibition of clean fielding and long kicking at its delightful best. Though Kerry lost subsequently to Offaly in the 1972 all-Ireland replay, they dominated the national football league, winning the final for the third year running by defeating their 1972 all-Ireland conquerors by 2-12 to 0-14. They were firm favourites to beat Cork in the Athletic Grounds in the Munster final of 1973; but they were in for a shock.

The wonderful successes of the Cork minors in the previous decade or more paved the way. From 1961 to 1972 Cork had won five all-Ireland titles in the grade, often defeating Kerry comprehensively in Munster finals. A new name too was creeping into the honours list in Munster senior football colleges titles, that of Coláiste Chríost Rí. Cork city football clubs were beginning to make their mark on the infant all-Ireland club championships, none more so than Nemo Rangers (Billy Morgan's club), which had already won its first all-Ireland club title in 1973, defeating St Vincent's (Dublin) in a replay on 24 June 1973.

In those winning Cork minor and under-21 teams one had noted the rise of names like Kevin Kehilly, Dónal Hunt, Séamus Looney, Denis Long, John Coleman, Jimmy Barrett, Ned Kirby, Con Hartnett, Declan Barron, and Brian Murphy; but one in particular—a closely cropped lanky youngster named Jimmy Barry-Murphy—really shone out like a beacon. He exuded style, was calm and collected, and possessed that wonderful innate gift of remaining cool in a crisis near the goal. Jimmy Barry-Murphy was the minor sensation of 1972 and walked straight into the Cork team of 1973.

Captain of the Cork team of 1973 was their goalkeeper, Billy Morgan, an inspiring figure for club and county, whose quiet exterior hid a steely resolve in a long career in goal that saw him represent his beloved red-and-white in three decades, from the sixties to the eighties, and who went on to change the whole attitude to Gaelic football in County Cork. It was fitting that such a man should lead Cork to its first Sam Maguire success since 1945.

Cork's path to glory began with a bang in their defeat of Clare on 17 June by 2-14 to 0-3. Next they hammered the national football league champions, Kerry, by 5-12 to 1-15. In truth Cork destroyed Kerry in the first half, rattling in goal after goal, the full-forward line of Jimmy Barry-Murphy, the tall Ray Cummins and Jimmy Barrett wreaking havoc. All those defeats of yore were exorcised; and in truth Kerry's final total of 1-15 didn't do justice to Cork's dominance, though it must be said in Kerry's favour that they never bent the knee fully. I travelled south to see this game and admired Cork's cheeky forward play as well as the uncompromising back play of Frank Cogan, Humphrey Kelleher and the versatile Brian Murphy, a dual star like Jimmy Barry-Murphy, Denis Coughlan, and Ray Cummins.

Later I was at Croke Park when Cork trounced Tyrone in the all-Ireland semi-final by 5-10 to 2-4. On this occasion Billy Morgan led by example, and Kevin Jer O'Sullivan was brilliant at right-half-back. Galway under Liam Sammon had qualified for the all-Ireland final, a repeat of the 1956 pairing. As usual, there was great excitement in both counties in the period before the final.

The status symbol on these occasions is being able to get an all-Ireland ticket and being able to show it in advance. It's a situation that obtains to the present day. If only an all-Ireland ticket could tell its story, as it wends its way among so many hands to the eventual recipient! I have passed on all-Ireland tickets over the years, answering many distress calls, but seldom if ever do I find myself beside the person to whom I gave the ticket for the adjoining seat. Sometimes they just barely know the name of the original recipient. The ticket craze gets worse with the years, despite the growth of television coverage, which—contrary to the general opinion at its inception—has helped enormously to propagate the allure of the game and to generate appeal among a wider audience.

Galway, having lost the 1971 all-Ireland final to Offaly, were intent on going one better this time; but early on in the game the genius of Jimmy Barry-Murphy, as he wriggled his way through the Galway defence for a seemingly casual goal, suggested that a new football star was born. This goal set Cork on the road to success, and they led at half time by 1-10 to 0-6, despite an inspirational point by the Galway centre-half-back, Tommy Joe Gilmore, who raced the length of the field before making what is regarded as one of the great all-Ireland final scores. The star of that first half, when Cork threatened to destroy Galway, was the midfielder Dinny Long. Unchallenged, he seemed to race through at will. Thankfully, Galway rallied in the second half and made a game of it, inspired by Joe Waldron and Johnny Hughes and a much-improved Morgan Hughes; and after Tom Naughton goaled, the battle was on in a game best remembered for an exhibition of old-style catching and kicking at its best.

But Cork weathered the Galway storm, inspired by some fine defensive work from Frank Cogan, Con Hartnett, Brian Murphy, and John Coleman. Before an attendance of 73,000, Cork ran out deserving winners by 3-17 to 2-13. It seemed as if they were on a winning streak, which might continue a trend in senior already achieved at minor level. But though they beat Kerry in the Munster final in a very wet Killarney in 1974, other football forces on the horizon were to dominate Gaelic football for well over a decade.

This was the winning Cork team:

Billy Morgan (*captain*)

Frank Cogan	Humphrey Kelleher	Brian Murphy
Kevin Jer O'Sullivan	John Coleman	Con Hartnett

Dinny Long   Denis Coughlan

Ned Kirby	Declan Barron	Dave McCarthy
Jimmy Barry-Murphy	Ray Cummins	Jimmy Barrett

On the face of it, this Cork team deserved richer rewards. Declan Barron was a high-catching centre-half-forward of quality, and Ray Cummins was a full-forward of vision. We had to wait until the late eighties for Cork's second coming, under their manager Billy Morgan. Trainers and managers weren't then the central figures they have since become. Doney Donovan quietly trained the Cork team of 1973 to success with little fuss and less attention; but the arrival of Kevin Heffernan and Mick O'Dwyer was to change all that.

25

THE INTRODUCTION OF CLUB ALL-IRELANDS, 1971

I n the early days of the GAA it was the champion club that represented the county in the all-Ireland inter-county competitions. Thus it was that clubs such as Limerick Commercials, Young Irelands (Dublin), Laune Rangers (Kerry), Tuam Krugers, Blackrock (Cork) and Tubberadora (Tipperary) represented their counties in all-Ireland finals.

Gradually the champion clubs broadened their choice to include the best players of rival clubs within the county, until the County Board structures took over county selections and chose teams that would include the best players from all affiliated clubs. The status of the club diminished, with the inter-county all-Irelands getting greatest prominence; but the importance of the club never disappeared altogether, and inter-club competitions within counties were always given proper recognition. But the role of the club versus that of the county became a bone of contention, especially among the top clubs, many of whose members played for both club and county.

From my earliest days, when I first heard the magic voice of Mícheál O'Hehir as he extolled such legends as Christy Ring, Mick Mackey, and John Doyle, he always linked the player to his club— 'And Big Tom O'Reilly of Cornafean rises high for the ball and clears to safety'—and I often wondered where the Glen was in Cork, what kind of places were Ahane, Holycross, Tarmon, and Dingle, not to mention Faughs of Dublin or Liam Mellows of Galway. O'Hehir really knew his players, and I was proud to hear him sing the praises of Brendan Nestor from my own home place of Dunmore, County Galway. Today Mícheál Ó Muircheartaigh is equally proficient in linking the stars with their place of origin.

Over the years great clubs built up wonderful traditions within their own counties, winning titles galore—clubs such as Thurles Sarsfields, Glen Rovers (Cork), Mount Sion (Waterford), Ahane (Limerick), St Vincent's (Dublin), Tuam Stars, Ballina Stephenites, many County Kerry clubs, Cooley Kickhams (Louth), and Cornafean (Cavan). From about the forties to the sixties many of these clubs began to spread their wings, seeking new pastures in inter-club tournaments and challenge games, and a succession of wonderful rivalries developed.

In the sixties the idea of establishing an inter-club all-Ireland competition grew apace. The GAA has always been slow to change, and despite the fact that official inter-club provincial championships came into being in the mid-sixties it wasn't until the Congress of 1970 in Galway that the motion to establish a club all-Ireland was passed. The proposer of that motion was my fellow-clubman from Dunmore MacHales, Bertie Coleman, who with some others, such as Brian McEniff of Donegal, had pioneered the movement for years beforehand and had even organised an unofficial all-Ireland as an experiment to establish its viability. Thus were the club all-Irelands born, which officially came into being in 1971.

To say they had teething problems would be an understatement. Cork had vehemently opposed their inauguration, though they were soon to be great supporters, and the county has since won more titles than any other. It took some time to fit them into the scheme of things, to drum up national support, to find a suitable date for the finals, and generally to give the competitions time to find their feet. But from the beginning the clubs themselves took the new challenge seriously. Here was the chance to attain all-Ireland glory for a club, an opportunity for small localities to get a place in the sun, to be able to play in Croke Park, to tog out in the same dressing-rooms as the well-known inter-county stars—to produce their own Matt the Thresher of *Knocknagow* fame, who would do anything 'for the love and honour of the little village.' Now the club finals on St Patrick's Day attract a huge attendance, and the competition is second only in importance to the inter-county all-Ireland championship.

Despite often adverse weather conditions, because of the time of year at which they are played, it is the intense passion of the games that grips the nation. Over the years there have been many great sagas involving Kiltormer and Cashel King Cormacs, Nemo Rangers and Austin Stacks, Kilmacud Crokes and Éire Óg, to name but three examples of three series. Eugene McGee, the well-known GAA columnist from County Longford, wrote in the *Irish Independent* of 22 February 1999, after seeing Ballina Stephenites defeat Doonbeg

(Clare) in dreadful weather the day before in Ballinasloe:

> The huge success of the all-Ireland club football Championship in recent years is based on a mixture of local identity and raw courage. In today's sports world these two qualities hardly ever come together in professional or semi-professional sport, but they have always been the core values of the GAA.

On the same day Jim O'Sullivan in the *Examiner,* reviewing St Joseph's Doora-Barefield's thrilling win over Athenry by 1-13 to 1-12 in the club hurling semi-final, wrote of 'Christy O'Connor's remarkable save for St Joseph's 90 seconds into injury time' and 'the agony for the Galway champions over the decision in the 57th minute not to allow what they insisted was a legitimate point,' while later 'the controversy was unfortunate against the background of a fiercely contested game which produced intense drama over the last twenty minutes.' Drama, games of epic proportions, passion, and local pride—all necessary ingredients of the continued success of the club all-Irelands.

In my own playing days with Dunmore MacHales we had an exciting club team that won the first official Connacht senior football club title, completed in 1964, but our team had fallen away when the all-Ireland club championship was introduced in 1971. But as a club we were very much behind the idea and were thrilled when Corrofin eventually won the title in 1998, becoming the first Connacht club to do so. This helped in no small way to inspire Galway to all-Ireland success later, in much the same way that Castlegar's success in 1980 (Connacht's first all-Ireland club title in hurling) led on to Galway's all-Ireland hurling success later that year.

In 1997 I wrote a book, *For Love of Town and Village,* exploring the exciting success of the All-Ireland club championship. In researching for the book I travelled the length and breadth of Ireland, and I remember my visits to rural communities such as Kilruane and Borrisoleigh in County Tipperary and commercial towns such as Baltinglass, Midleton, Port Laoise, and Killarney, all proud of their all-Ireland club success. I couldn't help but feel sorry for that wonderful rural club Clann na nGael (Roscommon), half way between Ballinasloe and Athlone. They had contested five finals in all, four in a row from 1987 to 1990, losing all five; and yet they keep on trying. Rathnure (Wexford) played in four finals, losing all four, bringing Blackrock (Cork) to a replay in 1974. My visit to Loughguile in the Glens of Antrim to recall their win of 1983 is one I'll always cherish;

there I met men with a great love of the game and pride in winning their county's only hurling all-Ireland in any grade.

The appendixes at the back of this book carry the cold statistics of the titles won in these club all-Irelands; but you need to meet some of the men who won these finals and hear them talk with intense pride of their clubs' achievements. Tony Doran (Buffers Alley and Wexford): 'Winning the all-Ireland with Buffers Alley was my greatest thrill.' John Fenton (Midleton and Cork): 'I remember one Wednesday evening in a group of twenty-five players training on a snow-covered pitch in Midleton when we could hardly see the ball.' Charlie Nelligan (Castleisland Desmonds and Kerry): 'Every day I walk down the street of my home town, Castleisland, I meet the lads I won the club title with.' John McGurk (Lavey and Derry): 'My greatest memory of the club final is of lifting the cup and seeing the whole parish of Lavey down below me in Croke Park.' Tony O'Keeffe (Austin Stacks and Kerry): 'Our win over Port Laoise in the semi-final was the greatest game I was ever involved in. The whole occasion was brilliant; see-saw stuff, and five times we were led. One of Tom Prendergast's goals was among the best I have ever seen. Sheer skill.'

Kickham's mythical character from Knocknagow is alive and well in modern Ireland.

26

OFFALY'S THREE TITLES AND A NEW FOOTBALL POWER

The arrival of Offaly as a football power was not quite as sudden as the Roscommon bolt from the blue in the forties. Offaly contested the Leinster football final for the first time in 1907, losing to Dublin, and didn't contest it again until 1945, when they lost to Wexford. But they made everybody sit up and take notice in 1954 when they defeated the celebrated Vincent's-powered Dublin team, which was about to blossom, in the Leinster senior football championship in Port Laoise by 2-5 to 2-4.

That team, captained by Seán Foran, had some great players, such as the Casey brothers, Paddy and Mick, Peter Nolan, a fine centre-half-back, Mick Furlong, Alo Kelly, and Noel McGee, among others. In the Leinster final of 1954 Offaly lost to Meath by 4-7 to 2-10; Meath later went on to win that all-Ireland. Offaly football had found itself, and though it took some time to climb football's highest mountain, the first Leinster crown was within sight. Though great men, like those mentioned, never won an all-Ireland medal, they all helped to sow the seeds for the future.

I have seldom seen a better Offaly player than Paddy Casey, who later emigrated to America; and some older County Offaly people remember with pride the excellent midfielder Seán Donegan, like Casey a star Leinster player.

Offaly's first senior trophy was the O'Byrne Cup, which they won in Leinster in 1955, when they defeated Louth in the final by 0-10 to 1-5. Men like Paddy Casey, Paddy Fenlon, Kevin Scally and Johnny Kinahan had all cut their football teeth in 1947 in Offaly's first successful Leinster minor title. Football successes just don't come out of the blue.

Offaly's big football day came in 1960 with the securing of two

Leinster titles on the same day: the minor for the second time, the senior for the first glorious time. In the minor final Offaly beat Louth, 1-12 to 1-5; and on a bleak day for Louth they also lost the senior final, by a single point, 0-10 to 1-6. In the all-Ireland semi-final Offaly almost caused a sensation after leading Down a merry dance before a controversial penalty decision eight minutes from time gave Down a lifeline and a goal, to draw by 1-10 to Offaly's 2-7. Offaly had led at half time by 2-4 to 0-3, with goals from that great servant Mick Casey and Harry Donnelly. Down won the replay, 1-7 to 1-5, and went on to all-Ireland glory.

Offaly kept up the initiative and won a second successive Leinster senior crown in 1961, defeating Dublin in the Leinster final by 1-13 to 1-8 and Roscommon in the all-Ireland semi-final by 3-6 to 0-6 to qualify for another tilt with Down. Interest in Gaelic football was now at its height, with two relatively new teams contesting the senior final and a record attendance of 91,000. Once again Offaly started brilliantly, with two goals in six minutes from Mick Casey and Peter Daly. But Down recovered in brilliant style, to lead at half time by 3-3 to 2-3 before eventually winning by 3-6 to 2-8 in a ding-dong game. Offaly had fought the good fight, went down bravely, and got a rousing reception in O'Connor Square, Tullamore, when they returned on the Monday after the game.

This was the Offaly team unlucky not to have gone the whole way, especially in 1960—but then the team lacked the quality and flair of Down's wonderful forwards:

Willie Nolan (*captain*)

Paddy McCormack	Greg Hughes	John Egan
Phil O'Reilly	Mick Brady	Charlie Wrenn

Seán Brereton   Seán Ryan

Tommy Cullen	Peter Daly	Tommy Greene
Mick Casey	Donie O'Hanlon	Harry Donnelly

I played many times against Offaly in the fifties, having as immediate opponents Mick Casey mostly, Tommy Cullen, and Tommy Greene. Mick Casey, known as 'the blacksmith from Rhode,' was strong and fair; his fame was legendary, and he served his county team for almost twenty years, from the forties to the sixties. Though he never won an all-Ireland medal, his name is sacred in County Offaly; he was one of the truly great players and a quiet man whom it was a pleasure to encounter on the field of play.

The spirit of Offaly football was up, and this was reflected in three Leinster minor titles in 1962, 1964, and 1965, with the Faithful County winning its first and only minor crown in 1964. I remember them defeating Cork by 0-15 to 1-11; and the great fetching skill of Willie Bryan at midfield and the jinking runs of Tony McTague in attack were as clear as daylight even then. Other members of that historic squad who were later to climb the Hogan Stand were Martin Furlong, Michael Ryan, Eugene Mulligan, Mick O'Rourke, and Jody Gunning (now a sports presenter on local radio). It isn't often you get so many minors delivering later at senior level. Furlong, Ryan, Mulligan, Bryan and McTague were all on the Offaly team beaten by Kerry, 0-10 to 0-7, in the all-Ireland senior football final of 1969. Better days, however, were round the corner.

The year 1971 started well. Paddy McCormack, known as 'the iron man from Rhode', alone spanned the years of close yet fruitless encounters against the up-and-coming Down team a decade earlier. But the experience gained in 1969 was a big help now. Captain of the team was the midfielder Willie Bryan, the impressive minor of 1964, now a man among men in senior ranks.

Offaly won their fourth Leinster senior football title in 1971, marching impressively to the all-Ireland semi-final with victories over Longford at Mullingar, 1-7 to 0-3, in May, over Laois at Port Laoise, 2-12 to 0-10, in July, and an easy win over Kildare in the Leinster final at Croke Park, 2-14 to 0-6. Cork had qualified in Munster, but in the all-Ireland semi-final at Croke Park on 22 August they were deservedly beaten, 1-16 to 1-11. Galway, having beaten Down, had qualified in the other semi-final.

Mick Dunne of RTE had invited Seán O'Neill of Down and myself to be his guests before the game and again at half time, interviewing us on the sideline in front of the Hogan Stand. The analysis of games was in its infancy then; nowadays it is perhaps carried too far. I opted for Offaly, and felt fairly pleased with myself.

There is great excitement in a county when its team reaches an all-Ireland senior final. People talk of little else. The elusive all-Ireland ticket becomes almost a status symbol. Plans are hatched for the weekend trip to Dublin: hotels or guesthouses are booked; train tickets are obtained; flags are made. I had a young family at the time, and I brought them often to games or training sessions. Pearse, now a professional golfer in America, was only six then but a seasoned campaigner; he said to me one morning as he set off for school, 'Dad, my favourite colours are maroon and white.' I knew the feeling! I'm sure that if anything it was more exciting still in County Offaly at that time.

Came the day, 26 September 1971, a wet and windy Sunday of the kind we never expect but that certainly, considering the time of year, we should always be prepared for. The eighty-minute all-Ireland final was now in operation, and teams had to pace themselves for this type of game. Galway, led by Liam Sammon at midfield and powered by T. J. Gilmore, Liam O'Neill, Billy Joyce, Jimmy Duggan, and the three-in-a-row hero Séamus Leydon at left-corner-forward, raced into a half-time lead of 1-6 to 0-4, backed by a strong wind and driving rain. But they squandered too many chances by playing their corner-forwards too far out from goal. Séamus Leydon, using all his experience, got Galway's goal. Was a five-point advantage good enough?

I was late back to my seat in the Hogan Stand, just in time to see Frank Canavan careering through for a point—Galway now six points clear. Exchanges were tough in that first half. The Offaly full-back line of Mick Ryan, Paddy McCormack and Mick O'Rourke took no prisoners. Six minutes after half time, with the heavens opening, Offaly made a few significant changes, which altered the trend of the game. John Smith came on for Kieran Claffey (a family that then and now were great contributors to Offaly football), moving to centre-half-back, with Nicholas Clavin going to midfield, where his great fielding in difficult conditions tended to counter Galway's supremacy; it was fitting that he should equalise for Offaly with twenty minutes to go. John Smith starred at centre-half-back too in a very dependable way; but Offaly's man of the game was their attacking right-half-back, Eugene Mulligan.

The final twenty minutes, played in a downpour, will be best remembered for Murt Connor's goal in the twenty-first minute, a match-winning score. A cross from Seán Evans, a very impressive side-step after fielding by O'Connor, and the net bulged. But Galway fought back, and in the twenty-third minute Séamus Leydon got his second goal. Level pegging again: 2-8 to 1-11.

After this it was all Offaly scores and Galway misses. First there was a point by Seán Evans, then a fifty by Tony McTague, a few Galway misses, and the final Offaly point from Kevin Kilmurray in the thirty-seventh minute. The score: Offaly 1-14, Galway 2-8. Offaly had won their first all-Ireland title.

Most of the Offaly fans were drenched from head to foot, but they cared little. Great were the celebrations of County Offaly folk everywhere as Willie Bryan lifted the Sam Maguire Cup in triumph, then brought it home to County Offaly the following day.

This was the winning team:

Martin Furlong

Michael Ryan   Paddy McCormack   Mick O'Rourke

Eugene Mulligan   Nick Clavin   Martin Heavey

Willie Bryan (*captain*)   Kieran Claffey

Seán Cooney   Kevin Kilmurray   Tony McTague

Jody Gunning   Seán Evans   Murt Connor

Substitutes: John Smith for Kieran Claffey, Paddy Fenning for Jody Gunning.

These men have all gone into folk history in County Offaly. But the journey wasn't over yet.

There was no talk of tiredness or mental fatigue in 1972. Offaly, now captained by Tony McTague, swept through Leinster, defeating Meath in June by 2-17 to 3-5 and Kildare in the final in July by 1-18 to 2-8 before beating Donegal in the all-Ireland semi-final in August by 1-17 to 2-10. It was Donegal's first time in Croke Park, and Offaly's experience of the big time stood them well. I travelled to the game from Gleann Cholm Cille, where I was holidaying with my family. We had watched Donegal training for the game; and though Brian McEniff and Martin Carney strove heroically, Offaly were better on the day. All Offaly's championship games in 1972 were played in Croke Park—another invaluable experience.

Kerry had qualified for the final with an easy enough win over Roscommon, but their wayward shooting prevented them from winning by a wider margin than 1-22 to 1-12. Offaly's stars against Donegal were Martin Furlong in goal, Paddy McCormack at full-back, and John Smith when switched to centre-half-back. A vital switch of Seán Evans (full-forward) and Willie Bryan (midfield) before half time saw both men rise to stellar heights. That peerless reporter Pádhraic Puirséal wrote in the *Irish Press*: 'The move really won the match for Offaly.'

So on 24 September 1972 to the final against Kerry, the final every county wants to win. I missed this game because my brother, Father Paddy Mahon, a close friend as well as older brother and one of the greatest Gaelic football aficionados I ever knew, died the night before the game. One of the visitors to his death-bed in Limerick Regional Hospital had been Mick O'Connell of Kerry. But I watched the game on television, and it never really ignited till the final ten minutes, when Johnny Cooney goaled to put Offaly ahead, 1-10 to 0-8. As John D. Hickey wrote in the *Irish Independent*, 'the smouldering match went instantly on fire and from then onwards burnt with ever increasing intensity.' Paddy Downey wrote in the *Irish Times*: 'Offaly were the better team for much of the game and must look back ruefully on the fact that they were never headed from start to finish, yet let their opponents away with a draw.' My own greatest memory of the game is of Brendan Lynch's goal immediately after Johnny Cooney's one. Lynch, older brother of Paudie, was a self-effacing player who shunned the limelight. He had skill in abundance and a great left foot. After Mick O'Dwyer's equalising point with three minutes to go, 'both teams came agonisingly close to defeat,' as Jim O'Sullivan wrote in the *Cork Examiner*. The referee, Fintan Tierney (Cavan), was blamed for not awarding a free to an Offaly forward who seemed to be fouled. Kerry were denied a goal by the upright.

A draw, 1-13 all, was a satisfying result in the end for a capacity attendance of 72,000—a record for the reconstructed Croke Park. The eighty-minute final was still in vogue. The replay was fixed for 15 October, three weeks after the drawn final, and Patsy Devlin of Tyrone was chosen to replace Fintan Tierney as referee—something pretty unusual, as the same referee as a rule is chosen to officiate at a replay of a drawn game; public opinion tended to sway the choice. Offaly weren't beaten yet.

On the eve of the replay I travelled to Mick O'Connell's wedding in Killygarry, County Cavan. The place was full of Kerry GAA personalities from former years, with Mick O'Dwyer representing the 1972 team and Mick's best friend, Ned Fitzgerald (father of the 1997 hero Maurice), acting as best man. I have many memories of a lovely day in County Cavan and was honoured when asked to read out a selection of telegrams and good wishes that came from far and near.

Right from the start the replay was a much better game. Offaly, facing the wind, were level at half time, 0-8 apiece, even though after eight minutes they had lost their star forward of the drawn game, Johnny Cooney, through injury, and the stalwart half-back Eugene Mulligan, eight minutes before half time, also through injury. Mick O'Connell was playing a fine game for Kerry, but so too was his opponent, Willie Bryan.

It was a gloriously sunny day that could have been borrowed from June or July. It was still anybody's game at half time, though Offaly played with great self-assurance and ease. A 'lucky' goal, as often happens in finals, was to change the whole complexion of the game early in the second half; though these 'lucky' scores tend to favour the brave.

Kerry led for the first time in the fifth minute of the second half and then moved two points clear after eight. Now a high speculative lob from far out by Paddy Fenning hopped in front of the Kerry posts and went untouched into the net. That score and the recovery of the lead fired Offaly into over-drive. Willie Bryan gave one of the greatest individual midfield displays ever seen in Croke Park, and Kerry were over-run on the score 1-19 to 0-13, a convincing victory for the Faithful County. It was the victory Offaly fans yearned for. Kerry would never be feared again, or any other county for that matter.

The passage of time hasn't dimmed the memory of the brilliance of Willie Bryan, whom John D. Hickey praised for his 'apparently always leisured movement and the wondrous refinement with which he used every ball, irrespective of which foot he considered it expedient to use.' Great players always seem to have time on the ball. Offaly's other stars included Michael Ryan, wonderful at corner-back, Martin Furlong, so safe in goal, as always, and Kevin Kilmurray, a brainy centre-half-forward; but in truth every Offaly player lifted his game after Pat Fenning's goal. Tony McTague, the captain, was mobbed after receiving the Sam Maguire Cup. He had scored 0-10, a top marksman from frees and play. One of the really top free-takers, Tony on a solo in full flight was a joy to watch. He had a wonderful side-step and jinked his way through many a defence.

This was undoubtedly Offaly's greatest display of Gaelic football, played before a record replay attendance of 66,000. Some 30,000 fans packed O'Connor Square, Tullamore, on the Monday to cheer their heroes home, and one of the loudest cheers was for the team trainer, Father Tom Gillooly, the man behind the double all-Ireland triumph.

This was the team that won the replay:

Martin Furlong

Michael Ryan   Paddy McCormack   Larry Coughlan

Eugene Mulligan   Seán Lowry   Martin Heavey

Willie Bryan   Seán Evans

Seán Cooney   Kevin Kilmurray   Tony McTague (*captain*)

Séamus Darby   John Smith   Paddy Fenning

Substitutes: Murt Connor for Seán Cooney, Nicholas Clavin for Eugene Mulligan, Mick Wright for Larry Coughlan.

The full-forward line for the drawn game read: Paddy Fenning, John Smith, Murt Connor. This was the only line changed for the replay.

Though Offaly retained the Leinster title in 1973, they fell to

Galway in the all-Ireland semi-final by 0-16 to 2-8 and didn't surface again as a football power until Eugene McGee took over as manager in the late seventies. He guided them to three Leinster titles in a row, 1980–82, overseeing wonderful rivalries between Offaly and Dublin and also some great games with Kerry. This was the era of Matt Connor, one of the most gifted of forwards, of his brothers Richie and Murt (a hero in 1971 and 1972) and cousins Liam and Tomás of Walsh Island; Johnny Mooney, Gerry Carroll, Pádhraic Dunne, Liam Currams, the dual star, the Fitzgeralds and the Lowrys. Martin Furlong was still in goal, while Seán Lowry and Séamus Darby were continuing links with the 1972 team. Darby was to place his name indelibly in GAA history—but more of that later.

The return of Offaly at this time was a welcome injection of a new force on the football scene. Kerry and Dublin had dominated the later part of the seventies, contesting four out of five all-Ireland finals, with Dublin winning six Leinster titles in a row, 1974–9. Though Dublin and Kerry brought Gaelic football to a new plane of popularity, the sameness of it all had grown somewhat tedious, and the welcome emergence of Offaly became the inspiration for other counties.

Kevin Heffernan and Mick O'Dwyer, in the new manager-mania, ruled the media waves. Dare anyone—even Eugene McGee, who had nurtured many fine UCD teams in Sigerson Cup and all-Ireland club competitions—sit at the same table! Dublin were eventually toppled in the Leinster final of 1980 by 1-10 to 1-8 for Offaly's seventh provincial senior victory. In this game Matt Connor scored a brilliant second-half goal, one of the greatest ever seen in a Leinster final and the real match-winner that day. Subsequently, in the all-Ireland semi-final, Offaly lost to Kerry, 4-15 to 4-10, when Matt scored an incredible 2-9; but in truth Kerry were by far the better team, and Offaly were still in the learning process.

In 1981 Offaly went a step further before losing in the all-Ireland final to Kerry by 1-12 to 0-8. This game was closer than the score suggests. Kerry in 1981 had brought off yet another four-in-a-row and were now set on the first five-in-a-row all-Ireland achievement. They seemed unbeatable, and even though Offaly were gaining in experience, the minefield in getting out of Leinster was far more difficult than getting over the annual game against Cork in the Munster final.

Since 1975 all inter-county senior football championship games were of seventy minutes' duration. As a result there was less pacing of games, but fitness of a high order was still necessary for teams to be able to keep up the momentum.

Offaly began the 1982 campaign on 13 June at Croke Park with victory over Louth, 0-17 to 0-8, then on 27 June a good win over Laois at home in Tullamore by 3-13 to 1-15, followed on 1 August by a convincing win over Dublin in Croke Park, 1-16 to 1-7. Galway, trained by Mattie McDonagh, had come racing out of Connacht, but on a windy August day Offaly overcame the westerners in a ding-dong battle by 1-12 to 1-11 to qualify for another all-Ireland tilt with Kerry, who were hot favourites to win a fifth final in a row—so much so that 'five-in-a-row' songs and T-shirts proclaiming the achievement were being produced in anticipation, though a wee bit prematurely I thought. In my preview of the game in my column in the *Galway Advertiser,* under the heading 'Offaly to create a shock,' I had gone against the grain and opted for Offaly. Public opinion was decidedly anti-Kerry; untypical of a county that always tended to take things easy, especially before finals, there was an unusual swagger to Kerry, and their supporters wouldn't hear of defeat.

Offaly had everything going for them. They were under no pressure. At an early stage in the game Liam Currams raced through from half-back for a fine point. This gave courage and hope to Offaly, who led at half time by 0-10 to 0-9. Everything was going nicely for them. Kerry proceeded to dominate the second half; and then the rain came down, and things seemed to go against Offaly. Kerry were leading when they were awarded a penalty, but Mikey Sheehy's shot was brilliantly saved by Martin Furlong. This put fire into Offaly, and the opportunities began to come their way. Matt Connor pointed two frees in the last five minutes, to bring Offaly within two points of Kerry's precarious lead. And then came Séamus Darby's famous goal, which has gone down in GAA history. The build-up, shown thousands of times on television, was innocent enough. A long ball floated in from midfield. A Kerry full-back at the time, Tommy Doyle, sailed up for it. He seemed to get a nudge in the back from Séamus Darby (who had earlier come on as a substitute), who fielded the ball and rocketed it into the net. The referee, P. J. McGrath (Mayo), gave no free. Croke Park went wild.

Kerry had their chances subsequently to level the game but failed to get the equaliser. The score: Offaly 1-15, Kerry, 0-17. Séamus Darby became a hero not alone in County Offaly but throughout the country. Kerry did no whingeing afterwards but accepted defeat like sportsmen.

In the following week's issue of the *Advertiser* my prediction was reproduced under the line 'Sam told you so.' Richie Connor, the Offaly captain, says in Brian Carthy's book *Football Captains* that he believes that 'Offaly's win would be put in perspective and be viewed as a wonderful team performance on the day.' It was very much a family occasion for Offaly, with five sets of brothers involved: the Connors (Matt and Richie), their cousins (Liam and Tomás), the Lowrys (Brendan, Mick, and Seán), the Fitzgeralds (Mick and Pat), and the Darbys (Séamus and Stephen). Liam Currams added his name to the list of dual all-Ireland winners. Besides Séamus Darby, Offaly had stars in Liam Currams, Pat Fitzgerald, Seán Lowry, Martin Furlong, Richie Connor, Brendan Lowry, and Johnny Mooney, though the latter wasn't quite as influential as he was in the semi-final against Galway.

This was the Offaly team:

Martin Furlong

Mick Lowry   Liam O'Connor   Mick Fitzgerald

Pat Fitzgerald   Seán Lowry   Liam Currams

Tomás O'Connor   Pádraig Dunne

John Guinan   Richie Connor (*captain*)   Gerry Carroll

Johnny Mooney   Matt Connor   Brendan Lowry

Substitutes: Stephen Darby for Mick Lowry; Séamus Darby for John Guinan.

Offaly's star dimmed somewhat after 1982, and there was much sadness throughout Ireland when that great forward Matt Connor was confined to a wheelchair as a result of a pre-Christmas road accident in 1984, when he was at the height of a wonderful career. During the nineties Offaly's football status reached its lowest level, and the team played second fiddle to the county's hurlers, who enjoyed great success and popularity. But when Tommy Lyons of Kilmacud Crokes took over the management of Offaly in the second half of the nineties the football star shone again. In 1997, under the prompting of Lyons, Offaly won its tenth Leinster crown, defeating Meath in a classic game before 46,000 spectators by 3-17 to 1-15; but they subsequently fell to Mayo by 0-13 to 0-7 in very wet conditions when much was expected of them. They went on in 1998 to win their first national football league title, defeating Derry in the final by 0-9 to 0-7.

One thing you can always say of Offaly footballers or hurlers is that they never drop the head, and, as they showed against Kerry in 1982, that pays. Bernie Robinson wrote a song in recognition of the county's renowned spirit, to the air of 'Slattery's Mounted Foot'.

Down from Rhode they came to gladden Offaly eyes,
Tenacious Johnny Mooney, the matchless Darby boys;
They thrilled the faithful followers, and how can we forget
That Darby shot like cannon-ball that rocked the Kerry net!

The Offaly anthem for years now has been 'The Offaly Rover',
sung first by Pat Delaney after the 1981 hurling triumph.

A rover I have been
And a rover I must stay,
But to the Faithful County dear
I shall return some day.
Uíbh Fhailí, I have missed you
And your heather-scented air;
Silently the peaceful Brosna
Calls your sons from far and near ...

27

HEFFO AND THE RISE OF THE DUBS

In September 1973 Dublin football was at its lowest point for twenty-five years. The glamour teams of the fifties, dominated to a great degree by St Vincent's, which won several national football league titles and an all-Ireland final, were a fading memory. Gone were the more businesslike and efficient teams of the sixties, which had added another all-Ireland senior title in 1963. Gone too were personalities such as Ollie Freaney, Jim Crowley, Des and Lar Foley, big John Timmons, Mickey Whelan, and Paddy Holden, as well as the élan and spirit that had characterised these teams. In place of a healthy extrovert personification of Dublin football there was a demoralised team just relegated to the nether division of the national football league, with little apparent commitment. Dublin football seemed doomed to the wilderness.

This gloomy prospect finally stirred the Dublin County Board to support the imaginative plans of its chairman, Jimmy Gray, and secretary, Jim King, to break the traditional arrangements for managing the Dublin senior football team. A three-man group—Kevin Heffernan, a former football star of the fifties, as manager, Dónal Colfer, and Lorcan Redmond—was appointed to have sole responsibility for Dublin's senior football fortunes for a period of three years. The group's objective was to restore Dublin's football pride by gathering a group of players who would give total commitment to that objective and to achieving the maximum potential from the panel of players within those three years. It was the wisest move Dublin ever made; and the objective was achieved sooner than expected.

In an article in the Dublin GAA Yearbook for 1976, Kevin Heffernan described how his management group set about achieving their objective.

Through a process of trial and error, extending over some months, we finally settled on a group of players in whose commitment we had total confidence. We then set about developing a team by:

(a) improving individual skills

(b) achieving maximum fitness

(c) developing field tactics most suitable to our particular team and Dublin footballers generally.

All these aspects were the subject of continuous discussion with players and these discussions were a prime factor in developing a united group and building team confidence.

In this way the Heffernan formula unfolded. In the years ahead the panel of players worked hard at the training sessions every Tuesday, Thursday, and Saturday, shirked nothing, and worked willingly and competitively to raise their personal performance. The results began to show almost immediately.

Dublin had an inauspicious start to the 1974 senior football championship, defeating Wexford in a low-key first-round game as a curtain-raiser to the replayed national football league final between Kerry and Roscommon. Immediately, Heffernan's management team called a retired and portly Jimmy Keaveney, who had watched Dublin beat Wexford from Hill 16, back into the Dublin panel. He answered Kevin's call and liked the buzz at the camp; and the roller-coaster to success began with good wins over Louth and the Leinster champions, Offaly. The crowds began to sense a Dublin comeback, and ever-increasing attendances saw Dublin defeat Kildare in the Leinster semi-final by 1-13 to 0-10 and Meath in the final by 1-14 to 1-9.

It was Kevin Heffernan who really fashioned the cult of the team manager in the modern GAA. He became the idol of Dublin's growing following, which came to be known as Heffo's army. He also became the darling of Hill 16, which became as never before Dublin's preserve, while the Dublin team came to be known as the Dubs. Even though the man himself never sought publicity, his every move was noted, and the return of the Dublin team was the sports story of 1974. It was especially so after Cork, the 1973 all-Ireland champions, were beaten in the all-Ireland semi-final by 2-11 to 1-8. Galway, beaten in two previous finals (1971 and 1973), qualified for the final after a good win over Donegal.

Great was the excitement and colour in Dublin before the final. Huge interest was generated, and Dublin's new strip of sky blue and navy (suggested by Jim King's secretary, Paula Lee), to replace the previous sky blue and white, seemed to work wonders. The colour on the Hill grew with every success. In truth the Dubs of 1974 made the game of football fashionable in Dublin; everybody wanted a ticket for the final. The all-ticket game was about to come upon us for the first time. In the middle of the Dublin euphoria a fringe element, aping the soccer thuggery of England, did their best to besmirch the genuine Dublin supporters who converged on the Hill; but the all-ticket game, when it arrived, got rid of that.

Dublin's team glistened with names that were to become household words. Paddy Cullen in goal, flamboyant and confident, had given loyal service, fronted by a solid full-back line of Gay O'Driscoll, Seán 'Doc' Doherty, and Robbie Kelleher. At midfield was a long-haired youngster named Brian Mullins, one of the all-time aces in Heffo's pack. But it was the forwards, one and all, who were to fashion the glory of the period, led by Tony Hanahoe and a less portly Jimmy Keaveney, possibly the team's most popular player and its absolutely dependable free-taker. The indefatigable Bobby Doyle, the stylish and courageous David Hickey, wonderful half-forward, Anton O'Toole, known affectionately as the 'Blue Panther', and John McCarthy, always dependable for scores.

Before an attendance of 72,000, Galway played well in the first half, inspired by Michael Rooney, Johnny Hughes, Billy Joyce, and Gay Mitchell, and led at half time by 1-4 to 0-5. They were very much in the game still when they were awarded a penalty twelve minutes into the second half. Liam Sammon struck it well, but Paddy Cullen sensed the right direction of the kick and turned the shot out for a forty-five with one outstretched hand. It was a super save and inspired Dublin to take over and score three unanswered points from Jimmy Keaveney (2) and John McCarthy (1). Galway weren't beaten yet and squared the game 1-6 to 0-9 with eleven minutes to go; but Dublin now took over and in a spell-binding finale scored five points, to send Hill 16 wild. This was to become a familiar scene for the future. There are few scenes better to behold than the crowded Hill 16 celebrating a Dublin victory. Full of colour and atmosphere, it is the place every Dublin supporter wants to be.

The score was Dublin 0-14, Galway 1-6. A new team had taken over in Gaelic football.

Jimmy Keaveney was the winners' top scorer, and Michael Rooney got Galway's only goal of the game. It was a huge disappointment for Galway fans to see their team lose three all-Ireland finals within four years.

This was Dublin's winning team:

Paddy Cullen

Gay O'Driscoll   Seán Doherty (*captain*)   Robbie Kelleher

Paddy Reilly   Alan Larkin   George Wilson

Stephen Rooney   Brian Mullins

Bobby Doyle   Tony Hanahoe   David Hickey

John McCarthy   Jimmy Keaveney   Anton O'Toole

Heffo's objective, born late in 1973, had garnered rich fruit in quick time. And the roller-coaster was only beginning.

After the heady days of 1974, 1975 fell a bit flat. Dublin embarked on an American tour, and on their return they lost the national football league final to Meath on a score of 0-16 to 1-9. The Leinster senior football championship was retained with style, with good wins over Wexford, then Louth in Navan before 31,000 fans by 3-14 to 4-7, followed by a comprehensive win, 3-13 to 0-8, over Kildare in the Leinster final. After that Derry were beaten 3-13 to 3-8 in the semi-final, and a young and exuberant Kerry team under its new trainer-manager Mick O'Dwyer had an easy win over Sligo in the other semi-final.

Would Dublin get their revenge for 1955 and 1959? The arrival of Mick O'Dwyer as manager had heightened interest. The former star half-back and forward has always been a charismatic figure, and the media loved him. If Heffo started the manager-mania, then O'Dwyer compounded it. Great was the speculation as the big day approached. But in the final, O'Dwyer's Babes swept aside the Dubs by 2-12 to 0-11. New stars such as Sheehy, Spillane, Power, Moran and Egan, under Mickey O'Sullivan's captaincy, had been launched on the scene to set up a rivalry unparalleled in GAA history.

Dublin needed to regroup, to get back the old appetite, to correct some chinks in the armour and set off anew. Even before 1975 was over they defeated Kerry in a smashing national football league game before some 25,000 fans by 2-11 to 0-13, with Paddy Cullen outstanding in goal. Pat O'Neill was in the team at half-back. The 1976 season was eagerly awaited.

Tony Hanahoe, another St Vincent's man close to Heffo's heart and a deep thinker on the game, had taken over as captain. In his own words,

I used to go to Croke Park from the age of ten and often met another little guy in a gaberdine coat, whom I grew to know later as Jimmy Keaveney. The two of us were often there hours before the officials opened the gates.

From such beginnings stars emerge.

Dublin's and Heffo's pride had been stung by the unexpected defeat in 1975 by the O'Dwyer Babes. Hanahoe told an interviewer for the Dublin 1977 Yearbook: 'We had a more determined attitude to win out in 1976.' Into the team for the league had come an exciting youngster named Kevin Moran. Another acquisition was the durable Pat O'Neill; and Dublin went from success to success, first of all winning the national football league, defeating Galway in the semi-final by 1-11 to 0-12 and Derry in the final by 2-10 to 0-15. Said Tony Hanahoe:

> We won the league on merit. We didn't train too much for it, as we had one primary aim—to win back the all-Ireland. But we won the league because we played every game to salvage our reputation.

With the national football league title regained after a lapse of eighteen years, it was all go for the championship. First there were easy wins over Longford and Laois, followed by a close win over Meath in the Leinster final by 2-8 to 1-9. Sighs of relief went up with seventeen minutes to go when Colm O'Rourke of Meath whizzed a penalty wide (yes, the same Colm of late eighties fame!). Then followed a disappointing semi-final win over Galway by 1-8 to 0-8 in an over-robust game totally out of character with the quality of play and sportsmanship almost always exhibited in this ancient rivalry. One noted the masterly midfield play of Bernard Brogan, the steadiness of Tommy Drumm at right-half-back, and the goal from Jimmy Keaveney that decided the game. Dublin's whole season had been geared for another all-Ireland crack at Kerry, and Kerry duly qualified for the final after two hectic games with Cork in the new Páirc Uí Chaoimh and an easy semi-final win over Derry.

The Dublin objective was achieved with a magnificent performance in the final and a comprehensive victory by 3-8 to 0-10 over the old enemy before a new record attendance of 73,000 for the reconstructed Croke Park. I will never forget the marvellous defence-splitting run of Dublin's centre-half-back, Kevin Moran, when, early in the game, he soloed right through Kerry's defence and sent a screamer for goal just inches wide. It would have been one of the most sensational goals ever scored; but it was as good as a score and inspired Dublin to success. The Dubs were never led, though they were pulled back to level terms twice in the first half. Brian Mullins was masterful at midfield, while David Hickey emerged as attacker supreme. But Kevin Moran in a superb half-back line of Drumm, Moran and O'Neill was the man of the match. The player who later became a soccer legend with Manchester United and Ireland gave a wonderful display of centre-half-back play at its best. The incessant running of Bobby Doyle was another contribution to possibly Dublin's greatest football triumph. The goal-scorers were John McCarthy, Brian Mullins, and Jimmy Keaveney.

Heffo's objective and that of his management team had been well and truly achieved. Dublin football was on top of the world, and to compound it all St Vincent's had earlier in the year become club champions of Ireland too.

This was Dublin's winning team:

Paddy Cullen

Gay O'Driscoll   Seán Doherty   Robbie Kelleher

Tommy Drumm   Kevin Moran   Pat O'Neill

Brian Mullins   Bernard Brogan

Anton O'Toole   Tony Hanahoe (*captain*)   David Hickey

Bobby Doyle   Jimmy Keaveney   John McCarthy

Substitutes: Fran Ryder for Tony Hanahoe, Paddy Gogarty for Bobby Doyle.

And so 1977 dawned. In the aftermath of the 1976 success, Heffo surprised everybody by stepping down as manager, because of pressure of work. The Dublin management stepped in quickly, placing Tony Hanahoe in the position, with the same two selections as before. As captain, manager and selector, Hanahoe had an onerous task, but the groundwork was done. Dublin would ever be in debt to the genius of Heffernan, who created the purposeful mobile style of play, holding on to possession and passing at will, backed by fitness of a high order.

Kerry were down but not out and won the 1976/7 national football league, defeating Dublin in the final by 1-8 to 1-6. But the Dublin roller-coaster continued in 1977 with a win over Kildare at Navan (1-14 to 2-8), a win over Wexford at Carlow (3-11 to 0-6), and a fourth successive Leinster final win over Meath in Croke Park (1-9 to 0-8).

Dublin now qualified to meet Kerry in the all-Ireland semi-final, and a crowd of 55,000 attended what has often been described as the classic of all Gaelic football games, won in the end by Dublin, 3-12 to 1-13, after Kerry had led at half time by 1-6 to 0-6.

I have a video recording of that game, which I replay now and again. It is certainly a classic—perhaps not the greatest game I've seen, but for excitement and commitment never excelled. What a joy to hear Mícheál O'Hehir describe it all so well once again!

It was neck and neck during the second half after John McCarthy goaled to make it level pegging. Four times subsequently the teams were level: 1-7, 1-9, 1-10 and 1-11 each. Then Kerry edged ahead and seemed set for victory. A number of classic O'Hehir expressions that one has tended to forget emerged: 'Just listen to that crowd roar,' and 'Oh, what a game,' after Seánie Walsh had levelled once again. But when David Hickey scored a super goal for Dublin, followed by Bernard Brogan's goal, the game was over for Kerry.

It was Dublin's sweetest victory. A long-haired youngster named Jack O'Shea was at midfield for Kerry. Anton O'Toole played a blinder. Brian Mullins caught some mighty balls but was in the wars after a high tackle on Ger Power. Kevin Moran too excelled; but one of my greatest memories of Dublin's determination is of Seán Doherty's wonderful catch in the Dublin goal-mouth and his holding onto possession as he fell to the ground; 'No surrender' was his motto.

Dublin were now favourites to retain their title against Armagh, who had emerged from the other semi-final after a replay win over Roscommon. There seemed no stopping the mighty Dubs. They went on to win the final easily over Armagh by 5-12 to 3-6, though not as easily as that score suggests. Armagh fought hard, though chasing the game from the start, inspired by Joe Kernan and Paddy Moriarty. Jimmy Keaveney shot a record 2-6 for a seventy-minute final. Dublin played the same team as in the 1976 final, with the substitutes Paddy Reilly, Alan Larkin and Jim Brogan replacing Pat O'Neill, Bernard Brogan, and Robbie Kelleher, respectively. They had now achieved two successive all-Irelands, had seized the initiative from Kerry, and went on to win the 1977/8 national football league final, defeating Mayo by 2-18 to 2-13.

Offaly were now beginning to emerge as a football force in Leinster. Still, Dublin went on their merry way, winning a fifth Leinster title in a row in 1978 and easily defeating Kildare in the Leinster final and Down in the semi-final.

Kerry again qualified to play Dublin in the final. This time, after a brilliant start in which Dublin seemed set to continue their mastery over Kerry, there came the now famous Mikey Sheehy goal from a free, which took Paddy Cullen unawares and led subsequently to almost complete Kerry domination, with the newcomer Eoin 'Bomber' Liston scintillating, especially in the second half. Kerry won easily in the end by 5-11 to 0-9.

It was really the end of this Dublin team, though after some team-building they emerged as 1979 Leinster champions with a heroic fourteen-man victory over Offaly, 1-8 to 0-9, inspired by Brian Mullins's do-or-die efforts. Kerry again defeated Dublin easily enough in the all-Ireland final of 1979 by 3-13 to 1-8. Gone from the team were many of the old faces, such as O'Driscoll, Doherty, and Keaveney. Dublin's unvaried mode of play had now become tedious and outdated; Kerry's more spontaneous skills and greater variety in approach had taken over. But let no-one dim the achievements of this great Dublin side because of their two final all-Ireland defeats to Kerry. The record shows that Dublin qualified for six successive all-Ireland finals (winning three) and five successive national football league finals (winning two) and won thirty-one All-Star Awards from 1974 to 1979; not forgetting the six Leinster titles in a row emulating Wexford and Kildare of yore.

These achievements, the masterminding of Heffo and the memory of a crowded Hill 16 agog with excitement in an extravaganza of blue are my memories of that wonderful era for Dublin football—and of course that classic 1977 all-Ireland semi-final.

28

MICKO'S MARVELS, 1975–81

To Ger McKenna, County Board chairman, raconteur and wonderful public speaker, must go the main credit for drafting in Mick O'Dwyer of Waterville as Kerry senior team manager before the national football league of 1974/5. It was in the aftermath of Cork's defeat of Kerry in Killarney in the Munster final of 1974, after the retirement of the trainer and former star Johnny Culloty of Killarney.

Mick had been in charge of the under-21 team and knew the potential of many of the prospective panel. He was eager to have a go. The national football league of that year went well enough but came to a sudden halt when Meath stopped the Kerry gallop, 0-11 to 0-5, in the quarter-final. Much work needed to be done, and it was now for the first time that many of the panel came face to face with O'Dwyer's training methods. Night after night he sent home weary bodies from Killarney: this young panel, the youngest ever to represent Kerry, were not going to fail for lack of fitness.

With twelve of the team under twenty-three and the oldest, Brendan Lynch, a 'veteran' of twenty-six, it was an eager bunch that ran onto the field at Clonmel on 15 June 1975 to take on Tipperary in the senior football championship.

Though Tipperary fought hard and gave Kerry a right game of it well into the second half, it was John Egan when moved to the forty who scored 2-2 between the fourteenth and seventeenth minute of the second half who spelt *finis* to Tipperary. Kerry won well, 3-13 to 0-9. Now for Cork in the Munster final!

Before that game, again at Killarney, O'Dwyer put his charges through twenty-seven consecutive nights of training; and when the team ran out in Killarney they were like greyhounds unleashed. Before a crowd of 43,000 they tore Cork apart by 1-14 to 0-7, with Mickey O'Sullivan, the captain, tireless in attack, ably helped by John Egan and John O'Keeffe, a pillar at full-back. It was Micko's first major achievement as a trainer, and he was eager to keep it going.

For raw recruits mostly, Kerry had an easy semi-final win over the lowly Sligo, who were contesting their second semi-final ever. Still, it was only in the last ten minutes that Kerry pulled away to score a staggering 3-2 and finish up winning by 3-13 to 0-5. Sligo had waited for such an opportunity for years, and it was a pity that men like Mickey Kearins (now at the end of a wonderful career), Barnes Murphy, Cathal Cawley and Mattie Brennan didn't win out in the west a few years earlier, or meet a less talented team on their Croke Park baptism.

John Egan got two of those late goals, and the youthful Pat Spillane got the other. Dublin, the all-Ireland champions, had stormed into another final, and memories of the great confrontations of 1955 and 1959 resurfaced as the battle between the two managers, Mick O'Dwyer and Kevin Heffernan, loomed. This was the start of a wonderful rivalry that was to dominate Gaelic football for well over a decade and in which these two teams tended to overshadow every other county. They set a headline in their professional approach to training, discipline, and tactics, and it took some time for other counties to follow the same route.

Came final day, and Kerry's young team were not given a chance by the pundits. The day before the final the Kerry captain, Mickey O'Sullivan of Kenmare, spoke in a television interview of this desire to lead Kerry to all-Ireland success. It was a precious interview, depicting the desire in every young Kerry youngster to be so honoured.

Next day the rain began to fall heavily on a crowded Croke Park. Kerry got the start they needed when John Egan, that compact man from Sneem, squeezed through in the third minute after a mix-up following a free by Mikey Sheehy, and goaled. Kerry never looked back after this. Mickey O'Sullivan was realising his dream with incisive runs, and in one of these in the seventeenth minute, in the words of Paddy Downey in the *Irish Times,* 'sustained a severe injury in an ugly tackle on the edge of the large penalty area after he had run fifty yards in possession.' O'Sullivan's dream ended as he was stretchered off to hospital. It was an amazing run, one of the most exciting ever in a final. O'Sullivan would have been wiser to get rid of the ball earlier, as the almost inevitable crash loomed.

But the sight of their inspiring captain being carried off seemed to galvanise the Kerry youngsters. Ger O'Driscoll came on as a substitute. Nineteen-year-old Ogie Moran at centre-half-forward, with wonderful acceleration, shot two capital points on the run to leave Kerry leading at half time by 1-6 to 0-4.

Kerry continued to dominate in all sectors. Brendan Lynch, the 'veteran', pointed a forty-five. John Egan continued to pulverise the Dublin defence, and Pat Spillane was at his confident best. (It often amazes me how young Kerry footballers seem to grow in stature in Croke Park, while other recruits to the Croke Park scene have legs of jelly and wish they were elsewhere.) John Egan's punched effort for goal came off the Dublin cross-bar; but then came the killer second goal by Ger O'Driscoll, who deflected a centre by John Egan for a goal. That was it. Kerry cruised home to win by 2-12 to 0-11, with Ger Power winning the 'man of the match' award but having little to spare over Pat McCarthy, an outstanding midfielder of the old style, Denis 'Ogie' Moran, whose speed and ball control were paramount, and of course the captain, Mickey O'Sullivan, before his unfortunate departure—not forgetting the brilliant John O'Keeffe at full-back.

The Sam Maguire Cup was presented to Pat Spillane in the absence of his injured captain, who was, however, released in time to join the festivities in the Garda Club in Dublin following the game. John D. Hickey in the *Irish Independent* eulogised the Kerrymen's 'speed in abundance, with the stamina of marathon runners and a dedication I have never seen excelled.' We had seen the birth of the nucleus of the greatest football team in the history of the GAA. They still had to mature somewhat, but on that wet September Sunday I knew I had witnessed something special.

This was the Kerry team:

Paudie O'Mahony

Ger O'Keeffe   John O'Keeffe   Jimmy Deenihan

Páidí Ó Sé   Tim Kennelly   Ger Power

Pat McCarthy   Paudie Lynch

Brendan Lynch   Ogie Moran   Mickey O'Sullivan (*captain*)

John Egan   Mikey Sheehy   Pat Spillane

Substitute: Ger O'Driscoll for Mickey O'Sullivan.

After the euphoria of the 1975 success there were high expectations in County Kerry of a continuation, but Dublin proved the masters in both the 1976 final and the famous 1977 semi-final. The Dublin v. Kerry rivalry was at its zenith. Even first-round national football league games, such as the Dublin v. Kerry game in Croke Park on 23 October 1977, drew an attendance of 25,000, to see Dublin winning again. That game saw Kerry introduce a tall (6 feet 3 inches) full-forward, slim and bearded, who made an instant impression. We were to hear more of Eoin 'the Bomber' Liston. Since 1975 Kerry had also introduced a big athletic midfielder named Jack O'Shea, and a lad from Tralee who could catch and kick as good as any Kerryman and became known as the 'Super Sub': Seán Walsh. The pieces in O'Dwyer's jigsaw were falling into place.

Kerry started the 1978 campaign by easily defeating Waterford in Killarney on 18 June, 4-27 to 2-8, with Mikey Sheehy and Pat Spillane bagging two goals apiece. Before an attendance of 45,000 in Páirc Uí Chaoimh, Kerry defeated Cork by 3-14 to 3-7. Charlie Nelligan from Castleisland was now in goal, and Tommy Doyle too was playing in his first Munster final. Two wonderful forward moves involving many Kerry players resulted in spectacular goals by Mikey Sheehy, the first a hand-passed effort, the second another deft flick.

The combination at speed was uncanny. Mick O'Dwyer perfected the delivery of the ball at close quarters by a forward gaining possession with his back to goal passing to a fast-advancing back, midfielder or fellow-forward racing at goal. Many times Eoin Liston or Tommy Doyle gained possession and passed the ball on to a flying colleague—Spillane, Sheehy, O'Shea, or Power—bearing down on goal. It was a gambit new to the game and O'Dwyer's special creation.

Declan Barron of Cork gave a man-of-the-match performance when switched to midfield. Cork's forwards were wild in their shooting, and Kerry won at ease, with Eoin Liston the star in his first Munster final. Pádhraic Puirséal in the *Irish Press* described Sheehy's second goal: 'Kerry answered with another sweeping "basketball" movement that left Sheehy with the easiest of tasks in palming the ball past Morgan.' But these palmed goals, which had now become a feature of Gaelic football, were not everybody's cup of tea.

In the semi-final Kerry continued their fine run with an easy win over Roscommon by 3-11 to 0-8 at Croke Park on 13 August, a day of torrential rain. Jack O'Shea gave a man-of-the-match performance at midfield, ably helped by John O'Keeffe, Tim Kennelly, a very mobile centre half-back, Paudie Lynch, solid as a rock, and Jimmy Deenihan, solid in the left corner. But the pundits still didn't rate Kerry too highly. Dublin in the meantime had powered their way into another final with easy wins over Carlow, Kildare, and Down, only Offaly giving them a close run in the Leinster semi-final, 2-9 to 0-12.

All was set for the great showdown, and Dublin were raging favourites after their 1976 and 1977 successes. 24 September 1978 has become an important date in Kerry football folklore: it was the day O'Dwyer's Marvels really came of age.

Tony O'Keeffe, the present Kerry county secretary, was a teaching colleague of mine in Moneenageisha Community College, Galway, at this time. At the tea break in the staff room on the Friday morning before the game he waltzed up to me, all smiles, showing me a quotation from that morning's *Irish Independent*. Jack O'Shea, Kerry's majestic midfielder—the best midfielder in the running game now so much in vogue—was quoted as saying, 'We'll eat them,' and this burst of confidence convinced Tony that Kerry would not be beaten.

Dublin started the final as if they were going to pulverise Kerry. There was only one team in it as Dublin, in absolutely confident mood, attacked in waves, Jimmy Keaveney scoring five points on the trot to lead 0-6 to 0-1. Then, against the run of play, Kerry counter-attacked, and after a movement involving Liston, Jack O'Shea, and Spillane, Egan squeezed the ball past the advancing Paddy Cullen for a well-taken goal. Jack O'Shea and John Egan then levelled the game with two fine points.

Three minutes before half time came one of the most talked-of goals in Gaelic football. The referee, Séamus Aldridge (Kildare), awarded a free in to Kerry after Paddy Cullen had cleared—a patently unfair decision; and while Cullen argued the toss with the referee, leaving his goal unguarded, Mikey Sheehy was handed the ball by Robbie Kelleher and, with spur-of-the-moment thinking, floated it over the retreating Paddy Cullen for a precious goal. Nobody expected it to be allowed, but it was, and Kerry went in at half time leading by 2-3 to 0-7 after Dublin had dominated the play for twenty-five minutes.

There was animated discussion under the Hogan Stand at half time. Was it a fair goal? Did Séamus Aldridge penalise Paddy Cullen unfairly? Is a forward entitled to take a quick free in such opportunist circumstances? Very few gave Mikey Sheehy the kudos he deserved. Years of practise at taking frees had given him the confidence to have a go; had he failed with the shot he might have been the laughing stock of County Kerry. In such instances, genius reveals itself. That shot decided the 1978 all-Ireland. Dublin would not be able to lift themselves again.

Dublin's defence collapsed in the second half, and Eoin Liston had a field day. Staying close to the square, he was monarch of all he surveyed. He scored his first of three goals after ninety seconds, and in the end Dublin were roasted with a score of 5-11 to 0-9. Liston, who scored 3-1 in one half, was a modest hero: 'I don't think I ever scored three goals in one half before.' Dublin collapsed like a pack of cards after their early dominance had been negatived, and Kerry's fitness, enthusiasm and all-round ability in the second half carved for them one of their greatest and most satisfying victories. Pádhraic Puirséal in the *Irish Press* wrote: 'Once fitness, flair and the luck of the day were all put together, it was impossible to see a weak link on this Kerry team.'

Charlie Nelligan

Jimmy Deenihan   John O'Keeffe   Mick Spillane

Páidí Ó Sé   Tim Kennelly   Paudie Lynch

Jack O'Shea   Seán Walsh

Ger Power   Ogie Moran (*captain*)   Pat Spillane

Mikey Sheehy   Eoin Liston   John Egan

Substitute: Pat O'Mahony for Jimmy Deenihan.

There is a poem by Liam Mac Gabhann entitled 'The Blind Man at Croke Park'. The following two verses are reproduced in tribute to all Kerry teams, especially that of 1978.

> Listen, asthore, for these eyes are sealed,
> Listen once more … When the Kerrymen take the field,
> Tell an old man who saw them in days of old,
> Do they walk proudly in their green and gold?
>
> Listen, asthore, when Kerry take the field,
> Tell me when they attack and when they yield;
> Say if they fail; asthore, I'm blind and old,
> Tell me they'll not dishonour the green and gold.

The Kerry steamroller continued in 1979 in even more emphatic fashion, first trouncing Clare at Milltown Malbay by 9-21 to 1-9, then an easy win over Cork in the Munster final at Killarney, 2-14 to 2-4. This was Kerry's fifth year in a row to defeat Cork in the Munster final. Ger Power in a man-of-the-match display before 46,000 spectators showed the way, and despite the score, Cork fought heroically, especially in the third quarter, before Kerry's all-round balance and combination engulfed them.

Monaghan, in their first all-Ireland semi-final since 1938, froze in Croke Park on 12 August despite getting any amount of possession and fell heavily to the Kerry machine by 5-14 to 0-7. This Kerry team made everything look so easy. Dublin once again had qualified at the other end, though lucky enough to squeeze past Roscommon in the other semi-final by 0-14 to 1-10 after another tough battle with Offaly in the Leinster final.

In the final, attended by a crowd of 72,000 in brilliant sunshine, Kerry continued their dominance with an emphatic triumph over Dublin, 3-13 to 1-8, to notch up all-Ireland senior football championship number 25. It was the day Mikey Sheehy scored 2-6 to equal Jimmy Keaveney's scoring record of 1977 for a seventy-minute final, his first goal, in the eleventh minute, being described by Paddy Downey in the *Irish Times* as 'the gem of the day'. Tommy Doyle replaced Ger Power, out of action with a hamstring injury, and he too combined brilliantly in a Kerry team whose varied football, mixing the long ball with the possession game, proved far superior to the unimaginative, painful and stereotyped short-passing chess-like build-up of the Dubliners, now a shadow of the team of previous years. They were missing Jimmy Keaveney, out through suspension, and hampered by an injury to the great-hearted Kevin Moran.

Paddy Downey in his report gave top billing to Pat Spillane and Seán Walsh. Even though Páidí Ó Sé was sent off by the referee, Hugh Duggan, with eighteen minutes to go for a foul on Anton O'Toole, it seemed to spur Kerry on. Was there any team to halt the Kerry machine?

Kerry's winning team, captained by Tim Kennelly, was the same one that played in the 1978 final, apart from Tommy Doyle at number 10 and with Vincent O'Connor replacing the injured John O'Keeffe.

Seán Walsh's fielding was a feature of this final. One catch of his in the twelfth minute of the second half, captured by the *Kerryman* photographer Kevin Coleman as he sailed over friend and foe to gain possession, is as good a pictorial demonstration of this wonderful skill as one could see.

The year 1980 wasn't quite as easy for Kerry. First Cork were well beaten in the Munster final at Páirc Uí Chaoimh by 3-13 to 0-12, with Eoin Liston in top form, scoring two vital goals at vital times, the first a deft flick at the end of the first half, the other a hand-passed effort past a helpless Billy Morgan from close range early in the second half. Hand-passed goals were becoming the norm for this Kerry team, something that drew a good deal of criticism from lovers of the game, perturbed that Gaelic football was over-influenced by some basketball techniques. But Kerry and O'Dwyer were playing within the rules, and making it pay.

Offaly had at last come through in Leinster against Dublin, and in a high-scoring semi-final Kerry defeated them on 10 August by 4-15 to 4-10. The game is best remembered for the personal tally of Matt Connor, whose 2-9 showed this player at his best, though much of Offaly's scoring came too late in the game to cause Kerry any real flutters. Three of Kerry's goals came from hand-passes, which caused Dónal Carroll in the *Irish Independent* to describe the game as 'an utter abuse of the hand-passing rules,' though he readily admitted to 'the winners' forwards playing copy stuff with off the ball running, jet-like acceleration and backup of an order few teams could aspire to match.' Kerry were worried about their defence and recalled the old reliables Jimmy Deenihan and Paudie Lynch for the final against Roscommon, who, after winning four Connacht titles in succession, had at last qualified for the ultimate showdown. Kerry, of course, were hot favourites; but they were in for a fright.

This was no ordinary Roscommon team but one with solid backs, a good midfield, and a forward line that included Tony McManus, Michael Finneran, and John O'Connor, all quality footballers. Kerry were forced to field without Eoin Liston, struck down on the Wednesday before the game with appendicitis, but he received an ovation from the attendance of 64,000 when he walked onto the field at Croke Park to join the Kerry team in posing for the team photograph.

This didn't faze Roscommon, who had a goal scored inside a minute. A piece of magic from Tony McManus laid on a goal for John O'Connor, and Roscommon went on to lead 1-2 to nil after eleven minutes. At this point some Roscommon players made the cardinal error of playing the man instead of the ball, and by half time the initiative had swung back to Kerry, after a goal by Mikey Sheehy left it level pegging, 1-3 apiece. Kerry pulled away in the second half to win by 1-9 to 1-6, but not until after a few scares when the score stood at 1-6 apiece and Charlie Nelligan and Páidí Ó Sé effected breathtaking saves from John O'Connor and Aidan Dooley, respectively.

It wasn't a great final in the swirling conditions. In fact it was a poor game, with much pulling and dragging, generating sixty-four frees in all. In Kerry's three-in-a-row success Tim Kennelly had the game of his life, with Paudie Lynch, Charlie Nelligan and Páidí Ó Sé also heroic. But it was a near thing, and Kerry knew it.

The winning team was:

Charlie Nelligan

Jimmy Deenihan	John O'Keeffe	Paudie Lynch
Páidí Ó Sé	Tim Kennelly	Ger O'Keeffe

Jack O'Shea   Seán Walsh

Ger Power (*captain*)	Ogie Moran	Pat Spillane
Mikey Sheehy	Tommy Doyle	John Egan

Substitute: Ger O'Driscoll for Ger Power.

Kerry began their four-in-a-row quest with an easy win, 4-17 to 0-6, over Clare in Listowel on 28 June, and in the Munster final at Killarney on 19 July they easily beat Cork, 1-11 to 0-3. An easy win, but the game ended on a sour note, with Billy Morgan, the Cork goalkeeper, being carried off after a heavy collision with Eoin Liston. Kerry had another easy semi-final win over Mayo by 2-19 to 1-6, with Mayo failing to raise a flag in the second half.

Earlier that year the GAA Congress had banned the hand-pass, but this didn't hamper Kerry one bit. Offaly had come though again in Leinster with a good win over Down. Because of a recurring knee injury, Pat Spillane had to cry off, to be replaced by Tommy Doyle. Offaly put it up to Kerry, and it was level pegging at half time, 0-5 each. The Kerry machine was on the slide. Offaly were still in it until Jack O'Shea scored a late goal after being set up in a marvellous Liston-Egan-Sheehy move. It's a goal that should be shown again and again. Kerry won in the end by 1-12 to 0-8.

The four in a row had been achieved, to equal the record set by Wexford (1915–18) and Kerry (1929–32). This, however, was the end of the road for this particular Kerry team, though many were to continue and to extend the O'Dwyer winning saga in what I describe as the 'second coming of Mick O'Dwyer'.

The 1981 team to win Kerry's second four-in-a-row was:

Charlie Nelligan

Jimmy Deenihan (*captain*)	John O'Keeffe	Paudie Lynch
Páidí Ó Sé	Tim Kennelly	Mick Spillane

Jack O'Shea   Seán Walsh

Ger Power	Ogie Moran	Tommy Doyle
Mikey Sheehy	Eoin Liston	John Egan

Substitutes: Pat Spillane for John Egan, Ger O'Keeffe for Mick Spillane.

A superb group of footballers—the best I have ever seen. Looking back now, I see them as poetry in motion, a unit made up of outstanding links, coached by a man who favoured flowing, sporting football of a kind played by himself in his own days with Kerry.

29

THE SECOND COMING OF MICK O'DWYER

After the loss to Offaly and the lost chance of winning five all-Irelands in a row, Kerry suffered another last-minute reverse in the Munster final to Cork in 1983. On a wet and thundery day in Páirc Uí Chaoimh, before a pretty sparse attendance of 17,000, a goal by Tadhg Murphy put paid to a record ninth successive provincial title win (all against Cork).

But another heartbreak didn't dent the Kerry or O'Dwyer spirit. Replacements were required, as some of the old warriors of the seventies were nearing the end of the road, and the flame just needed to be rekindled in others. The arrival of the GAA's centenary year, 1984, gave all a necessary spur.

First Kerry won the 1983/4 national football league, defeating Galway in the final at Limerick in April by 1-11 to 0-11. A good start. In the Munster senior football championship they easily defeated Tipperary in Tralee, 0-23 to 0-6, and in the Munster final defeated Cork in Killarney by 3-14 to 2-10, with Eoin Liston scintillating and the newcomer John Kennedy kicking four good points. Ambrose O'Donovan, a raw recruit from Gneeveguilla, was a young and inspiring captain who grew in stature as the year progressed. In the semi-final Kerry had a very easy win over a weak Galway team by 2-17 to 0-11. Seán Walsh was now at full-back, with Páidí Ó Sé beside him in the right corner. Tom Spillane, the youngest of an illustrious trio of brothers, had taken over from Tim Kennelly at number 6, with Ger Lynch on his left. The younger Spillane stole the show against Galway.

Dublin, with a new-look team, qualified for the final, and the prospect of another Kerry v. Dublin contest awakened memories of battles in the fifties and seventies. Only Brian Mullins and Anton

O'Toole remained of the men of 1974. Were we to witness a rebirth of the old rivalry of the mid-seventies? Dublin, as all-Ireland champions of 1983, were favourites and were eager to win two successive titles.

Before 68,000 spectators, Kerry outclassed Dublin with a score of 0-14 to 1-6, being far superior in the basic skills of catching and kicking, whereas Dublin were far too tactical and, apart from a brief spell in the second half after a fine goal by Barney Rock, never threatened the Kerrymen. Mikey Sheehy was out of the Kerry team through injury, and Ger Power, as versatile as ever, was drafted in at right-corner-forward to fill the vacancy. Pat Spillane was at his indomitable best, Seán Walsh unbeatable at full-back, Páidí Ó Sé as tight as tuppence at corner-back, Jack O'Shea in all his glory at midfield, and all the youngsters working together well. Paddy Downey in his description of the game in the *Irish Times* paid tribute to Kerry's 'football ability of a high order, fitness, speed, concentration and indomitable spirit which all combined to form a withering force that ragged Dublin could not withstand.' Kerry and O'Dwyer were back on top.

This was Kerry's centenary year team:

Charlie Nelligan

Páidí Ó Sé   Seán Walsh   Mick Spillane

Tommy Doyle   Tom Spillane   Ger Lynch

Jack O'Shea   Ambrose O'Donovan (*captain*)

John Kennedy   Denis Ogie Moran   Pat Spillane

Ger Power   Eoin Liston   John Egan

Substitute: Timmie O'Dowd for John Egan.

John Egan was never again to play for Kerry. A most unassuming man, he is still held in the highest regard as one of the all-time great Kerry forwards and is considered one of the greatest exponents of the solo run. Very difficult to dispossess, he had an almost uncanny ability to shield the ball while in full flight.

The year 1985 began for Kerry with an easy win over Limerick at Listowel in June, 2-18 to 0-9. Then in July at Páirc Uí Chaoimh the Cork challenge was overcome, 2-11 to 0-11, when, as Seán Kilfeather wrote in the *Irish Times,* 'Kerry's suspected problems with Old Father Time surfaced fleetingly but not fatally,' and 'two stunning goals from Liston and Sheehy scuttled Cork's chances.' But Cork had got closer than the score suggests and might have carried the day but for the brilliance of Tom Spillane at centre-half-back and his elder brother, Pat the indefatigable, in attack.

Kerry were firm favourites to account for Monaghan in the all-Ireland semi-final on 11 August, but they almost got the shock of their lives. Seán Kilfeather in the *Irish Times* was ecstatic about the game, which he described as

of quite outstanding excitement and high quality—a game of intensity, skill and sportsmanship in which Kerry and Monaghan provided ample evidence that Gaelic football can still brighten the dreariest of summers. Not since the epic semi-final of 1977 have we seen the likes of this.

Before an attendance of 22,000, Monaghan fought back on four occasions in the last thirteen minutes to draw level. Finally, almost with the last kick of the game, Éamonn McEneaney of Monaghan showed nerves of steel in drilling over a 55-yard free for the equaliser: Kerry 1-12, Monaghan 2-9. Kerry were glad to earn a replay; but the Monaghan coach, Seán McCague (now president of the GAA), and the team captain, Eugene Sherry, knew Monaghan had missed their chance, and both were bitterly disappointed not to have won.

In the replay on 25 August, Kerry crushed Monaghan, 2-9 to 0-10, before an attendance of 54,000. They were ahead by 2-3 to nil after twenty-five minutes, despite having Eoin Liston sent off after twenty minutes. Jack O'Shea starred; Pat Spillane had a wondrous first half. Liston and Power bagged the goals, Power's the 'gem of the day,' while the high fielding of Timmie O'Dowd and the defensive qualities of Páidí Ó Sé and Ger Lynch were vital ingredients in the success.

But Kerry were beginning to behave like spoiled children, especially in their attitude to the official team photograph, not having the full team involved and making it almost impossible for the photograph to be taken, something that offended ordinary members as well as the GAA authorities. This was the first time a county team had acted in such a manner in relation to GAA custom and the first time professionalism raised its ugly head. They were still winning on the field of play, but other forces were now impinging on their approach to success, and Monaghan had almost caught them napping. Would Dublin—who had come through after two rousing games with Mayo—put a halt to the Kerry gallop?

Before the 1985 final the Kerry team again took on the establishment by openly endorsing a washing-machine manufacturer in full-page advertisements in Sunday newspapers, which included rather crude photographs of many players in different stages of undress. This exercise in poor taste did nothing to heal the growing rift between the Kerry team and the GAA or the rank-and-file supporters, who didn't wish to see a Kerry tail wagging the GAA dog. There had been collisions in the past—as in 1982, when Kerry wore a strip produced by a multinational company instead of an Irish manufacturer—but that had been sorted out. The 1985 collision was more serious. It may all seem petty now; but for the first time Dublin had most of the neutral support behind them when they took the field against Kerry for the final of 1985.

Before an attendance of 69,000 on 22 September 1985, Kerry went on to defeat Dublin again by 2-12 to 2-8, first running away with the game and then surviving a wonderful Dublin rally in a match of an exemplary sporting nature.

Paddy Downey in the *Irish Times* wrote:

> Choose any cliché you like to describe Kerry's dire situation with only five minutes to go in an extraordinary all-Ireland final, their backs were crushed against the wall, they had one foot in the grave, they were barely hanging on by their finger-nails when with a mighty explosion of guts and skill they dismantled Dublin's fierce chilling and surging charge for the scores that retained the Sam Maguire Cup and Kerry's twenty-ninth title.

Páidí Ó Sé was Kerry's captain in 1985, as true a Kerryman as ever wore the green and gold. But being captain didn't change Páidí's approach. Kerry led 1-8 to 0-2 at half time, mainly through the brilliance of Jack O'Shea (described by Paddy Downey as 'a colossus in the first half, a saviour in the last five minutes'), the magnificent Eoin Liston (what a wonderful ball-winner and distributor!), Ger Lynch, giving his best display ever in the green and gold, Tommy Doyle, Páidí as captain, Tom Spillane continuing his great form, and Timmie O'Dowd.

In my GAA memorabilia I have a file of all-Ireland senior final programmes in which my instant impressions are written. The men who stood out for Dublin in that memorable second-half revival were Noel McCaffrey, giving a man-of-the-match performance at centre-half-back, and his two flankers, Pat Canavan and Dave Synnott, with John Kearns and Tommy Conroy also starring. Joe McNally scored two goals in the second half, the second one leaving only one point in it with seven minutes to go. It was up to Kerry now. Mikey pointed a free after a foul on Ogie; Barney Rock responded with a point from a fifty-yard free. But a wonderful point from Pat Spillane, followed by points from Timmie O'Dowd and John Kennedy, saw Kerry through for their twenty-ninth title. Close, but the play of champions.

It was a game of fine sportsmanship played on a warm and overcast day, and Dublin especially recalled for those present the glory days of 1974–7, before Kerry exerted dominance—easily the best game between the counties since 1977. The Kerry mix of the new and the old was still ringing true. But how long more could the O'Dwyer magic last?

The team in the final was much the same as in 1984. The forward line was:

Timmie O'Dowd	Denis 'Ogie' Moran	Pat Spillane
Mikey Sheehy	Eoin Liston	Ger Power

Substitute: John Kennedy for Ger Power.

When the GAA selected Kevin Heffernan and Liam Sammon at the end of 1985 to manage the first official Ireland team to travel to Australia for the International Series under Compromise Rules, there was widespread indignation in County Kerry and not a little surprise outside it that Mick O'Dwyer, with his wonderful record of success at this level, was bypassed; but one had to appreciate that for some time the genial Waterville man had been in the van of confrontation with the association that was now being expected to confer a singular honour on him. Jack O'Shea, Kerry's midfield maestro, was to be honoured with the captaincy of the team, which won that series in 1986 and acquitted itself well in Australia, a success that did Heffernan, Sammon and all concerned proud. O'Dwyer later coached the All-Star football team on an American visit in 1990.

1986 saw Kerry bounding out of Munster again, first beating Tipperary in Clonmel by 5-9 to 0-12, then Cork in the Munster final in Killarney by 0-12 to 0-8. In the semi-final in August they got a fright early on from an eager Meath team and were helped no end in the seventeenth minute of the first half by an incident in the Meath goal-mouth that yielded a very easy goal. Ogie Moran lobbed the ball towards Ger Power on the edge of the Meath square, but in their eagerness to deal with the shot Michael McQuillan, Mick Lyons and Joe Cassells collided, sending each other sprawling and presenting the onrushing Power with the ball and the simplest of tasks in shooting to an empty net. Though Meath rallied immediately, the stuffing had been knocked out of them. There was another Kerry goal twelve minutes from the end, involving Ogie Moran, Pat Spillane, and Jack O'Shea, who flicked the ball on to Willie Maher for yet another classic goal of the type we had now come to expect from this Kerry forward machine. Kerry emerged victorious, 2-13 to 0-12. Meath were taught a cruel lesson on the road to greater things; they would be back, older, wiser and more experienced. Elsewhere, Tyrone beat Galway with a late penalty to qualify for their first all-Ireland senior final.

Kerry were firm favourites to win the three-in-a-row, their thirtieth title in all and for a precious quintet—Páidí Ó Sé, Ogie Moran, Pat Spillane, Mickey Sheehy, and Ger Power—a record eight all-Ireland medals, 1975–86. Páidí and Ogie were among the starting fifteen in every winning final; Pat Spillane came on as a substitute in 1981. Denis 'Ogie' Moran, one of the least heralded of Kerry's stars yet a footballer of grace, speed, skill, and charisma, had the unique honour of playing in the same position, centre-half-forward, on all winning all-Ireland teams. Not gifted with great physique and often used over the years as a versatile play-anywhere footballer, Ogie is highly regarded inside and outside County Kerry. He was one of his county's most loyal sons, though domiciled in Limerick most of his life. But I'm jumping the gun.

All neutrals were supporting Tyrone, a county passionate about Gaelic football. Was Sam Maguire on his way to County Tyrone for the first time? As chairman of the Galway Football Board I was proud to see our county win its fifth minor all-Ireland crown in the curtain-raiser to the big game. Our party were in our seats on the top deck of the Hogan Stand just in time to see the start of the senior final. As expected, Kerry raced ahead and led by 0-3 to nil. Tyrone, getting over early nerves and exerting control at midfield, where Plunkett Donaghy and Harry McClure were on top, went in at half time deservedly leading by 0-7 to 0-4. Was an upset on the cards?

Kerry introduced Timmie O'Dowd for Ambrose O'Donovan in the second half, but Tyrone started in rampant fashion, and a goal by Paudge Quinn in the first minute put them ahead, 1-7 to 0-4. Then, in the third minute, Eugene McKenna was fouled in the small square, and Kevin McCabe, who had goaled from a penalty at a crucial stage against Galway in the semi-final, to the dismay of all Tyrone and neutral fans, blasted the ball over the bar and in a sense blasted Tyrone's chance of creating history.

But it's the old dogs for the hard road. Kerry took heart, and the pendulum swung in their direction. Instead of a 2-7 to 0-4 deficit it was 1-8 to 0-4, and plenty of time for Pat Spillane, Timmie O'Dowd, Jack O'Shea and Ger Power to create and take scores. Pat Spillane was inspired, and his flick-on goal from a Ger Power centre was vintage Kerry. Six minutes later, after another Power pass, Mikey Sheehy bulged the net again to level the score. After that it was plain sailing for Kerry, and they won by 2-15 to 1-10. If Tyrone had goaled that penalty it might have been different.

The Kerry team differed little from that of 1985. Willie Maher had replaced Timmie O'Dowd at right-half-forward, but O'Dowd came on as a substitute during play. It was not an altogether promising win but eventually a convincing one that signalled the end of Kerry's greatest era. Cork, with Larry Tompkins to inspire them and Billy Morgan as manager, were about to take over in Munster.

As we left Croke Park in 1986 it was hard to believe that Kerry would not win another all-Ireland until 1997. Mick O'Dwyer stayed on for some time, remained perhaps too loyal to his old guard, then eventually moved away before taking charge of Kildare in the nineties. But his position as Kerry's supremo in their greatest era remains sacred. Of this team we can truly say, 'Ní bheidh a leithéidí arís ann.'

> Plough and spade and seine-boat shaped them
>   for the deeds they were to do;
> Street and school and mountain heard their victory cry.
> Now their memories are like rainbows
>   o'er the meadows of the mind,
> The alive who'll live for ever and the dead who'll never die.
>   (Sigerson Clifford, 'Kerry's Footballers')

30

THE AUSTRALIAN CONNECTION

I n 1964 the Central Council of the GAA agreed to issue an invitation to an Australian football team to play a game in Ireland, but nothing much came of it. But about the same time Harry Beitzel, managing director of an Australian public relations and management consultancy and a former prominent umpire in Australian football, watched a broadcast of an all-Ireland final while on a business trip to London and was intrigued by the similarities between the Australian and Irish codes. He decided to bring them together, despite getting little encouragement from the Victoria Football League.

There are solid grounds for believing that the development of Australian football owed much to the influence of emigrant Irishmen. It is the only specifically Australian sport and boasts some of the oldest football clubs of any code in the world: Geelong and Melbourne were formed in 1858 and 1859, respectively. From humble beginnings, Australian football has grown in popularity to be the country's most successful national sport, now embracing teams from Perth, Adelaide, Sydney, Brisbane, and Victoria, the heartland of the sport.

Australian and Gaelic football are similar in their methods of catching, screening, running with the ball, punting, and passing. But the Australians use an oval ball, play on a round pitch, can lift the ball from the ground, play in quarters rather than halves, tackle differently, and use point posts similar to those used by the GAA until 1913.

Harry Beitzel, who was also well known as a television panellist and radio commentator on Australian football, set about organising a trip to Ireland in 1967 with a Victoria team that he called the 'Galahs', captained by one of the sport's legends, Ron Barassi. The sole concession granted to the Australians was being allowed to pick the ball off the ground; otherwise it was GAA rules all the way.

Meath had been crowned all-Ireland champions for the third time the previous month, and a match between the two teams was arranged. Beitzel had let it be known in the weeks before their arrival that they were coming to win. No-one knew what to expect when the team of muscular athletes in sleeveless guernseys (jerseys that if anything exaggerated their strength, athleticism and brawn) raced onto the field before a crowd of 23,000 on 12 October 1967. As the Australian team marched round the field, led by a smiling and confident Ron Barassi, somehow those present felt that history was about to be made.

The men from Australia took Meath apart with a display of high fielding and long kicking, racing to a 3-16 to 1-10 win. The brilliant Barry Davis won the *Irish Independent* 'Sports Star of the Week' award for his wonderful display. Royce Hart scored 2-2, and Hassa Mann popped over six points. Other names, such as those of Ken Fraser, Don Williams, Bob Skilton, Graham Chalmers, and Ian Law, would remain etched in GAA folklore. A new vista opened as the Australians hunted in packs through the field, overwhelming the Irish champions.

A game the Galahs had arranged in London fell through, and at short notice the GAA arranged for the Connacht champions, Mayo, to provide the opposition in Croke Park the following Saturday. A large attendance of 20,000 travelled to see the amazing Australians, who didn't disappoint the appreciative spectators, winning well by 2-12 to 2-5. They received an ovation as they made a lap of honour around Croke Park before scooting off to catch a plane for America, where they were due to play a New York team in Gaelic Park the following afternoon. But even the super-fit Galahs succumbed to fatigue and jet lag, and they were well beaten by 4-8 to 0-5 before 9,000 fans. New York had a very strong team at that time and were justifiably proud of being able to put a halt to the Australian gallop.

Meath, stung by their defeat, set about organising a trip to Australia the following March for a five-game series against local opposition, well chronicled in Peter McDermott's book *Gaels in the Sun.* Harry Beitzel had issued the invitation to Meath before the first game in Croke Park; they grabbed the opportunity, and their tour was an outstanding success, with victories in Perth (6-6 to 0-3); in the Melbourne Cricket Grounds against the Galahs by 3-9 to 0-7, sweet revenge against a team that included many of the pioneers from 1967, such as Davis, Deen, Dugdale, Nicholls, Frazer, Barassi, and Dwyer; in Sydney (3-14 to 1-3); in Adelaide (6-5 to 1-9); and finally in Melbourne at the Carlton Oval against the Galahs, again by 2-9 to 1-7, easily the best game of the series. There were 18,000 at the

Melbourne Cricket Grounds and 12,000 at the Carlton Oval to see men like Mattie Kerrigan, Tony Brennan, Paddy Mulvaney, Ollie Shanley, Pat Reynolds, Mick Mellett and of course Red Collier redeem the pride of Gaelic football. I was staying in the Gresham Hotel in Dublin on the eve of the Railway Cup finals and rose early to listen to Mícheál O'Hehir's superb live broadcast and the obvious pride in his voice at Meath's success.

The Australians were back for a second visit to Ireland in 1968 in another tour organised by Harry Beitzel, but this one didn't create quite the same stir. The Galahs drew with Kerry at Killarney, 1-12 each, and would step up their programme with a win of 1-11 to 2-7 over the all-Ireland champions, Down, who had returned to Dublin the previous Friday from an American tour. In between the Kerry and Down games the Galahs drew with Meath and defeated the Combined Universities.

Kerry kept the contact alive with an ambitious world tour in 1970. In Australia they won all five games played; they also played in New Zealand and San Francisco.

Despite these pioneering efforts, the high hopes at the time of establishing a regular international outlet did not materialise immediately. But the contacts were not lost, and another Beitzel group was back in Ireland in 1978 to play UCD, Dublin, and Kerry, while Kerry under Mick O'Dwyer undertook another world tour in 1981, visiting Australia during October and winning all three games there. Kerry in fact never lost to an Australian team, being the only Irish winners of Australia's 1978 tour, with a score of 3-9 to 0-16.

The link that had been established so excitedly was now almost threadbare. During the seventies and eighties the Victoria Football League was more concerned with the expansion of their own league so as to embrace the whole of Australia than with the promotion of an international series; but all was not lost.

At the GAA Congress of 1982 in Kilkenny, Dr Pat O'Neill, a prominent Meath delegate of the time, received overwhelming support for his motion that the GAA appoint a committee to investigate the concept of a permanent relationship between Australian and Gaelic football. This was the imaginative proposal that set the scene for the whole series of internationals that were to begin in 1984 and are now in their very successful state. In 1982 another imaginative connection was made with the visit of a schools team from Victoria for games with Dublin schools. This new dimension was further cemented when a Dublin Colleges team visited Australia in 1983.

How to draw up compromise rules for the first international test series between the two countries was the task that faced those organising the visit of the Australian team to Ireland in 1984, the centenary year of the GAA. The selectors for the first Irish team were Peter McDermott (Meath), Liam Sammon (Galway), Jody O'Neill (Tyrone), and Éamonn Young (Cork), while John Todd was the Australian coach, a man who ruffled a few feathers in his comments before and after the games.

The first compromise rules agreed were as follows. For scoring, the ordinary Gaelic football goal-posts would be used but with an extra set of posts erected six metres outside these. The normal goal would merit six points and the normal point over the cross-bar three points, and there would be one point for the ball going between the normal goal-post and the external post. Marks were allowed for players gaining clean possession. The pick-up off the ground was allowed. A player in possession was permitted to run six steps and could solo or hop the ball while running. Free kicks could be taken from the hands or the ground, but penalties had to be kicked. There would be a panel of twenty-one players, fifteen to play, with unlimited substitutions permitted. Substitutes would be allowed for players sent off during any game.

Playing time was agreed at eighty minutes, divided into four quarters, with an interval of two minutes between quarters and five minutes at half time. Two referees, one from Australia and one from Ireland, would operate in different halves of the field.

These rules, which were printed in the programme for that initial tour, made no reference to the tackle, something that caused no end of confusion in earlier games and was to flare up in the very first test in Cork. Pulling a player down in Gaelic football yields a free to the person in possession; in the Australian code a person tackled in possession is deemed to have fouled if caught in possession. The emphasis in Australian football has always been on speeding up play. So a conflict was inevitable from the beginning on this issue alone.

The Australians, captained by Stephen Malaxos, won the first test in Cork by 70 points to 57, after an ugly brawl in the third quarter, with Gary Pert and Robert 'Dipper' Dipierdomenico outstanding and Ross Glendinning and Craig Bradley scoring ten points apiece. Eoin Liston scored thirteen points for Ireland before a crowd of 8,000. The attendance increased to 13,000 a week later in Croke Park when Ireland won by 80 points to 76, with Colm O'Rourke of Meath scoring eighteen points.

A huge crowd of 32,000 came to Croke Park to see the decisive third test, won by Australia by 76 points to 71. This was another tough affair, with three players sent off and six booked and another massive punch-up involving many players. Stephen Malaxos and John Platten were the Australian stars; Jack O'Shea and Colm O'Rourke, who scored twenty-four points, starred for Ireland.

But the entire series, while creating interest, especially for the final test, left a poor taste here in Ireland, and the free-for-alls were not welcomed by fans. The tackle was not yet clearly defined. The round ball and the rectangular pitch were to Ireland's advantage, but the different refereeing interpretations of the tackle left fans and players guessing.

Australia had won the first test series. Ireland needed a more structured approach and a single coach to take on the unpopular John Todd, who accused the Irish of being 'wimps'.

The stage was set for a return visit. This took place in 1986 and featured the first international tour by a panel of Gaelic footballers representing Ireland. This time the planning was much more intense, and the whole screening and training programme, under Kevin Heffernan of Dublin as coach-manager, was much more professional. Ireland won two of the three tests played, to win the series, losing the first test by 64 to 57, winning the second by 62 to 46, and winning the third by 55 to 32 before 10,000 spectators in Adelaide. The star of the series was nineteen-year-old John O'Driscoll of Cork. Once again there were unseemly scenes in the first test, with five players in all sent off.

The final test was broadcast live in Ireland, and the public showed great interest in the win and took pride in the displays of Jack O'Shea, Brian McGilligan, Greg Blaney, John O'Driscoll, Jimmy Kerrigan, and Pat O'Byrne of Wicklow. The first test, in Perth, was a bruising affair. Happily, sportsmanship improved for the two final tests.

The third series of tests took place in Ireland in 1987, and Australia recovered from a poor start to take the series for the second time, Ireland winning the first test by 53 to 51 but losing the second by 72 to 47 and the final test, before 27,000 spectators, by 59 to 55. This third test was another bruising affair. Eugene McGee was the Irish team manager, with Neil Kerley in charge of Australia. Tony McGuinness for Australia won the 'Man of the Match' award for the final test.

The rules regarding tackling were much more clearly defined; all the other rules were much as before. But the rule on tackling as interpreted by the two referees, Paddy Collins (Ireland) and Rick Kinnear (Australia), was not to the satisfaction of either team.

Ireland, again under the management of Eugene McGee, made their second visit to Australia in 1990 and got off to a great start, winning the series by defeating Australia 47 to 38 in the first test and by a fine 52 to 31 in the second, with Jack O'Shea outstanding. A crowd of 18,000 showed up for the first test, in Waverley Stadium, Melbourne, but there was a disappointingly poor attendance of just 7,000 for the second test in Bruce Stadium, Canberra. Jim Stynes played for the Ireland team for this series, while the Kerryman Seán Wight played for Australia.

In the years following Harry Beitzel's pioneering venture quite a number of young footballers from Ireland opted to travel to Australia and try their luck at the new game, just as happens with soccer hopefuls who go on to play for clubs in England. Most returned after a year, but Jim Stynes became one of the true greats of the Australian game, while Seán Wight also attained star status. The lure of semi-professionalism is very enticing and is one that is likely to increase.

The third test, won by Australia by 50 points to 44 in Perth, was a bit of an anti-climax, with the series already won. Fewer than 8,000 attended the game, and the interest generated back home didn't compare with 1986, when players like John O'Driscoll were the talk of the country.

There followed a lull in the Irish-Australian link where international series were concerned, but many of the old contacts were maintained. The Victoria Football League, which hitherto governed the sport, now ceded this position to the Australian Football League, whose main aims were the expansion of the game within Australia, the creation of new clubs, and the development of stadiums, to be given priority over embarking on the establishment of another international series with Ireland.

In 1998 a four-year two-test international series was established, to be reviewed after its completion in 2001. The Australian Football League were keen to promote the series when it would be hosted by them in 1999, and the GAA also pledged it their full support. So the 1998 series was born, and the GAA placed every resource at the disposal of the manager, Colm O'Rourke, and his selectors, Mickey Moran and John O'Keeffe, while the Irish players took it seriously and prepared well. Colm was anxious that the brawls that were so much a part of previous series would have no place, and the Australian coach, Leigh Matthews, and the AFL rowed in with that. Passion, yes, but none of this he-man stuff that had become associated with the hybrid game and earned it headlines for all the wrong reasons.

And the series remained true to the wishes of those in charge. The rules were more on less as in previous series. The tackle was defined. Each team management was allowed a runner to facilitate changes in personnel and switches. Fifteen players and five interchange players were allowed. Players were permitted to carry the ball up to ten metres without bouncing it or playing it on. There would be a round ball, as before, and an official from each team would act as timekeeper and scorer and operate the hooter to signal the end of each quarter.

In Croke Park for the first test 22,000 fans saw Ireland dominate the game from the start, superbly led by John McDermott of Meath, only to be pipped at the post by Australia with 62 points (2-13-11) to Ireland's 61 (2-13-10). The fitter Australians lasted the pace better, with the fit and strong Nathan Buckley running and scoring at will.

The crowd liked what they saw. There were none of the brawls associated with earlier tests, and Jarlath Fallon, Seán Lockhart, Séamus Moynihan, Peter Canavan and Glen Ryan were able to keep up with their professional opponents.

In the second test a week later a big attendance of 35,000 saw Ireland win the series, winning the second test by 67 points to 56 (aggregate 128 to 118). The game grew in stature, and Colm O'Rourke's gambit of favouring short passing instead of using the long through ball allowed Ireland to dominate. Both sets of players enjoyed the international experience, and the Australians vowed to win back the series in Australia in 1999.

Would the Australian public take to the hybrid game this time? Hitherto the Irish public had shown more interest, but the AFL guaranteed a serious effort in the promotion of the 1999 series in Australia. They were true to their word. We in Ireland were not prepared for the change in attitude of the Australian followers until we switched on our televisions on the morning of Friday 8 October to see a packed Melbourne Cricket Grounds, with 64,000 fans assembled (a bigger crowd than assembled for either of the 1999 all-Ireland finals) and Ireland deservedly winning the first test by 70 points (2-16-10) to 62 (0-16-14). The crowd warmed to the game too, and here at home we were proud of the great play of Jarlath Fallon (Galway), the Meath contingent of John McDermott, Darren Fay, and Trevor Giles, of Finbar Cullen of Offaly, and of Joe Kavanagh of Cork; and when Ciarán Whelan of Dublin rocketed a goal, a cheer greeted it in many an Irish home.

Once again Nathan Buckley starred for Australia, and the local team seemed to favour the selection of skilled rather than brawny players—though some of their close marking of men like Peter Canavan (Tyrone) and Jarlath Fallon was somewhat intimidating. If they can become more familiar with the round ball and can shoot straighter they will pose even bigger problems.

The next stop was Adelaide a week later, when Ireland won the series, drawing the second test by 52 points (1-11-13) to 52 points (2-12-4). Ireland made a great comeback in the final twenty minutes before a capacity crowd of 45,000. The smiles on the faces of Colm O'Rourke (operating the same management structure as in 1998) and John McDermott, the captain, on the presentation podium afterwards told it all. Michael Donnellan took off in the final quarter and inspired Ireland to a sensational finish, though the winners of the series were strangely off form in their shooting. Anthony Tohill of Derry was another player to shine.

Whither now? It's safe to say that the future of the international link looks extremely bright. Though the distance is huge, modern travel has made access and contact much easier, and links at under-age and college level are being strengthened. The connection established in 1967 is at its highest level now.

It would be wrong to think that either game will replace the other, but already Gaelic football has learnt from and adopted some Australian influences, such as the quick free and the option of taking frees from the hand. The mark and the tackle are still bones of contention. Sometimes it pays to hold the ball in the Irish code, whereas the reverse is true under the Australian rules.

The establishment of an international series on a firm footing has been the great achievement. There will be advances and refinements in the years ahead. Let us hope that the GAA will promote future series in Ireland with the same force and acumen as obtained in Australia in 1999 and that an atmosphere similar to that in Melbourne and Adelaide will prevail.

In the meantime the originator of it all has not been forgotten. The Harry Beitzel Medal is awarded to the man who, in the opinion of the judges, is the 'fairest and best' player of each series. So far these have been Jimmy Kerrigan (1984), Robert Dipierdomenico (1986), Tony McGuinness (1987), Jack O'Shea (1990), Nathan Buckley (1998), and Séamus Moynihan (1999).

31

Seán Boylan and the Re-Emergence of Meath

He arrived without a fanfare to take the reins of Meath football when it was at a low ebb. Previously involved with the Meath hurlers as a player, he had helped the footballers as physiotherapist and herbalist on their few big days.

The year was 1982, and Seán Boylan, the Dunboyne herbalist, came into the job because it seemed that nobody else wanted it. He's still there, bringing Meath to their greatest heights as footballers and in the period 1982–96 guiding the team to six Leinster championships, three all-Irelands, one Centenary Cup, and three national football league successes.

From the moment Seán took over, Meath looked up. The first time I noticed the change was at a national football league semi-final against Armagh in Croke Park on a very cold and wet Easter Sunday in 1983. Meath went down by a few points but left a lasting impression. Then followed an O'Byrne Cup success and two stirring first-round championship games with Dublin (draw and replay) in Croke Park, which Meath lost narrowly in the end, mainly because of a series of goalkeeping errors, which tended to afflict their efforts at the time.

These games were the beginning of one of the greatest rivalries the sport has ever seen, Croke Park battles that drew massive attendances, always creating drama in knife-edge finishes, culminating in that wonderful four-game saga of 1991. It was Seán's unusual and varied training regime that really took his players' fancy; it produced a fit, contented and determined group of players and soon began to make sense. He has man-management skill of a high order and before long earned the respect of all for his approach. In his book *The Final Whistle,* Colm O'Rourke, one of Meath's top players, writes about the 'respect he instilled in his charges for the County Meath and the jersey you pulled over your head.'

The Meath team became used to running through the sand dunes at Bettystown, up and down the Hill of Tara, and around the all-weather track at Summerhill. They rowed in the canal, ran in the swimming-pools at Navan and Gormanston in special buoyancy suits to help sore limbs and to generate flexibility, and paddled in the ice-cold sea, as well as training in the normal football routine in quiet Dalgan Park, close to Navan.

When Dublin won the 1983 all-Ireland, Meath knew that success for themselves wasn't too far away. The first breakthrough came in the novel open-draw Centenary Cup of 1984, when Meath defeated Monaghan in a fine game of Gaelic football. But despite this, Meath didn't show again until 1986, when Boylan—now joined by Pat Reynolds and Tony Brennan, both former stars, as selectors—introduced new blood, which, allied to experience, saw the green and gold win Leinster honours by defeating Dublin by 0-9 to 0-7, before losing to Kerry in the semi-final by 2-13 to 0-12. Lack of experience tended to inhibit Meath against a Kerry team almost at the end of its tether. In their anxiety to clear a ball, three Meath defenders—Joe Cassells, Mick Lyons, and the goalkeeper, Mick McQuillan—clashed, allowing Ger Power the freedom to pick a spot in an empty net.

In 1987 Meath benefited from that experience and began the year with a good win over Laois, 1-11 to 2-5. It was an anxious game for the winners, who came good in the end to avenge a sore defeat of two years previously. Martin O'Connell, who had become disillusioned by being played anywhere instead of in his favourite half-back position, was back in the squad, if not yet on the team. Then followed an easy win over Kildare, 0-15 to 0-9, with Brian Stafford emerging as the cool-as-cucumber full-forward, combining ace free-taking talent with a wide range of football skills. On this day Brian accounted for 0-10 of the total. Martin O'Connell also was back on the team, this time at corner-forward, in for the injured Colm O'Rourke.

Meath now faced Dublin in another Leinster final, and they recorded a 1-13 to 0-12 win over their old rivals, with Martin O'Connell finally back in his true position of number 7 and performing brilliantly. Two wins in a row over Dublin in the Leinster final made Meath fans happy.

Another good win over Derry in the semi-final, by 0-15 to 0-8, saw Meath reach the all-Ireland final against Cork, who had beaten Galway well in a replayed semi-final after taking over from Kerry (at last) in Munster, with the former Kildare players Larry Tompkins and Shay Fahy very much in the van.

Meath now began to experience the euphoria that grips counties when an all-Ireland final is reached. They hadn't been in a final since 1970—seventeen long years in the shadows. Cork, inspired by Tompkins, had beaten Kerry as well as Galway in a replay and were the sensation of 1987 after so much big-game exposure.

Meath's training ground in Dalgan Park grew more thronged as final day approached. Liam Hayes in his readable book *Out of Our Skins* writes about the scene on the night of 10 September:

> It was crazy tonight. Like a bloody circus. People everywhere inside and outside the low wire which surrounded the field.

But they got used to it, as teams tend to.

In the final, Cork, after a very bright opening in which they led 0-7 to 0-2 after twenty-one minutes, were pegged back, first by an inspirational block of a goal shot from Jimmy Kerrigan by the teak-tough Mick Lyons, then an inspired punched goal by Colm O'Rourke and a delightful point by David Beggy, to leave Meath in front at half time, 1-6 to 0-8. They ran out easy enough winners in the end by 1-14 to 0-11. Brian Stafford was cool, calm and collected at full-forward, scoring 0-7 (four from play). Mick Lyons and Robbie O'Malley shone in defence, while Liam Hayes had a blinder at midfield and was selected as RTE 'Man of the Match'.

This was the winning team:

Michael McQuillan

Robbie O'Malley   Mick Lyons (*captain*)   Terry Ferguson

Kevin Foley   Liam Harnan   Martin O'Connell

Liam Hayes   Gerry McEntee

David Beggy   Joe Cassells   P. J. Gillic

Colm O'Rourke   Brian Stafford   Bernard Flynn

Substitutes: Colm Coyle for Joe Cassells, Pádhraic Lyons for Martin O'Connell.

Colm Coyle had returned from America before the semi-final and was recalled to the Meath panel almost immediately. This was a fine Meath team, captained by Mick Lyons. They played a 'no frills' brand of football with a refreshing return to the long kick and the skill of high fielding, essential to the team's success. Every member of the team fitted in to Seán Boylan's pattern, with Bernard Flynn an exceptional corner-forward in the Mickey Sheehy mould. Seán

Boylan's great wish had been achieved. And more was to come.

As time went on, the Meath appetite seemed to grow. The national football league title for 1987/8 was secured with a good win in the final over Dublin in a replay, 2-13 to 0-11. The show went on with a third successive Leinster title win over Dublin by 2-5 to 0-9. This was the day Charlie Redmond kicked a Dublin penalty over the bar with the last kick of the game, a shot that, if goaled, would have drawn the game.

After Meath had beaten Mayo in the semi-final by 0-16 to 2-5 it was to be Cork again as opponents in the final. But Meath were fortunate to draw, with a score of 0-12 to 1-9, getting a doubtful free at the end to level the game through the trusted boot of Brian Stafford. Cork were incensed at the finish: they had been the better team and had lost the lead because of a free they felt was undeserved.

For the replay Meath let it be known that they were not to be shoved around, as they felt they had been in the drawn game. Controlled aggression is what Seán Boylan asked for; he got a bit more than that, and Gerry McEntee was the first casualty of this new plan, being sent to the line for an incident involving Niall Cahalane six minutes into the game. Despite the handicap, Meath managed to defeat Cork by 0-13 to 0-12 in a game played in a bad spirit. But they deserved to win, if only for the inspirational play of Martin O'Connell. Once again Brian Stafford scored 0-7 and, as always, was as sporting as the day is long.

There was bad blood between Meath and Cork for some time afterwards; and Meath didn't endear themselves to neutrals, either during the game or subsequently, as they tried to defend their approach. Cork overdid the complaining and would have done themselves more service by remaining silent. The only change on Meath's team from 1987 was Colm Coyle at number 5 instead of Kevin Foley. Joe Cassells, a wonderful servant of Meath football, had the great honour of lifting the new Sam Maguire Cup aloft for the first time. Seán Boylan, the amiable herbalist with the ready smile, had notched up title number 2. Meath had joined the ranks of great teams—teams capable of winning two all-Irelands in a row.

They continued on their merry way, winning another national football league title in 1989/90 and the Leinster title in 1990 and 1991 before losing out to Cork and Down, respectively, in the all-Ireland final; but the great days for this team were over. Dublin were beginning to champ at the bit, and one by one all the old reliables— Lyons, O'Rourke, Hayes, O'Malley, Harnan, McEntee, Cassells, Stafford, Beggy, McCabe, Flynn, and Gillic—tended to move on.

On 30 July 1995 Dublin defeated Meath in the Leinster final for the third successive year—this time by 1-18 to 1-8. It was the swan song of Colm O'Rourke, Brian Stafford, Robbie O'Malley, and P. J. Gillic. One felt sure that Seán Boylan would call it a day too—but not a bit of it. He stayed put, picked up the pieces, and set off again, depending on the ever-reliable Martin O'Connell, Colm Coyle, now much more level-headed in approach, and a new bouncing star in Tommy Dowd to inspire a whole host of former minor stars, such as Graham Geraghty, Trevor Giles, Conor Martin, Darren Fay, and Enda McManus. Added to all this, Meath had a potential match-winner in the new midfield star John McDermott, one of the best the county has ever produced in the position.

So began 1996, Meath again unheralded but starting well by hammering an expectant Carlow team by 0-24 to 0-6, then Laois by 2-14 to 1-9, with Trevor Giles scintillating both days, taking over the mantle of Brian Stafford as ace free-taker. Then followed a hard-earned win over Dublin in the Leinster final by 0-10 to 0-8, with the captain, Tommy Dowd, leading by example.

In the all-Ireland semi-final, Tyrone were well beaten by 2-15 to 0-12 and whinged too much afterwards about two or three incidents in which their players picked up injuries after close physical contact. Two of these involved Martin O'Connell, and both, to my eyes, were accidental. The injury suffered by Peter Canavan was different; he is a player who gets more than his share of close and often excessively physical treatment. Again Meath didn't win any friends, but one had to admire the birth of a new team, whose stars were Giles, McDermott, Fay, and the always reliable O'Connell and Dowd.

Mayo, under John Maughan, had come bouncing out of Connacht, beating Galway and Kerry with style and generating excitement in County Mayo and a hope that their great football famine was at an end.

Graham Geraghty had been Meath's star in the semi-final win over Tyrone, but it was Mayo who stole the show, led by Liam McHale at midfield. A rather hopeful kick at goal by Colm Coyle hopped over the bar for an undeserved equalising point on the stroke of time, to leave the score Meath 0-12, Mayo 1-9.

Mayo decided they would not be intimidated by Meath's rugged approach in the replay, and therein lay their downfall. The now infamous 'One in, all in' approach led to a melee and almost total involvement in a brawl that disgraced the occasion and the game. As a result of this fracas Liam McHale and Colm Coyle got the line when many others might also have been pinpointed. Mayo were not as dominant in this game, but once again the Meath spirit of 'never say die' prevailed as they came from behind in a see-saw finish for the full-forward, Brendan Reilly, to score a remarkable winning point late in the game. One couldn't but feel sorry for Mayo, who missed the bus the first day and who, in opting to take on Meath physically, chose the wrong option. Mayo's style of football is open, fast, and spontaneous, and the rough stuff is foreign to their style.

Meath play a tougher brand of football but don't deserve the unpopular status to which many neutrals assign them. I like the Meath approach, except when one or two individuals besmirch it. One heavy head-high tackle on Mickey Linden in the 1991 all-Ireland final is a case in point, when the Meath player responsible was lucky to stay on the pitch. Seán Boylan had done the incredible again; and he is still in charge. Trevor Giles was selected as Footballer of the Year, and Meath were a force again.

The 1996 winning team was:

Conor Martin

Mark O'Reilly	Darren Fay	Martin O'Connell
Colm Coyle	Enda McManus	Paddy Reynolds
Jimmy McGuinness	John McDermott	
Trevor Giles	Tommy Dowd (*captain*)	Graham Geraghty
Colm Brady	Brendan Reilly	Barry Callaghan

Evan Kelly was selected at number 13 in the drawn game.

32

BILLY MORGAN AND CORK'S TWO-IN-A-ROW

The age of the team manager had really arrived when Cork deservedly won two consecutive all-Ireland titles in 1989 and 1990. Heffernan, O'Dwyer, McGee, Boylan, and now Morgan.

Billy Morgan, the steely Nemo Rangers goalkeeper, had captained Cork to success in 1973 and in no small way masterminded Nemo Rangers' run of all-Ireland club successes, first as captain and later as coach. It was inevitable that he should be placed in charge of the Cork senior footballers, and almost as inevitable that success would come their way too. Billy was helped in his great ambition by the decision of the two former Kildare stars Larry Tompkins and Shay Fahy to throw in their lot with Cork and become key figures in the Cork renaissance. Tompkins, who had emigrated to America, later returned to live in County Cork and lent his allegiance to Castlehaven. Fahy, an army officer stationed in Cork, had become, like Tompkins, disillusioned with Kildare football and felt confident that something was on the way in Cork.

Everything started to happen almost immediately. Kerry were beaten in four successive Munster finals, something unheard of in the past, and were really trounced in the last of these by 2-23 to 1-11. Meath proved the bogey team in 1987 and 1988; but that was to change too.

It took some motivation on Morgan's part to get the engines revving again after the 1987 and 1988 losses to Meath, but a winter holiday in the Canary Islands helped strengthen their resolve. Morgan and the selection team of Bob Honohan, Michael Farr, Seán Murphy and Dave Loughman decided on a definite easy-training approach to the national football league, hoping to get promotion to division 1. They topped division 2 and went on to win the national football

Galway completed a magnificent three-in-a-row in 1966 and dominated the game in the middle years of the decade. This team played in the All-Ireland semi-final v. Cork. **Front Row** (*from left*): S. Cleary, M. Newell, J.B. McDermott, C. Dunne, E. Colleran (Captain), J. Geraghty, J. Donnellan. **Back Row**: S. Leydon, N. Tierney, M. McDonagh, J. Duggan, L. Sammon, J. Keenan, C. McDonagh, P. Donnellan.

James McCartan of Down, one of the best players of his or any other era.
(G.A. DUNCAN)

Dermot Earley of Roscommon (*right*), one of the finest players in the modern era not to have won All-Ireland honours.

The Offaly team of 1971 which brought the Sam Maguire Cup to the Faithful County for the first time. **Front Row** (*from left*): S. Cooney, T. McTague, W. Bryan (Captain), E. Mulligan, M. Heavey, J. Gunning. **Back Row**: P. McCormack, M. O'Rourke, M. Connor, K. Claffey, N. Clavin, S. Evans, M. Furlong, M. Ryan, K. Kilmurray. (CONNOLLY COLLECTION/SPORTSFILE)

The less fashionable counties often produce outstanding players. Sligo's Mickey Kearins (no. 14), seen here tussling with Mayo's Ger Feeney, was one such.

Cork's winning captain, Billy Morgan, climbs the steps in the Hogan Stand in 1973 to become the first Leesider to claim the Sam Maguire Cup since 1945.

The Dublin team, All-Ireland champions of 1974. **Front Row** (*from left*): B. Mullins, G. Wilson, P. Reilly, S. Doherty (Captain), D. Hickey, G. O'Driscoll. **Back Row**: S. Rooney, A. O'Toole, R. Kelleher, J. Keaveney, T. Hanahoe, P. Cullen, J. McCarthy, A. Larkin, B. Doyle. (CONNOLLY COLLECTION/SPORTSFILE)

Tony Hanahoe in action in the 1974 All-Ireland final against Galway. It was the Dubs' first championship win in eleven years and the start of one of their greatest eras.

Brian Murphy of Cork (left) challenges Pat Spillane of Kerry in the Munster final of 1976. (DONAL SHEEHAN)

The Kerry team of 1977: NFL champions. **Front Row** (*from left*): M. Sheehy, J. Deenihan, G. O'Keeffe, P. Ó Sé, J. O'Keeffe (Captain), G. Power, J. Egan, B. Walsh. **Back Row**: D. Moran, P. Lynch, P. Spillane, C. Nelligan, T. Kennelly, S. Walsh, J. O'Shea. (CONNOLLY COLLECTION/SPORTSFILE)

This Dublin-Kerry All-Ireland semi-final of 1977 was one of the finest Gaelic football matches ever played. (CONNOLLY COLLECTION/SPORTSFILE)

Seán Walsh of Kerry and Brian Mullins of Dublin rise for the ball.

Jack O'Shea, one of the all-time greats, demonstrates the art of fielding. (CONNOLLY COLLECTION/SPORTSFILE)

The Offaly team that denied Kerry their bid for a historic five-in-a-row by winning the 1982 All-Ireland final. **Front Row** (*from left*): M. Fitzgerald, P. Fitzgerald, M. Furlong, R. Connor (Captain), J. Guinan, M. Lowry, C. Conroy. **Back Row**: S. Lowry, G. Carroll, J. Mooney, L. Connor, L. Currams, P. Dunne, T. Connor, M. Connor. (CONNOLLY COLLECTION/SPORTSFILE)

Two views of Séamus Darby's goal that won the 1982 title for Offaly. (COLMAN DOYLE)

The Kerry team that completed a three-in-a-row in 1986. **Front Row** (*from left*): E. Liston, T. Doyle (Captain), P. Ó Sé, A. O'Donovan, M. Spillane, G. Power, D. Moran. **Back Row**: J. O'Shea, T. Spillane, M. Sheehy, C. Nelligan, G. Lynch, W. Maher, P. Spillane, S. Walsh. (CONNOLLY COLLECTION/SPORTSFILE)

The Meath team of 1990, winners of the Leinster title and All-Ireland runners-up. Under the brilliant management of Seán Boylan, Meath have won more championships in the 80s and 90s than any county except Kerry. **Front Row** (*from left*): P.J. Gillic, T. Ferguson, B. Flynn, K. Foley, R. O'Malley, L. Hayes. **Back Row**: C. O'Rourke, C. Brady, M. Lyons, T. Dowd, D. Smyth, M. O'Connell, B. Reilly, B. Stafford, D. Beggy. (CONNOLLY COLLECTION/SPORTSFILE)

Seán Boylan, the Dunboyne herbalist who has piloted Meath to almost twenty years as a major force in the game. (SPORTSFILE)

September 1992. Anthony Molloy becomes the first—and so far the only —Donegal captain to lift the Sam Maguire Cup. (INPHO)

Pure romance. The Leitrim team that won the Connacht championship in 1994 before
going down bravely to Dublin in the All-Ireland semi-final. **Front Row** (*from left*):
G. Flanagan, P. Kieran, P. Donoghue, D. Darcy (Captain), F. Reynolds, A. Rooney,
P. Kenny. **Back Row**: J. Honeyman, M. Quinn, C. McGlynn, L. Conlon, M. McHugh,
S. Quinn, N. Moran, G. Dugdale.

Peter Canavan of Tyrone, one of the very finest footballers of the 1990s.

Ulster teams dominated the championship in the first half of the 1990s. Donegal and Derry (shown here) won in 1992 and 1993, respectively, with Down victorious in 1991 and 1994. In addition, Tyrone were unlucky to lose to Dublin by a single point in 1995.

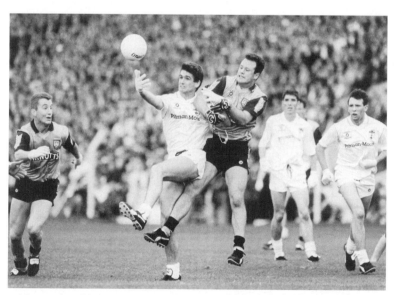

Kildare and Dublin in action in the Leinster championship of 1998. The great Kildare revival of that year brought them all the way to the All-Ireland final, where they finally met their match in an inspired Galway team.

The Galway team that bridged a 32-year gap by bringing the Sam Maguire Cup back across the Shannon in 1998. **Front Row** (*from left*): S. de Paor, M. Donnellan, R. Silke (Captain), D. Savage, M. McNamara, N. Finnegan, T. Mannion. **Back Row**: P. Joyce, T. Meehan, S. Walsh, J. Fallon, K. Walsh, S. Ó Domhnaill, G. Fahy, J. Divilly.

league without unduly stepping up the training schedule, defeating
Kerry well in the semi-final and Dublin in the home final before
travelling to New York and winning the final proper (after two legs on
aggregate, Cork 3-21 to New York's 2-14). But the victory was won at
a huge price. The All-Star full-back Colman Corrigan suffered damage
to a knee ligament that hampered him for some time.

But league success built up morale for the championship, despite
the injuries, and Cork went on to record their first three Munster titles
in a row, first of all by beating Tipperary easily 0-22 to 0-6 and then
defeating Kerry in Killarney after a close game by 1-12 to 1-9, a game
in which Larry Tompkins scored 0-7 and John O'Driscoll scored a
spectacular first-half goal. Denis Allen, the Cork captain, was ecstatic
afterwards.

> I have been on Cork teams which scored 0-15 in Killarney and
> lost. It is true we played in fits and starts today, but when all is
> said and done, we achieved what we set out to do, and that was
> to beat Kerry for the third year in a row.

Everything was rolling along nicely.

Much has been written, and rightly so, of the Munster hurling
final magic of Thurles, but Kerry v. Cork Munster finals in Killarney
are special events too. It's great to spend the weekend in Killarney for
such an event. Rival supporters mingle in pubs the night before and
sing together 'The Banks of My Own Lovely Lee' and 'The Rose of
Tralee'. There is never any rancour.

Dublin had stripped Meath of their Leinster and all-Ireland titles,
and an attendance of 60,000 thronged Croke Park for the Dublin-
Cork semi-final, an extraordinary game in many ways. Dublin raced
into a seven-point lead, but two penalty goals from the superb ball-
player John Cleary brought Cork back to lead by a point at half time.
Dublin, now reduced to fourteen men because of the sending off of
Keith Barr, still battled royally, and it was only in the last five minutes
that they wilted to the score 2-10 to 1-9.

Mayo, under John O'Mahony, had come out of Connacht, then
conquered Tyrone and with a midfield axis of T. J. Kilgannon, Liam
McHale and Willie Joe Padden were expected to push Cork to the
limit. And they did just that.

Cork started well, playing into a slight breeze, and went into a
four-point lead, but Mayo rallied to within two points at half time.
After play resumed, Mayo had an inspirational goal from Anthony
Finnerty to put them ahead of Cork for the first time. Cork edged

ahead again; but the Mayo fire was still aflame, and they went ahead by a point with eighteen minutes to go. Then the Cork goalkeeper, John Kerins, narrowed the angle severely on Anthony Finnerty so that he missed from close range. The Corkmen were inspired, none more so than Dave Barry, who was truly brilliant; and a final salvo of four unanswered points from Paul McGrath, two from the late Mick McCarthy and a final one from the dual star Teddy McCarthy left the score Cork 0-17, Mayo 1-11.

Mayo had fought the good fight; but Cork had won at last. Billy Morgan summed it up in a Cork Yearbook article:

> The hard work, the worries, the fears of three successive final defeats, the long years since 1973 were over. Cork had won the 1989 final. Life would never be the same again. I felt very happy, happy and thankful that I, Billy Morgan, was part of a magnificent effort by players, selectors, Board officials and a tremendous public to bring another great honour to Cork. The welcome home from the cheering crowds in the South Mall on Monday night crowned a wonderful weekend. What a fine bunch of men.

The following are Billy's fine bunch of men, champions of 1989:

John Kerins

| Niall Cahalane | Stephen O'Brien | Jimmy Kerrigan |
| Michael Slocum | Conor Counihan | Tony Davis |

Teddy McCarthy   Shay Fahy

| Dave Barry | Larry Tompkins | Barry Coffey |
| Paul McGrath | Denis Allen (*captain*) | John Cleary |

Substitutes: Danny Culloty for Shay Fahy, Mick McCarthy for John Cleary, John O'Driscoll for Barry Coffey.

The 'fine bunch of men' included some quality footballers, such as Niall Cahalane, a wonderful servant of Cork football, Stephen O'Brien, a lion-hearted player, Conor Counihan, solid centre-half-back, and Tony Davis, a quality wing-half-back. Teddy McCarthy's great spring and fielding ability complemented Shay Fahy's grafting. In a lively forward line Larry Tompkins was the arch-orchestrator, one of the really great players of modern times. During one of those Killarney Munster finals Mícheál Ó Muircheartaigh painted the picture as only he can.

Arriving in Killarney yesterday, the first man I met was Larry Tompkins, heading for Fitzgerald Stadium with a bag of footballs on his back. He was going to practise a few frees from all angles, and reminded me of the *spailpín fánach* of old. It's wonderful what a star player will do to achieve perfection.

In April 1990 Meath once again proved to be a spanner in Cork's works, defeating the all-Ireland champions in the national football league quarter-final; but a hugely successful American trip in May, which included impressive victories over the All-Star teams, built up morale and set the tone for another lash at the all-Ireland. First there was an easy win over Limerick by 4-15 to 1-3, followed by Cork's easiest win ever over Kerry in the Munster final by 2-23 to 1-11. This was despite a desperate Cork injury crisis involving Teddy McCarthy, Tony Davis, Barry Coffey, John O'Driscoll, and John Cleary, which meant the recall of the dual performer Denis Walsh, Paddy Hayes, out of action for eighteen months, and the retired Colm O'Neill.

Larry Tompkins, now captain, led by example, and Colm O'Neill ran riot, scoring eleven points to Larry's five, with Mick McCarthy and Johnny Culloty scoring invaluable goals. What could have been a dark day turned out to be one of Cork's greatest, with four Munster final victories over Kerry in a row, a complete reversal of old traditions.

Roscommon were overcome in the semi-final by 0-17 to 0-10 after moments of anxiety early on, when Niall Cahalane was superlative at full-back. Switches that brought Shay Fahy from full-forward to midfield and Mick McCarthy into the attack worked wonders. In the other semi-final Meath defeated Donegal by 3-9 to 1-7. Would these Meathmen prove the bugbears once again? But inspiration of a different kind surfaced now, with Cork's hurlers winning the all-Ireland hurling title after an epic game with Galway. The double was on, and Teddy McCarthy was the man who could achieve the unique honour of winning the all-Ireland in both codes in the same year.

Everyone was now fit for the fray and dying to be involved. The announcement of the Cork team to be selected by Christy Collins, Bob Honohan, Seán Murphy, Billy Morgan and Dave Loughman was awaited with interest and anxiety. This was it:

John Kerins

Tony Nation   Niall Cahalane   Stephen O'Brien
Michael Slocum   Conor Counihan   Barry Coffey

          Shay Fahy   Danny Culloty

Dave Barry   Larry Tompkins   Teddy McCarthy
Paul McGrath   Colm O'Neill   Mick McCarthy

From the outset Cork took the game to Meath, with Shay Fahy outstanding at midfield. The full-forward Colm O'Neill, a lovely ball-player always, was early in the wars with his opponent, Mick Lyons, and was unlucky to see a piledriver for goal rebound off the crossbar and unluckier still to be sent off in the thirty-first minute of the first half for an untypical retaliation. Were Cork going to go under to the Meath bogey again? Still they kept in front and led at half time by 0-6 to 0-5. Though the future looked gloomy, there were positive signs all across the field. Stephen O'Brien, playing at full-back, was sound, and Niall Cahalane was containing the Colm O'Rourke menace. Barry Coffey was at his best at left-half-back.

The heads never went down in the second half. In fact the loss of O'Neill seemed to lift Cork, and two crucial points from Shay Fahy and Paul McGrath just after half time resuscitated any flagging spirits. Larry Tompkins, despite suffering a crippling leg injury, soldiered on in an act of superhuman bravery, and Cork held on for a heroic and deserved win by 0-11 to 0-9. They had called in three substitutes: John O'Driscoll for Mick McCarthy, Paddy Hayes for Dave Barry, and John Cleary for Paul McGrath.

The double had been achieved. Meath had been beaten at last; and Teddy McCarthy had achieved a unique place in GAA history. Larry Tompkins, despite damaging the cruciate ligament in his knee, scored four points in all; he didn't play again until well into 1991. He was ecstatic afterwards when being presented with the Sam Maguire Cup. So were Cork's army of supporters. The footballers of Cork, often the poor relations in the county, had come of age, had secured two all-Irelands in a row, and had courageously delivered the double.

The first part of the journey home by train on the Monday evening was relaxing, but it became exciting as Mallow and Cork approached. Éamonn Young in his book *Rebels at the Double* described the scene.

> The big open bus moved steady and slow, through the thousands that gathered in MacCurtain Street, the Bridge and

Patrick Street. Red and white was everywhere; men sang, women clapped and youngsters who should have been in bed an hour before, were lifted on to the shoulders of ecstatic Daddies.

It was a wonderful homecoming, and the city went beautifully mad.

We'll leave the last word to Liam Mulvihill, director-general of the GAA, who wrote in the Cork 1991 Yearbook:

> In achieving the double again in 1990 (it happened once previously in this century) Cork have confirmed the county's status as the brightest jewel in the GAA crown.

33

THE END OF GAELIC FOOTBALL'S GREATEST SAGA

There have been some wonderful sagas in the history of Gaelic football, such as the series involving Roscommon and Sligo in 1925. Some old-timers who saw the wonderful three-game series between Meath and Louth in 1949 still recall it as vintage football. Counties Meath and Louth are neighbours, and the rivalry has always been keen, and never keener than in 1949. Meath, on their way to their first senior title, overcame the then Leinster senior champions, Louth, after three hectic games. The details too bear recording: 3 July, Croke Park: Meath 1-5, Louth 1-5 (Paddy Meegan got the equalising point for Meath on the stroke of full time); 10 July, Croke Park: Louth 3-6, Meath 2-9 (Louth scored 2-1 in a hectic finish to tie the game); 24 July, Croke Park: Meath 2-5, Louth 1-7 (the winning point from long range by Paddy Connell of Meath at the end of the game).

Though the rivalry between Meath and Louth still exists, it has been surpassed by the Meath-Dublin one, which has been the main football rivalry in Ireland for some time. Huge numbers attended the 1949 Louth-Meath series, but they pale in comparison with the unique popularity of the 1991 Meath-Dublin saga.

This Meath-Dublin rivalry really began in the fifties. An attendance of 48,000 established a record for the Leinster final in 1955, when the native Dubliners, powered by the wonder club St Vincent's, overwhelmed the all-Ireland champions. I was present in the old Cusack Stand for my first Leinster football final on a gloriously sunny July day.

That 1955 record was bettered in 1964, when 57,000 fans saw Meath defeat Dublin. In 1984 another bumper Leinster final crowd of 56,000 saw Dublin come out on top. They were on top again in 1989 before an attendance of 57,000.

All these crowds were for Leinster finals; so when Dublin were drawn against Meath for a first-round Leinster championship game on 2 June 1991 in Croke Park, the previous first-round attendance record of 30,000, set up in 1953 by the same counties, was going to go, and for a couple of reasons. The first was the Dublin v. Meath rivalry, now at its zenith in the wake of Meath's all-Ireland successes of 1987 and 1988 and Dublin's continued eminence in the game. The second was the high profile of sport in the wake of the success of Jack Charlton's soccer team on the international stage. Gaelic football was under threat, while support for the Irish soccer team was euphoric. A Meath v. Dublin first-round senior football championship game was the spark that would ignite the flames of passion. But nobody was quite prepared for the fairy-tale story about to unfold.

Tommy Howard of Kildare was selected as referee. Few took any notice of the appointment, but long before the series ended the quiet-spoken Kildare postman became a household name and even today his identity is only a two-mark question in a table quiz.

The press dubbed the first game the 'clash of the titans', and, as expected, a record crowd of 51,000 came to Croke Park, expecting a Dublin win and thinking that an ageing Meath team was on the slide. The former Dublin goalkeeper Paddy Cullen was in charge of Dublin, while Seán Boylan was still in charge of Meath—both charismatic and articulate characters.

Charlie Redmond was in inspired form for Dublin, who deservedly led at half time by 1-7 to 1-2. Liam Hayes, Meath's captain, sparked the revival from midfield, but as time ticked away Dublin led by 1-12 to 1-11. But Meath's persistence paid off when David Beggy dispossessed the otherwise brilliant Mick Deegan and set up P. J. Gillic for the levelling point. The ball hopped over the bar, eluding both John O'Leary and Tommy Dowd, and almost entered the net. It wasn't a great game; exchanges were toughly contested, and there were many bookings.

But for the second game a week later at Croke Park, with the pairing capturing the imagination of the country, a crowd of 61,000 was in attendance, and huge queues formed along the footpath outside Croke Park looking for tickets.

Barney Rock, left out for the first game, was back for the second and scored eight splendid points from frees. Again Dublin set the pace and seemed assured of victory when Vinny Murphy got possession nearing the end of normal time and, instead of punching the winning point, had his goal shot saved by the Meath goalkeeper, Michael McQuillan, to leave the score 0-10 apiece. In extra time Meath moved ahead by three points, but Jack Sheedy fisted home a centre by Barney Rock from a free to level the score to 1-11 each. Incredibly, there were no further scores. Limbs visibly ached. Even the referee, Tommy Howard, got cramp. Mícheál Ó Muircheartaigh was at his almighty best, and crowds leaving GAA venues throughout the country were enthralled as they listened in groups around car windows or stopped at the side of the road to savour the excitement of it all.

The second replay was fixed for Croke Park two weeks later, 23 June, and there was yet another record attendance of 64,000. Tommy Dowd was dropped by Meath, but back into the panel came Colm Coyle and Gerry McEntee. The queues gathering near Croke Park for tickets were even bigger.

Dublin led by 0-5 to 0-4 at half time and with fifteen minutes to go were in double figures, 0-10 to 0-5. Seán Boylan introduced Gerry McEntee, and the revival had begun. That lovely corner-forward Bernard Flynn rose to a centre from Colm Coyle and punched to the net. Brian Stafford pointed from play and then in injury time slotted over the equaliser from a free. Meath 1-7, Dublin 0-10. More extra time! Would it ever end?

Early in extra time Colm Coyle scored a goal, but minutes later Paul Clarke equalised for Dublin. Points were swapped, and at the break of extra time it was level again: 2-9 to Dublin's 1-12. In the second period of extra time four points were shared again, and it took a fine point by Paul Curran nearing the end to save the day for Dublin. The score: Dublin 1-14, Meath 2-11. All agreed that the third game was the best of the three, with some great passages of play and some brilliant individual displays. Brian Stafford scored 0-10 altogether in game number 3, and yet some critics were not enamoured of his display.

Saturday 6 July was the date fixed for the third replay. By now this Dublin v. Meath thing was the subject of conversation everywhere. Mick Lyons of Meath, their durable and teak-tough full-back, was spoken of with awe in Dublin. Even bigger queues for the cherished tickets were now to be seen. The game was of course all-ticket, and the GAA decided to allow live television coverage of this unique event, feeling sure there would be no diminution in attendance.

Saturday dawned beautifully sunny—the perfect day for the showdown. I was taken by the crowds of young Dublin supporters clad in the distinctive Dublin jersey of sky blue and navy and wasn't surprised to hear that almost fifty thousand of these were sold in the weeks beforehand. An amazing attendance of 62,000 was present, and the colour on Hill 16 and at the canal end was brilliant. It was the perfect day.

The game lived up to the occasion. There was drama right up to the throw-in; a freak accident in the dressing-room deprived Meath of the services of the dependable Terry Ferguson, son of the former Dublin star Dessie.

Tommy Dowd and Pádraig Lyons were back in the Meath line-out. Though Meath started well, Dublin gradually got on top and led deservedly at half time by 0-7 to 0-5. As the second half progressed, Dublin moved further ahead, with Paul Bealin dominant at midfield, Niall Guiden popping over some lovely points on the run, and Dublin's half-back line of Tommy Carr, Keith Barr and Éamonn Heery dominant. Fourteen minutes into the half Tommy Carr, an inspiring figure in the entire series, went off injured, with Dublin leading 0-11 to 0-6; but this setback didn't faze Dublin, who kept on playing vintage football. When the corner-forward Bernard Flynn of Meath also limped off it looked blue for these great-hearted warriors, and they must have doubted their powers of comeback now as Dublin moved six points ahead. Were they going to be swamped after all?

The dependable Brian Stafford pointed a free, and then in the fifty-fourth minute came a badly needed Meath goal when Colm O'Rourke, loyal servant over many years, placed Brian Stafford, who drove past John O'Leary: 0-12 to 1-7. We had a game again. But just when we expected Meath to be inspired, back came Dublin immediately with two telling points from Mick Galvin and Niall Guiden. The Hill went wild with delight, arms aloft, and their own peculiar clap-clap-clap rhythm. Then Mattie McCabe pointed for Meath, keeping them in the game: 0-14 to 1-8.

Now a penalty for Dublin. Surely this was the end for Meath? But, lo and behold, Keith Barr sent it narrowly wide. Instead of being deflated, Dublin came back for another Niall Guiden point: 0-15 to 1-8, four points ahead, and just a few minutes to go. Stafford again pointed a free. Dublin stormed forward again, and the substitute Vinny Murphy, instead of taking the insurance point, opted to pass to Declan Sheehan, only to see Martin O'Connell collect. Just two minutes remained. Eleven passes after that O'Connell interception, Kevin Foley found himself facing an empty Dublin net and eternal glory; he gladly booted home the equaliser. Now it was 2-9 to 0-15.

This is how that fairytale goal came. O'Connell found Mick Lyons, who gave the ball to Mattie McCabe. On to Liam Harnan, who booted it downfield to Colm O'Rourke. O'Rourke was fouled by Mick Kennedy, and he took a quick free, finding David Beggy on his left. One hop and one solo and he transferred to the half-back Kevin Foley. On from him to P. J. Gillic, who flicked it on to Tommy Dowd. Dowd

---

took the ball at speed, and this injection of pace threw Dublin. Dowd transferred to O'Rourke, but he kept on running and took the return pass, also at speed. It seemed as if Tommy himself would score, but he passed to Kevin Foley on the edge of the square with the goal at his mercy. The rest is history.

From the kick-out, Mattie McCabe placed his captain, Liam Hayes, who kicked a cross-field pass to P. J. Gillic. He passed to David Beggy, and it was obvious that the fleet-footed Beggy would pop over the winner. It all happened so quickly; the Hill went silent.

Dublin had one final chance to level the score, but Jack Sheedy's long-range free drifted wide. The saga was over. Meath had done the impossible yet again. Their followers were ecstatic; Dublin's were shell-shocked.

This was wonderful sporting entertainment from amateur players; it was a pity there had to be a winner. It was a moment to savour, the end of a never-to-be-forgotten saga that has gone into the annals of Gaelic football. If the GAA felt any threat from Jack Charlton's World Cup exploits, their fears died that day. Gaelic football got a fillip as new followers were attracted to its thrill-a-minute nature. The Leinster Council had a financial bonanza from it all and decided to reward both teams with a donation of £30,000 to their holiday funds, as well as an extra £55,000 apiece on the amount due to the competing counties and an additional £25,000 to the other Leinster counties. Michael Delaney, secretary of the Leinster Council, was thrilled with it all. The atmosphere from early morning was magic, and Ireland got a chance to celebrate its own sporting entertainment. It was Gaelic football's greatest day.

This was the Meath team that played on that wonderful occasion:

Michael McQuillan

Robbie O'Malley   Mick Lyons   Pádraig Lyons

Kevin Foley   Liam Harnan   Martin O'Connell

Liam Hayes   P. J. Gillic

David Beggy   Colm O'Rourke   Tommy Dowd

Colm Coyle   Brian Stafford   Bernard Flynn

Substitutes: Finian Murtagh for Pádraig Lyons, Gerry McEntee for Finian Murtagh, Mattie McCabe for Bernard Flynn.

And the Dublin team:

John O'Leary

| Mick Deegan | Gerry Hargan | Mick Kennedy |
| Tommy Carr | Keith Barr | Éamonn Heery |

Jack Sheedy   Paul Bealin

| Charlie Redmond | Paul Curran | Niall Guiden |
| Declan Sheehan | Paul Clarke | Mick Galvin |

Substitutes: Ray Holland for Tommy Carr, Joe McNally for Paul Clarke, Vinny Murphy for Charlie Redmond

34

THE NORTHERN RENAISSANCE

Derry won two successive Ulster titles, in 1975 and 1976; but that feat wasn't achieved again by an Ulster team until the nineties, when Tyrone did likewise in 1995 and 1996.

It wasn't always that way, especially when Cavan ruled the roost, on one occasion winning seven Ulster senior titles in a row (1939–45). Nowadays competition is very keen, and Fermanagh alone have yet to win an Ulster senior football title.

Gaelic football is almost a religion in Ulster. Even in the darkest hours of strife it has been an inspiring force; and though competition is extremely keen, the whole province rows in behind the Ulster champions in Croke Park. Clones on Ulster final day is a special place, and watching rival sets of supporters enjoying themselves together in the Diamond is a particular pleasure. Ulster people have every right to be proud of the province's top sporting occasion, and the recent modernisation and development of St Tiarnach's Park in Clones, which regularly hosts attendances of over 30,000 for Ulster finals, is a credit to the province.

After Down's all-Ireland win of 1968 came a drought in Ulster football even more noticeable than the downward trend in the standard of the game in Connacht. This was just before the dawn of the Dublin and Kerry dominance; and when these two counties died, supremacy passed over to another Munster v. Leinster rivalry with Meath and Cork. But in the mid-eighties there were signs of an Ulster revival when Monaghan won a national football league title in 1985 in an all-Ulster final with Armagh; four Ulster teams had contested the semi-finals, the others being Down and Tyrone. Later that year Monaghan were decidedly unlucky not to defeat Kerry in a drawn all-Ireland semi-final, 2-9 to Kerry's 1-12, before losing out in the replay.

The following year Tyrone reached the all-Ireland for the first time and gave a good fright to Kerry before losing in the end by 2-15 to 1-

10. And that score doesn't do justice to Tyrone's effort. Kevin McCabe pointed a penalty kick that, if goaled, would have put Tyrone nine points ahead in the second half. Kerry were too experienced not to take heart from such a miss and, inspired by Pat Spillane among others, raced to a convincing win in the end. Tyrone had got a glimpse of 'Sam', and Ulster was on the march.

Ulster's road to national glory began with Down, the county yet to lose an all-Ireland senior final; and the force behind their momentum in regaining national status was their team manager, Pete McGrath— a most unlikely and, at the start, unwanted choice when selected to take charge in October 1989. Pete in his younger days was a MacRory Cup (Ulster colleges senior football) star with St Colman's College, Newry, and went on to play for Down for a few years in the seventies, before being discarded for being too small. Then he branched into coaching at under-age level. In 1978 he went back as a teacher to his old school, St Colman's, where he joined a former college team-mate, Ray Morgan, to coach them to five MacRory Cup and three all-Ireland Hogan Cup successes. In 1987 he managed the Down minors to all-Ireland success, a team that included James McCartan and Conor Deegan; and when all efforts to find a senior manager failed, Down finally turned to Pete McGrath to take the baton.

The players were slow to accept him, but Greg Blaney, a lad he had coached in St Colman's, knew of his passion and devotion and good coaching techniques and backed him fully. Almost immediately results followed, and Down reached the national football league final of 1990, before falling to Meath, 2-7 to 0-11.

The build-up to 1991 by Down wasn't too impressive. Poor league results with the loss of six games, despite good scoring totals, led to relegation; and prospects for a first-round date on 9 June against Armagh in Newry didn't look rosy. Armagh had beaten Down in an Ulster semi-final replay in 1990 and so were confident of success again. But in a close game, Down, with the bustling Peter Withnall at full-forward, flanked by Mickey Linden and James McCartan (son of the Down hero of the same name), came good to win by 1-7 to 0-8 after Mickey Linden had goaled from a penalty after a mere seven minutes. The first hurdle had been crossed.

The previous Sunday, Dublin had played Meath in the first game of that wonderful four-game saga, and the Down panel and management, who had spent the weekend in Gormanston College, took in the game. Little did they know then that they would be meeting the winners later on.

Down's next engagement was against Derry in Armagh on 30

June. This was another close one, and they had to depend on the sharpshooter Ross Carr to score the equalising point with virtually the last kick of a pulsating game: 0-13 to 1-10. It wasn't just any old free. The ball was placed some fifty-five yards from goal, to the right of the posts and into the breeze in injury time. But the trusted left boot delivered a replay. Down had played a wonderful first half and led by 0-9 to 0-4 at half time. They even went ahead, 0-11 to 0-4, with Linden, Blaney and Kane flying; but disaster struck when Blaney was sent off for a second bookable offence. Derry, inspired by McGilligan and Tohill, slowly took over and eventually seemed to have the game won after a magnificent solo point from Éamonn Burns, before Ross Carr did the needful.

In the replay at the same venue Down won well by 0-14 to 0-9, with Ross Carr scoring 0-9 in a man-of-the-match performance to qualify Down for an Ulster final date with Donegal in Clones on 28 July.

The Ulster final was won easily enough by 1-15 to 0-10, with the Anglo-Celt Cup going to Down for the eleventh time after an absence of ten years. Even Peter McGrath, who seldom allows a smile in the heat of battle, was grinning broadly long before the end, saying:

> We were told we didn't have the bottle any more. It became an albatross around our necks but was removed that day with some style.

Paddy O'Rourke, the captain, had played in 1978 and 1981 and regarded the third Ulster medal as 'the sweetest of all.' Mickey O'Sullivan, the Kerry team manager, who was present in Clones, was impressed with Down's display. Within fifteen minutes Down led by 1-7 to 0-2, the goal coming from a fine centre by Greg Blaney and finished with flair by the exciting Mickey Linden, a speedy corner-forward who in 1991 took the GAA world by storm. Down led 1-9 to 0-5 at half time, then let Donegal back into the game with some wild shooting. Then the Down goalkeeper, Neil Collins, not for the first time, dive-blocked what seemed a certain goal, and Down swept upfield for Barry Breen to pop over a point. It was all Down after that. Greg Blaney, whose father, Seán, had been an outstanding college and county star, was selected as Man of the Match.

In 1996 Danny Murphy, a prominent Down and Ulster official, brought me on a visit to St Colman's College in Newry, that wonderful nursery of Ulster and Down football. The president of the college, Canon Stephenson, a loyal Armagh man, took me on a tour of the college, where I admired the photographs of all the teams that won the MacRory Cup and all-Ireland finals. He showed me a MacRory Cup team of the forties captained by Seán Blaney and then further down the corridor another MacRory Cup team captained by his son, Greg, some thirty years later. I often think of that day as the perfect example of the tradition that permeates the GAA. 'Briseann an dúchas trí shúile an chait.'

After Clones it was on to Croke Park to meet the old rivals, Kerry, who had never yet beaten Down in a senior football championship game. Down kept that record intact, beating Kerry comprehensively in the end by 2-9 to 0-8. Before an attendance of 42,000, Down came back from a penalty miss by Mickey Linden after only seven minutes for Peter Withnall to score his first of two goals. Still Kerry, with an ageing team (Pat Spillane and Jack O'Shea were almost at the end of illustrious careers), were still level, 1-5 to 0-8, with just eight minutes remaining. Then came a magical point by Mickey Linden after being put through by the midfielder Barry Breen, followed by Withnall's second goal, and victory.

Down were in another final. Could they preserve their record of never losing a senior all-Ireland? Even against Meath, who with all the draws and attendant publicity had become a real glamour team and the talk of the country, it was an exciting time as both teams prepared for the fray under a glare of publicity. Our own Galway team of 1956 were guests of the GAA for the occasion and were introduced to the crowd in a 'last hurrah' farewell to Croke Park, a feature of the all-Ireland final scene introduced the previous decade. It is a lovely if emotional occasion and has now become one of the added highlights of all-Ireland day. Two of that team's substitutes, Aidan Swords and Joe O'Neill, had passed on; so the tears weren't far away as we made our way to the Hogan Stand before the senior final.

Meath were all the rage. And why wouldn't they, after playing nine championship games in Croke Park, often rising from the dead almost, to survive? Down were generally disregarded, despite their 100 per cent all-Ireland record. It was a lovely position to be in going into a final; and no-one knew that better than Pete McGrath.

As is their wont, Down didn't travel to Croke Park till the day, assembling in Newry and travelling by coach to Portmarnock for a light lunch before heading for Croke Park. Rumours that one of Meath's best players, Colm O'Rourke, was out with a viral infection were confirmed. He would not be starting, and it was doubtful that he would come on as a substitute if needed.

It took Down some time to settle; but as soon as the forwards started to buzz, free kicks were won. Even when Mickey Linden received a dangerous facial attack in which he lost a tooth, he bounced back up, and Down led by 0-8 to 0-4 at half time. Meath didn't score after the eighteenth minute.

Down went mad in the first fourteen minutes of the second half, scoring 1-6 (1-5 from play), with James McCartan in devastating form and Meath almost mesmerised. A goal by Barry Breen from a pass by Mickey Linden in a movement involving McCartan, Withnall, Blaney and Linden in the fourth minute left the score 1-11 to 0-5. It couldn't be as easy as this!

It got even better. Points by Carr, McCartan and Blaney left Down 1-14 to 0-6 ahead with sixteen minutes to go. Down called an old servant, Liam Austin, to help counteract Gerry McEntee; and a mighty Meath cheer heralded the entrance of Colm O'Rourke, who immediately set the Meath attack ticking. In the closing twenty minutes Meath battled as only they can, scoring 1-8 to Down's 0-2 in a brilliant comeback that yielded a dramatic second half. The Down goalkeeper, Neil Collins, was their saviour with a point-blank blocking of a goal special by Bernard Flynn. But Down kept plugging away, their final two points coming from Éamonn Burns and Gary Mason, giving them a cushion of six points.

Meath still chipped away at the lead. Mickey Linden had a chance to wrap it up but failed. In the end, despite Meath's courageous fight back, Down triumphed by 1-16 to 1-14. Paddy O'Rourke was presented with the Sam Maguire Cup by the president of the GAA, his fellow-Ulsterman Peter Quinn of Fermanagh in his first year of office, and then was chaired on the shoulders of delirious fans across Croke Park, as was the team manager, Peter McGrath, the unobtrusive hero who took the job nobody wanted.

Down had kept their all-Ireland final record intact; Sam was going across the border to County Down for the first time since 1968.

This was Down's winning team:

Neil Collins

Brendan McKiernan   Conor Deegan   Paul Higgins

John Kelly   Paddy O'Rourke (*captain*)   D. J. Kane

Barry Breen   Éamonn Burns

Ross Carr   Greg Blaney   Gary Mason

Mickey Linden   Peter Withnall   James McCartan

Substitutes: Liam Austin for Barry Breen, Ambrose Rodgers for Peter Withnall.

Down's great forward line helped in no small way to deliver the team's fourth all-Ireland victory. It was nice too to see that in the heat of battle nearing the end, with Meath coming so close, a place on the Down team was found for both Liam Austin and one of Down's most celebrated and charismatic players, Ambrose Rodgers. It's touches like this that make Down so special.

The selection of the 1991 All-Stars football team caused some controversy, with just four Down players honoured: Conor Deegan at full-back, Barry Breen at midfield, Ross Carr at right-half-forward, and Greg Blaney on the forty. Meath's great nine-game championship programme had gained them five places, including the entire full-forward line of Colm O'Rourke, Brian Stafford, and Bernard Flynn. County Down folk felt aggrieved, especially over the non-selection of Mickey Linden and James McCartan; but then the bigger prize had been won, and All-Stars would follow in other years.

In the 1992 championship Down, after beating Armagh, fell to the champions, Derry, by 0-15 to 0-12, thereby starting a trend that lasted throughout the decade of all-Ireland champions biting the dust the year after all-Ireland success. The pressure of winning takes its toll on appetite and reserves—that and the modern over-emphasis on celebration.

Worse was to follow in 1993 when Derry came to the Marshes in Newry and on a May day of driving rain humiliated Down in the championship in their own territory by a whopping eleven points: 3-11 to 0-9. Pete McGrath in a television interview afterwards was embarrassed at the performance of his team and said they owed an apology to their supporters for their display—a remark that alienated him from some of his players, who felt sick with themselves for their own ineptitude but felt that such criticism should have been expressed behind closed doors. Other problems were to surface between management and team over selection, and matters came to a head when two of the stars of 1991, Greg Blaney and James McCartan, opted out of football; but, as with teams elsewhere, sanity eventually prevailed: meetings were arranged, matters were thrashed out, and on 16 February 1994 Blaney and McCartan returned to training. It was the beginning of a fresh assault on the all-Ireland crown.

D. J. Kane, Down's captain, was another man of fibre. Despite difficulties off the field, Peter McGrath had been searching around for new talent and after a number of experiments had decided on a selection to get over the enormous task of beating Derry in their own Celtic Park in the first round of the Ulster senior football championship. Derry's strongest sector was their midfield partnership of Brian McGilligan and Anthony Tohill. A new midfield pairing of the 1991 full-back Conor Deegan and the impressive Gregory McCartan was tried and proved exciting, while the former midfielders Barry Breen and Éamonn Burns were slotted into the half-back line in trial games. James McCartan was given a more roving role in the half-forward line, and the newcomers Mícheál Magill, Brian Burns and Aidan Farrell were all fitting in well. And Down had two place-kickers of great quality: Ross Carr and Gary Mason, both very effective from different sides of the field. Ross Carr's trusted left foot was used for frees on the right, and Gary took those on the left-hand side. It's a marvellous option to have in a team.

The eagerly awaited Down v. Derry game in Celtic Park, Derry, on 29 May turned out to be a classic: all action, great scores, brilliant displays, and played at a fast pace. In an era when epic games were few and far between, this one was fit to stand alongside any, ahead even of the 1977 semi-final between Dublin and Kerry. Martin Breheny in his book *All in the Game* described it as 'not only one of the games of the year but of the decade.' Raymond Smith in the 1995 edition of *The Football Immortals* rated it 'the finest exhibition of Gaelic football since the Dublin versus Kerry all-Ireland semi-final of 1977.'

After a wonderful first half after which Down led by 0-10 to 0-8, both teams were cheered off the field. Then seventeen minutes into the second half Fergal McCusker goaled to put Derry in front by 1-11 to 0-12. They failed to press home the advantage, and Down, inspired by a marvellous point by James McCartan after a weaving solo run, went on to seal their victory by 1-14 to 1-12 with a goal from Ciarán McCabe (substitute) and a pointed free from Gregory McCartan. The gambles had paid off. The half-back line was a tower of strength; midfield more than coped with Derry; and Mickey Linden, with 0-6 to his credit, gave a virtuoso performance as Man of the Match. Down were on their way again; Derry went down like champions.

The Mourne men's path to success continued with good wins over Monaghan, 0-14 to 0-8, in Armagh on 19 June and Tyrone in the Ulster final at Clones on 17 July, 1-17 to 1-11, without reaching the heady heights of the Derry game. Features of the provincial final win before 31,000 in the 'new-look' Clones were the leadership and purposeful defensive play of the Down captain, D. J. Kane, and yet another top-class game by Mickey Linden. As well as collecting the Anglo-Celt Cup, D. J. Kane won the Man of the Match award.

Dublin had come out of Leinster, defeating Meath in the final and moving on to beat a very game Leitrim in the all-Ireland semi-final. Meantime Down came to Croke Park and decisively beat Cork in the semi-final by 1-13 to 0-11 when the midfielder Conor Deegan was a mighty force and the young hopeful Aidan Farrell scored Down's vital goal before 44,000 fans. Gary Mason scored 0-6; Mickey Linden and James McCartan buzzed, as always; Greg Blaney was the unobtrusive orchestrator; D. J. Kane continued to lead from the front.

Down were in another final—their first against Dublin in Croke Park. Could they preserve their 100 per cent record?

The New Stand to replace the old Cusack Stand was in the process of construction, with work well advanced and the lower and middle tiers in operation.

This final, before a crowd of 59,000, was in many ways similar to that of 1991, though Down never jumped ahead of Dublin in quite the same way that they raced away from Meath three years before. A great goal by James McCartan in the seventeenth minute set Down on their merry way, and by the fiftieth minute they were clear: 1-12 to 0-9. They failed to score in the final twenty minutes as Dublin edged back point by point; then in the sixty-second minute there was a penalty to Dublin for a foul on Dessie Farrell, when a goal would have the two teams level. The shot by Charlie Redmond was brilliantly saved by Neil Collins, and that finished it for Dublin, who lost in the end by 1-12 to 0-13. It was heartbreaking for Charlie, who had failed to goal penalties in the 1988 Leinster final against Meath and in the 1992 all-Ireland final against Donegal. Fate wasn't kind to the likeable Charlie.

The Man of the Match was Mickey Linden, who tormented the Dublin defence endlessly, gave the pass for McCartan's goal, and made life hell for his opponent, Paul Curran, who had been chosen by Dublin to counteract Linden—a huge blunder in giving an over-defensive role to a player of wonderful attacking flair. Tom O'Riordan in the *Irish Independent* the day after the final described the Mayobridge man as 'the best forward in the game.' Mickey had a personal tally of 0-4 in as good a corner-forward display as has ever been seen on final day. A sportsman from head to toe, Mickey, despite close attention from defenders, never retaliates and is a role model for youngsters everywhere.

For Paddy Downey of the *Irish Times,* the doyen of GAA writers, this was the last final, and as a tribute to him I reprint his opening paragraph.

> Ulster still says 'no surrender'. The Ulster I speak of is the historical province of nine counties, not the State which inappropriately claims the name. It was Down who said 'no

surrender' on behalf of their province at rain-sodden Croke Park when with a little luck on their side they beat Dublin in an enthralling final.

Paddy paid tribute to Mickey Linden, of course, whom he described as 'mercurial'. There was praise too for the 'indefatigable Gregory McCartan' and 'the old general Greg Blaney,' and for 'Michael Magill— a regal figure in defence.'

I was present on the Monday for the reception for the four final teams hosted by the GAA. The ovation of the day was given to Paddy Downey, when Jack Boothman, then president of the GAA, made a presentation to the genial reporter who had made so many friends throughout a lifetime of loyalty to the GAA. There was a flair to his writing that is still missed. He was the last of the old school of sports journalists who covered the scene from the time when the press was king into the radio and then television age. In paying tribute to Paddy we remember also John D. Hickey, Pádhraic Puirséal, Con Kenealy, Mick Dunne, Paddy Mehigan, Dónal Carroll, and Seán Óg Ó Ceallacháin, all of whose reports were read and re-read throughout the country.

Paddy was presented with a carving on 300-year-old bog oak with the figure of a hurler and a footballer on either side of a seated figure writing—a most appropriate present. Paddy was overcome by it all. 'I've been involved in the GAA all my life,' he said. 'I have an interest in other sports too, which I like, but I love the GAA games.' It was a moment to savour, and Down were part of it all. Paddy had seen Down win five all-Irelands from five attempts. D. J. Kane had kept the record intact.

Pete McGrath allowed himself a smile or two. At the time of writing, the bold Pete has been appointed to continue as manager of Down for another two-year term. Don't be surprised if he works the miracle again, even after another upheaval.

This was the winning Down team:

Neil Collins

| Michael Magill | Brian Burns | Paul Higgins |
| Éamonn Burns | Barry Breen | D. J. Kane (*captain*) |

Gregory McCartan   Conor Deegan

| Ross Carr | Greg Blaney | James McCartan |
| Mickey Linden | Aidan Farrell | Gary Mason |

Substitute: Gerard Colgan for Conor Deegan (seventy-one minutes).

35

Tír Chonaill Abú!

Gaelic football was always big in County Donegal, especially in south Donegal—in Gaoth Dobhair and Gleann Cholm Cille, Letterkenny and Ballybofey; but because of emigrant ties, with Scotland in particular, the county was always deeply interested in soccer too.

It took some time for Donegal to win their first Ulster title in any grade. The first significant success at provincial level came in 1956 when they won the Ulster minor football championship for the first time. Better times lay ahead at senior level too, and Donegal reached the Ulster final for the first time in 1963. The Ulster senior football championship was eventually won for the first time in 1972, when Donegal, captained by Frankie McFeely, defeated Tyrone in the final by 2-13 to 1-11, before losing to Offaly in the semi-final by 1-17 to 2-10.

In 1972 a Donegal team that included Brian McEniff, Donegal's first All-Star, at right-half-back and the top scorer in the championship that year at left-corner-forward, Joe Winston (with a fine total of 0-26), won the Ulster senior football championship. There were euphoric scenes in the Diamond in Donegal when the Anglo-Celt Cup was borne in triumph home to the Hills for the first time.

I was holidaying in Gleann Cholm Cille at the time, and I travelled the long route to Dublin for the county's first appearance in a semi-final. It was a hugely exciting time, and the pride in this first achievement was palpable. Croke Park was reached at last.

And so Donegal's football resurgence continued. There were more Ulster titles in 1974, 1983, and 1990, and Brian McEniff, either as player or manager, or both, was associated with all of them. In another grade Donegal achieved all-Ireland under-21 titles, first under Tom Conaghan in 1982 and again in 1987 under P. J. McGowan, defeating

Roscommon in the 1982 final by 0-8 to 0-5 and Kerry in the replayed 1987 final by 1-12 to 2-4.

The path to all-Ireland senior football championship success seemed easier to traverse. A winning formula had been evolved, and young men like Matt Gallagher, Anthony Molloy, Dónal Reid, Martin McHugh, Charlie Mulgrew, Joyce McMullan and Sylvester Maguire, all from the 1982 under-21 team, and John Joe Doherty, Barry Cunningham, Paddy Hegarty, Tommy Ryan, Barry McGowan and Manus Boyle from the 1987 under-21 team had got the winning way: they had won an all-Ireland medal and were in the 1992 senior football panel, eager to go after Ulster title number 5 and Sam Maguire at last.

Brian McEniff was team manager again for the umpteenth time. A man passionate about football and his native county, he had learnt all the tricks of the trade, had seen and was part of four semi-final defeats in 1972, 1974, 1983, and 1990. Would 1992 be the year of victory?

The *Donegal Democrat* played its own part in the build-up to Donegal's rise to the top. After the under-21 triumph in 1987 its sports editor, Gerry McDermott, prevailed on the *Longford Leader* columnist Cormac McGill, a staunch Donegal man, to write a weekly column under the pen-name 'The Follower'. It became a clarion call, a rousing weekly diet of hope, an optimistic appraisal of the scene, and a popular and readable column linking supporter, team member and management in the huge desire to bring Sam to the Hills.

When the senior football championship of 1992 dawned, Brian McEniff was in charge of a seasoned outfit, well experienced in top national football league competition and well used to playing in Ulster finals. In the national football league preceding the championship, Donegal were ousted by Dublin in deflating circumstances. Comfortably leading the Dublin men by four points with two minutes remaining in the quarter-final at Breffni Park, Cavan, Dublin scored two goals in ninety seconds to rob the Donegal men. It couldn't get worse than that.

The championship began in the same Breffni Park on Sunday 23 May, and Donegal were never so lucky as in drawing this one with a score of 1-15 to 1-15. The back-turned-forward Damien Reilly was Cavan's hero, first with a brilliant left-footed volley point to draw level, just after Martin McHugh curled over a wonderful free kick from fifty yards for what seemed the winner, before Reilly pointed again to force a replay. On a dreadfully wet Whit Sunday in Ballybofey, Donegal won easily by 0-20 to 1-6, with Anthony Molloy and Brian Murray rampant at midfield and Matt Gallagher outstanding at full-back, completely blotting out Cavan's danger man Fintan Cahill before an attendance of 16,000. Despite the rain, delighted Donegal fans trooped out of Mac Cumhaill Park in happy mood.

Then followed a good win over Fermanagh in the Ulster semi-final at Omagh by 2-17 to 0-7, a flattering enough result, with the losers still there with a chance entering the second half. But when the injured Martin McHugh came on Donegal went on song, and even Matt Gallagher sailed up for a point late in the game. Tony Boyle also starred.

Donegal were now in their fourth successive Ulster final. Their opponents were Derry, who had been impressively crowned national football league champions in the spring and came to Clones with a huge support fully expecting an Ulster title to add to their national football league success.

Ulster final day in Clones was a very special experience, the greatest atmosphere I've ever experienced before the game: a sunny day, huge crowds teeming down the Fermanagh Street incline, both teams' supporters expectant of glory; Derry, the national football league champions, eager to continue the good times, Donegal feeling that this was their year. The Follower in the *Donegal Democrat* caught the mood perfectly as he looked back in agony at all the near misses of the past and, despite Derry being the raging favourites, felt deep down that Donegal's day was nigh.

Before an attendance of 35,000, the game lived up to expectations after a dreary enough first half, which ended with scores level at 0-5 each. Donegal, facing a mountainous climb, failed to take advantage of the scoring goal. With whatever wind and sun advantage there was, they lost John Cunningham, sent to the line for two bookable offences just before half time, and Tony Boyle, ace full-forward, injured mid-way through the half. Anthony Tohill's challenge on Boyle was more awkward than premeditated but it incensed Donegal's huge following in the packed arena. Tohill himself was injured in the clash an retired subsequently. It was a mountain to climb of savage proportions. Brian McEniff dug deep at half time and sent out fourteen men prepared to die for the honour and glory of Donegal.

That second half was one of the finest I have ever seen. Damien Barton put Derry ahead; James McHugh equalised; Tommy Ryan put Donegal ahead again and repeated the act to put two points between the sides. Donegal were rocked by a Derry goal in a move involving Coleman, Gormley and Séamus Downey. At this point every Donegal player on the field was playing out of his skin, none more so than Martin Gavigan at number 6, Anthony Molloy at midfield, and Martin

Beag McHugh in attack. Gavigan raced up in attack but was fouled, and Declan Bonner equalised. Then Martin Gavigan again brought off a mighty catch but was fouled again, and Martin McHugh lofted over from forty-five metres into the wind. Gripping stuff!

Derry drew level four times in all in the second half, but the tide was with Donegal, and Martin McHugh, with some smashing points, sealed Donegal's victory on the score 0-14 to 1-9. One point in particular bears recalling. Bursting through several defenders on the left, he shot a miracle point across his right shoulder over the bar. He could almost have walked on water that day. There followed marvellous scenes of Donegal joy, with Brian McEniff feted everywhere. The football played by both teams was a credit to them—catching, kicking and scoring at its best.

Donegal had won their fifth Ulster crown in their greatest football display so far. Word seeped through to Clones that Clare had beaten Kerry in the Munster final—another good omen for Donegal. The Follower's eyes had seen the glory; but bigger battles lay ahead.

The next test was against Mayo in the all-Ireland semi-final on 16 August, when Donegal, despite playing poorly, won by 0-13 to 0-9 in a disappointing game when the winners shot sixteen wides. Still one had to admire the skilled full-back play of Matt Gallagher, the sweeping never-say-die runs of the left-half-back, Martin Shovlin, ungainly in gait but stout of heart; the power of Molloy and Murray at midfield; and the sparkle of Tony Boyle at full-forward. Manus Boyle, who came on as a substitute, steadied the northerners with his accurate and confident free-taking.

Donegal were in their first final and had triumphed at senior level in Croke Park at last. Joy was unconfined. The Follower in his *Democrat* column wrote:

> Could money ever buy the pleasure, the joy and the excitement of Sunday last around 4.52 p.m. after Máirtín Beag had tapped the ball over the bar from a penalty to make victory secure with the last kick of the game. I cried like a child and I want another chance to shed tears again in the final.

In the other semi-final, Dublin defeated Clare after a day of wonderful atmosphere when Clare took over Croke Park and gave Dublin a hard game before losing by 3-14 to 2-12. Dublin in Croke Park in the final were the toughest opposition you could get, especially after that league quarter-final defeat in Breffni Park. Call it larceny if you will, but it helped to make Dublin raging favourites.

How Brian McEniff smiled at his good fortune! Now followed the long five-week wait for the final on 20 September. Still, it couldn't be long enough for Donegal's legion of fans as they planned an invasion of the capital city for the final.

So at last all-Ireland day dawned for Donegal and Dublin. In savouring Donegal's first all-Ireland senior final, the Follower in the *Democrat* paid tribute to all the officials and former stars over the years who had ploughed the furrow—men like Seán Ó Cinnéide, Frank Muldoon, Hugh Daly, Paddy McGill, Michael Gillespie (officials all) and former stars such as Columba McDyer, the Railway Cup heroes Red Jack and Hiúdaí Beag, Séamus Hoare, P. J. Flood, Seán Ferriter, John Hannigan, Seán O'Donnell, Peadar McGeehan, the Coyles of Gaoth Dobhair, Frankie McFeely, Bernard Brady, Mickey McLoone, Séamus Granaghan, Anton Carroll, Mickey Griffin, and Des Houlihan.

Rumours circulated underneath the Hogan Stand. That great servant Martin Shovlin, though selected, hadn't recovered from injury; John Joe Doherty was in for him. A huge doubt surrounded Joyce McMullan's participation, but happily the rumours were groundless and this fleet-footed forward was there for the big day in his customary left-half-forward position. Would Matt Gallagher be able to contain Vinny Murphy, Dublin's ace forward?

Anthony Molloy won the toss and decided to play into the Hill, a move whose wisdom was questioned when Donegal seemed to be nervous and at sea early on and their opponents, playing with ease, were two points up after five minutes. Then Martin McHugh steadied the ship with a point after his brother James had struck the cross-bar earlier. Now a penalty to Dublin after nine minutes. Were Donegal in for a hiding? Poor Charlie Redmond, not for the first time, continued his ill-luck with penalties, and you could almost hear the Donegal sighs of relief around Croke Park. Undaunted, Dublin swept back for a fine point by Vinny Murphy. James McHugh and Jack Sheedy exchanged points, and then Declan Bonnar, with absolute confidence, pointed a free to leave it 0-4 to 0-3 in favour of Dublin after eighteen minutes.

You could almost see a change in confidence coming into Donegal's play. Now they dictated the show, running at Dublin, beating their opponents, using their short-passing game to perfection, and deservedly leading at half time by 0-10 to 0-7.

Donegal continued where they left off, with Manus Boyle as confident from frees on his side as Declan Bonnar was from the right. The reliable triangle of Gavigan, Molloy and McHugh was unbeatable.

After fifty-eight minutes Donegal led by 0-15 to 0-9, giving Dublin a lesson. Paul Bealin stopped the Dublin rot at midfield, and Tommy Carr did his level best to motivate his team in his usual way, but Donegal had grasped the initiative. Matt Gallagher, though never kicking a ball in the entire game, had come to grips with the Vinny Murphy menace, while his two corner-backs, Barry McGowan and Noel Hegarty, were brilliant. Manus Boyle in his first full game of the 1992 campaign was the star of the show, scoring 0-9 in all (four from play) in a dream game. Donegal were coasting at the end and thoroughly deserved their 0-18 to 0-14 victory.

It is wonderful to be part of a special first-time win, in this instance the first in Gaelic football in Croke Park since Down's first triumph in 1960. The crowd, apart from disappointed Dublin fans, remained to hear Anthony Molloy's emotive speech as he received the Sam Maguire Cup from his fellow-Ulsterman Peter Quinn. Out in the quadrangle behind the Hogan Stand as the team emerged they received a deserved ovation as they mixed with ecstatic fans before returning on the Monday in a wonderful nostalgic journey to Donegal and the Hills.

On a visit to County Donegal recently I called on the team's most loyal fan, 83-year-old Jim Hannigan of Stranorlar. Jim, a former star club player, has been going to all-Irelands since 1937. He remembers the 1992 final with pride and emotion.

> That day was very special and a brilliant game too, though I'd have to say the drawn 1938 final Galway v. Kerry is the best final I've seen. I've seen Donegal down the years from the time of Red Jack Gallagher to Séamus Hoare—a great goalie—to Pauric McShea, so adaptable and versatile; but Barry McGowan in the 1992 final showed quality, athleticism, consistency, and brains—a great reader of the game.

Brian McEniff, the manager and part of all Donegal's previous Ulster senior triumphs, earned for himself a special place in Donegal folklore, as indeed did all the team, from the goalkeeper, Gary Walsh, to the two Boyles, the gifted full-forward Tony and the man with the magic feet, Manus, not forgetting the substitute Barry Cunningham. The heading to the Follower's piece in the *Democrat* after the final read, 'Sam—tá fáilte romhat'.

This was the winning team:

Gary Walsh

Barry McGowan   Matt Gallagher   Noel Hegarty

Dónal Reid   Martin Gavigan   John Joe Doherty

Anthony Molloy (*captain*)   Brian Murray

James McHugh   Martin McHugh   Joyce McMullan

Declan Bonner   Tony Boyle   Manus Boyle

Substitute: Barry Cunningham for Brian Murray.

36

DERRY FOLLOW DONEGAL'S EXAMPLE

Hardly had the dust settled on Donegal's first all-Ireland title than their opponents in Ulster were eager to topple them. Donegal continued their good form into 1993 before losing the 1992/3 national football league final in a replay to Dublin; but other forces were quietly plotting their downfall in the minefield that is Ulster football, where few county senior teams have won successive Ulster senior football titles recently.

After Derry's initial Ulster senior final victory in 1958, further successes came at minor all-Ireland level in 1965, 1983 and 1989 and at under-21 level in 1968. The victories of the sixties were a result of a wonderful two-year period of success by St Columb's College, Derry, while those of the eighties were increasingly indebted to the wonderful influence of St Patrick's College, Maghera, which won eight Ulster colleges titles from 1977 to 1990 and two all-Ireland colleges senior football titles in 1989 and 1990 from five Hogan Cup final appearances.

At senior level, Derry won Ulster titles in 1970, 1975, 1976 and 1987 to complement the 1958 success. While in the national football league they had a fine victory in 1991/2 to add to their initial victory in the 1946/7 competition.

Another plus for Derry was the appointment of the former Derry footballer Éamonn Coleman as manager in November 1990. A product of the successful minors of 1965, he won an all-Ireland under-21 medal with many of the same team in 1968 and played for the seniors for several years. In 1989 his son Gary captained Derry to its third all-Ireland minor win, having as team-mates Anthony Tohill, Éamonn Burns, and Dermot Heaney, men who helped to shape events in 1993.

Éamonn Coleman was always a man to call a spade a spade. A strict disciplinarian, he could ruffle feathers easily, but his team responded to him, and with another former Derry star, Mickey Moran, acting as coach and trainer, the men from County Derry were in good hands. Results improved steadily, culminating in that fine national football league victory in 1991/2 and the wonderful Ulster final epic with Donegal in Clones in 1992. Would 1993 be the year to cross the Rubicon?

The 1993 Ulster championship campaign began impressively for Derry when they trounced Down in their own town of Newry by 3-11 to 0-9. Anthony Tohill at midfield was majestic. The tall 21-year-old from Swatragh had developed into a superb athlete and in catching the throw-in at the start of each half in Newry had pointed the way for a team that responded magnificently and handed Down its biggest championship defeat since 1952. Dermot Heaney's first-half goal set Derry on their way, and two second-half goals by Richard Ferris and Éamonn Burns sealed a comprehensive performance. Derry were not to be under-rated any more.

Derry qualified for the Ulster final on 20 June with a good win over Monaghan in Casement Park, Belfast, 0-19 to 0-11. It was a workmanlike if not brilliant performance, with Enda Gormley (0-7), Anthony Tohill (0-5) and Joe Brolly, who came on as a substitute (0-3), being the top scorers and Damian McCusker once again keeping a clean sheet in goal.

Donegal had come through to the final after a replay win over Armagh in the semi-final but with crippling injury problems affecting some of the stars of the previous Ulster and all-Ireland finals. Tony Boyle and Noel Hegarty were out, and those stalwarts of 1992, Martin Gavigan and Anthony Molloy, were injured. I travelled to Clones for the 1993 final and visited the former Ulster final hero Frank McGuigan in his home in Ardboe on the eve of the game, a gloriously sunny day—quite a contrast with the following day, which dawned miserably wet and poured cats and dogs all day long.

The eighteenth of July will be remembered by all who were drenched that day in Clones. The pitch, in the throes of reconstruction, was not a suitable venue. The real deluge came about mid-day: inches of water lodged on the freshly laid pitch, and in fact the minor final should have been cancelled.

Conditions improved slightly for the senior final—or did we just imagine it? Players skidded and skated around, and scores were at a premium. Derry put in a spirited display to win the game, 0-8 to 0-6. Anthony Tohill's brilliant burst after half time won this game. He was fouled immediately after the throw-in to start the second half and scored a magnificent 55-yard free to make it 0-5 each. In the next six minutes or so he carried the game to Donegal in a *tour de force,* winning great ball and laying on precious points for Damien Cassidy, Damien Barton, and Enda Gormley. Donegal only managed one point in the second half against a defence in which everyone starred, especially Tony Scullion at full-back and Henry Downey, the captain, further out. Kieran McKeever at corner-back was as tight-marking a defender as you could get, while Gary Coleman was a gutsy defender, capable of subduing much taller opponents.

But it was Tohill's day, in one of the finest individual displays I have ever seen. It was a pity that Donegal should lose in such dreadful conditions, so depleted without Tony Boyle and Noel Hegarty and with Martin Gavigan and Anthony Molloy able to come on only as substitutes. Derry didn't grumble, and their joyous fans danced in the mud of St Tiarnach's Park as Henry Downey lifted the Anglo-Celt Cup aloft. Derry's team looked strong, with a fine midfield of Tohill and that great workhorse Brian McGilligan. Their forwards didn't move the ball as fluently as Down did in 1991 or indeed Donegal in 1992, but in general their team was strong in all departments and seemed set for glory.

Any time you play Dublin in Croke Park you're at a disadvantage. That's the way most counties view it—other than Kerry or Meath. Still, Donegal upset any myth of invincibility in their first all-Ireland in 1992; and though Dublin were anxious to redress this, Derry were up for it when travelling south to meet Dublin in the semi-final. They started well, with three points in seven minutes, then fell away, and Dublin led by 0-9 to 0-4 at half time and should have led by more. But Derry revived, inspired by the effervescent brilliance of the extrovert Joe Brolly and the introduction of the former star Dermot McNicholl from the dug-out. He had captained the all-Ireland champion minors of 1983; now was his chance to grab the headlines again.

Slowly Derry reduced the gap, inspired by a magnificent half-back line of John McGurk, Henry Downey, and Gary Coleman, all of whom ran at Dublin. With seven minutes to go, Séamus Downey was fouled, and Enda Gormley made it level pegging, 0-13 apiece. Henry Downey and Charlie Redmond now exchanged points in a thrilling last five minutes of gripping excitement. Then came the move started by Brolly, on to McNicholl and to the overlapping John McGurk (now at right-half-forward). He shot a curling ball off his left foot and it swung beautifully over the bar for the winning point, 0-15 to 0-14.

That point set the seal on a wonderful family contribution to Derry football—a family of six McGurk brothers totally committed to Gaelic football, their native Lavey and County Derry. All three half-backs scored in this wonderful fight-back. Tony Scullion starred when moved to full-back; McGilligan and Tohill rose to it when needed in the second half; Brolly was the attacking star.

Sam was within sight again for the first time since 1958. The long journey home was a happy one. Now for the final against Cork.

Derry started poorly. Cork were 1-2 up after six minutes, the goal coming from Joe Kavanagh. John McGurk settled them with a point; Brian McGilligan tapped over another. Eleven minutes after McGurk's score, Derry scored 1-4, all from play without reply, Séamus Downey getting an opportunist goal with a fisted effort. Tony Scullion and Henry Downey were magnificent in defence. The score after eighteen minutes read Derry 1-5, Cork 1-2. Before half time Niall Cahalane was lucky to be left on after felling Enda Gormley, who responded positively by scoring two quick points from play. Then Tony Davis got the line for a heavy tackle, more the victim of Niall Cahalane's let-off than his own sin. Derry led by 1-9 to 1-6 at half time. Cork were visibly upset, and Cahalane was not his usual ebullient self.

Switches for both teams were decided on at half time. Cork brought on Danny Culloty to partner the brilliant Shay Fahy at midfield, while Éamonn Coleman got the old reliable Dermot McNicholl ready to replace Damien Cassidy. Cork had the aid of the wind and the spur of winning with fourteen men, something they had achieved against Meath in the final of 1990. This extra player, which used to be a decided advantage and often resulted in runaway wins for the fifteen-a-side team, had been turned on its head many times in modern days. Tactically it was possible to counter the numerical advantage. Referees also tended to favour the disadvantaged side, and neutrals tended to root for the underdog.

John O'Driscoll, who had starred against Mayo in the semi-final, shot a great goal ten minutes into the second half to put Cork ahead, 2-8 to 1-10. The fat was in the fire. Amazingly, this was to be Cork's last score, and for eleven long minutes Derry didn't score either. But Scullion and McKeever were mopping up everything in defence. Henry Downey, after a shaky start, was in absolute command and sallied out of defence with confidence. Gary Coleman was superb. The loose man John McGurk linked up well as the extra marauder. At last the pressure told when Enda Gormley swung over the equaliser. Then Tohill pointed a free, and John McGurk shot another left-footed special.

With five minutes to go, the sharpshooter Gormley pointed a fine free to leave the score 1-14 to 2-8 in Derry's favour. Then a repetition of the emotional scenes of the year before: tears spilling from old faces; men and women who had soldiered down the years, washing jerseys, marking pitches, ferrying players, following their beloved Derry, waiting for their first big day in Croke Park, when they would be crowned High Kings of Gaelic football. Sam Maguire was crossing the border again, and scenes reminiscent of Down's first triumph in 1960 were re-enacted. Henry Downey in his acceptance speech said: 'We needed this all-Ireland a lot more than Cork.'

The journey home to Derry on the Monday was memorable. The first stop was Drogheda, where Joe Brolly sang 'Back Home in Derry'. Next stop Dundalk; then the Carrickdale Hotel near the border at Newry—to Armagh—Moy—Dungannon (Sam was travelling a new route, and everyone knew it)—Cookstown—Moneymore—Magherafelt; and finally Maghera at 3 a.m., where twenty thousand loyal souls waited faithfully for their heroes to return. The rest of Ireland was delighted to see Sam go to another new team for the first time. There's nothing like a first-timer for the health of a game or a competition.

This was the winning team:

Damien McCusker

Kieran McKeever	Tony Scullion	Fergal McCusker
John McGurk	Henry Downey (*captain*)	Gary Coleman

Anthony Tohill   Brian McGilligan

Dermot Heaney	Damien Barton	Damien Cassidy
Joe Brolly	Séamus Downey	Enda Gormley

Substitutes: Dermot McNicholl for Damien Cassidy, Éamonn Burns for Séamus Downey.

37

WONDERFUL BREAKTHROUGHS BY CLARE AND LEITRIM

Much has been said and written and there has been much pontification about the domination of the all-Ireland senior football championship by the few—Kerry, Dublin, Galway, Meath, and Cork—at the expense of the many—Carlow, Sligo, Waterford, Wicklow, Fermanagh … But the provincial successes of Clare in Munster in 1992 and Leitrim in Connacht in 1994 bred hope in every other county and generated a fresh enthusiasm and two very special Croke Park all-Ireland semi-final days that wafted a beautiful breath of fresh air through the GAA.

There had been breakthroughs at provincial final level before, such as Carlow's success in Leinster in 1944 and Longford's sole success in the same province in 1968. These successes were very much cherished both in County Carlow and in County Longford; but the hype attached to the Clare and Leitrim breakthroughs was much greater. It's the times we live in, I suppose. But it wasn't by accident it happened for either county.

Though Gaelic football has always been second to hurling in the scheme of things in County Clare, certainly in popular perception, west Clare at least has always been football territory, with traditional strongholds of the game in Milltown Malbay, Quilty, Doonbeg, Kilrush and Kilkee since the foundation of the GAA. There were always men in County Clare with a passion for the promotion of Gaelic football. One such man was the well-known army officer Noel Walsh from Milltown Malbay, a long-time Clare football selector who, with others, campaigned for years for the introduction of an open draw in the Munster senior football championship. Their argument was that the seeding system that kept Kerry and Cork apart was grossly unfair, killed incentive, and offered no hope to the so-called weaker counties, including Clare.

Eventually the exponents of the open draw got their way in Munster in 1991. Here was the chance for the other counties to threaten the Kerry-Cork preserve. But in 1991 Clare found themselves on the same side of the draw as Kerry and Cork and lost out to Kerry by 5-16 to 2-12 in Ennis; but they saw their move vindicated when the no-hopers Limerick put it up to Kerry in the 1991 Munster final, before losing out on the score 0-23 to Limerick's 3-12. The expected rout hadn't materialised. The open draw was in.

Another huge factor in the surge of Clare football was the appointment of another army officer, John Maughan of County Mayo, as team manager in October 1990. Maughan, a former college star with Carmelite College, Moate, had seen a glittering career with Mayo halted by a leg injury. Noel Walsh had no small hand in persuading him to come on board, and the Mayoman's total commitment to the job and his standards of discipline made an instant impact. Noel Walsh summed up this contribution in the magazine *Hogan Stand* of 21 August 1992:

> We were at a low ebb when John joined us. Being so young (in his twenties then) he was an unusual choice but this has worked to his advantage. He identified with them and they with him. He ran up all the sand-hills and suffered it all with them and they gave him the response he required. His organisation is superb. He gave his players great belief in themselves and brought them to a peak of fitness no one ever dreamed of.

Instant success didn't follow, but Maughan set about his task with gusto, and after the championship defeat to Kerry in 1991 Clare became involved in the all-Ireland B championship (for specific teams beaten in the first round of the all-Ireland proper, a competition inaugurated in 1990) and duly won it, defeating Longford in extra time by 1-12 to 0-9.

This was a big feather in Clare's cap; and further progress was made when they won promotion to division 1 of the national football league and also earned a league quarter-final tilt with mighty Meath in Ballinasloe in the spring of 1992. Everybody sat up and took notice when Clare, despite having Gerry Killeen sent off in the tenth minute, carried the game to Meath, led going into the last ten minutes, and finally fell bravely by 0-8 to 0-6 to their much more experienced rivals.

The Mayo army man couldn't wait to get going in the 1992 Munster senior football championship, especially after Kerry were drawn against Cork in the preliminary round. The omens were good.

Clare were poised to pounce in 1992, and on 21 June in Limerick they duly accounted for Tipperary by 2-11 to 2-7, while at the same venue Kerry beat Limerick by 1-14 to 1-11.

Nobody outside County Clare expected them to beat Kerry in the Munster final at Limerick on 19 July. A goodly crowd of 26,000, consisting mainly of Clare supporters, was in attendance. Clare enjoyed much possession but were a bit nervy, and Gerry Killeen's sixth-minute penalty was easily saved by Peter O'Leary. Tom Morrissey and Aidan Maloney were dominant at midfield, and despite their inexperience Clare led at half time, 0-7 to 0-6.

After half time, Maurice Fitzgerald, with two points, edged Kerry ahead. But instead of caving in, Clare now took the game to Kerry in all departments, with Séamus Clancy, Noel Roche (veteran of countless defeats to Kerry over the years), Tom Morrissey (catching like a champion), Francis McInerney (a captain courageous with a lion's heart), Gerry Killeen and Aidan Maloney in the van. Then in the fifty-first minute came Colm Clancy's goal to put Clare three points up.

Jack O'Shea, at the end of a great career, did his best to revive Kerry, but the Clare surge was on, and when the substitute Martin Daly fisted a second goal in the fifty-ninth minute, the writing was on the wall. But no-one in Limerick or elsewhere listening to Marty Morrissey's commentary on RTE or Malachy McMahon on local radio could relax until the final whistle sounded. Would it ever come? Marty Morrissey uttered the immortal words as Clare won by 2-10 to 0-12: 'There won't be a cow milked in Clare tonight.' Limerick Gaelic Grounds went mad, and Clare people all over the world cried tears of joy—their first Munster football title in seventy-five years, and beating Kerry too at long last.

After the game, Jack O'Shea, one of Kerry's greatest players ever, announced his retirement from inter-county competition, but the news received scant attention from a public captivated by Clare's bravery and belief in themselves. In 1979 a Clare team including Noel Roche had been hammered in the Munster senior football championship in Milltown Malbay by 9-21 to 1-9 by a Kerry team including Jack O'Shea and all Mick O'Dwyer's stars of that wonderful time. Now his day had come, after fifteen years of striving. Noel Walsh's dream too had come true. John Maughan was king of County Clare.

The tour of the county, which lasted for two days after the game, was fantastic. Every town and village that had given players to the squad was visited: Liscasey, Coolaclare, Kilrush, Kilkee, Doonbeg, Corrofin, Rineen, Quilty, Milltown Malbay. Noel Walsh reported:

> The place went mad. Half way between Lehinch and Rineen the way was blocked and a famous ambush of 1921 re-enacted with the hillside set ablaze to welcome Francis McInerney and the Cup. A somewhat more subdued reception eventually in my native Milltown Malbay, where I was so proud to bring the cup home to the town I love so well. Where I got the feel of the leather first. Where I kicked the ball back from behind the goal to the big fellows. There was music, song and dance in the air. It was equivalent to an Odyssey and a great privilege to be part of it.

There are some wonderful memories from that time. One was the delight of all neutrals at the emergence of a new football power to challenge the old order. The word that Clare were beating Kerry spread around Clones during that wonderful game between Donegal and Derry in the 1992 Ulster final. Another is of a trip from Galway to play golf in Lehinch the week before the semi-final date of Clare v. Dublin and seeing the saffron-and-blue flags on practically every house and vantage point in County Clare and the obvious pride and joy in every face. The final one is the mighty cheer that erupted in Croke Park on 23 August when Francis McInerney led his team out onto the field to take on Dublin, and the sea of colour that engulfed the place when Clare supporters in the massive crowd of 58,000 for once dwarfed Dublin's huge support.

It was one of the greatest of all Croke Park occasions, and Clare fought heroically before failing in the end by 3-14 to 2-12. In fact at one point in the second half Clare fought back, to close the gap to two points, but the highly talented Vinny Murphy punched to the net from a free by Keith Barr, and that was that.

The Clare team was not content to lose with grace, and though they have not maintained the same momentum since, they helped in no small way to spearhead the hurling revival in the Banner County and are still capable of taking on the best at any level in league or championship. And they gave hope to all aspiring counties that even if you have to wait for seventy-five years of toil and tribulation and effort, your persistence can be rewarded in the end.

Leitrim's breakthrough was similar to Clare's but much more gradual. The open draw, apart from a fixed game against London in the preliminary round involving all the other Connacht counties in rotation, was in vogue for Connacht, but still it seemed always to be Galway or Mayo or Roscommon coming out on top. Like County Clare, County Leitrim has always had a fine Gaelic football tradition, but in a county with a small and declining population they were up against it. But the spirit never weakened, despite persistent defeats at the hands of Galway, Mayo, and Roscommon.

The gradual climb back to the top began in 1975 when Leitrim won the Father Manning under-16 competition and in 1977 won their first Connacht under-21 football title, before losing to Kerry in the semi-final after a brave fight. Then in 1983 Leitrim almost upset Galway's apple-cart in the Connacht senior football championship when Mickey Quinn's superlative midfield display almost won the day, a feat they repeated at the same venue in 1987, once again falling to Galway.

Then followed a low point, and after a disastrous start to the 1989/90 national football league they lured in an outside team manager from County Cavan, P. J. Carroll, a man with tremendous motivational talents and a high degree of organisation and enthusiasm, and almost immediately things began to look up. Within a year Leitrim won promotion to division 3 of the national football league and, like Clare, captured the all-Ireland B title in their initial year of 1990, trouncing Sligo in the final at Roscommon by 2-11 to 0-2. It was Leitrim's first all-Ireland football title and a massive springboard for the future.

In the subsequent national football league, Leitrim came very close on two occasions to gaining promotion to division 1. Their new-found success had awakened tremendous interest, and huge crowds flocked to support them at games both home and away. It wasn't unusual to have thirty or forty busloads of fans leaving the county on trips to venues such as Belfast in the heart of winter. A flame had been lit in Leitrim football, and Declan Darcy, Mickey Quinn, Pat Donohue, George Dugdale, Noel Moran, Pádraig Kenny and Gerry Flanagan were becoming household names.

Leitrim were now gaining in confidence with the experience of competing at a higher standard. P. J. Carroll had taken them as far as he could, and into the managerial seat came John O'Mahony of County Mayo, who had piloted his native county to an all-Ireland tilt with Cork in 1989 and lifted Mayo to a higher plane than for many years. Roscommon, Leitrim's near neighbours, were now the team they couldn't overcome when the chips were down, being beaten by them successively in the Connacht senior football championship from 1990 to 1992. Then, on 30 May 1993, Leitrim came to Tuam and beat

Galway for the first time in forty-four years, by 1-12 to 1-11. It was no fluke either. Galway cruised into a lead in the crucial stages late in the game, but Leitrim edged back point by point to level before Aidan Rooney scored the winning point late in the game.

The explosion of joy from Leitrim's growing support took over Tuam. All the ghosts of the past were exorcised. All those beatings, losing four Connacht senior football finals in a row, 1957–60, when men like Packy McGarty, Cathal Flynn, Josie Murray, Jimmy O'Donnell, Bernie Doyle, Leo Heslin, Tony Hayden and Jim Reynolds kept coming back, were remembered now as Leitrim supporters danced with joy. The unbelievable had happened.

Then, just when their cup overflowed, the old bogey team, Roscommon, defeated them in Carrick-on-Shannon by 1-12 to 1-10 in the Connacht semi-final, for the fourth successive year. Would those demons ever be beaten?

But the draw for the 1994 Connacht senior football championship didn't favour Leitrim at all. First they must beat Roscommon in their own Hyde Park in the first round, before taking on Galway in Carrick-on-Shannon, scene of the near-wins of 1983 and 1987. But at last the Roscommon jinx was laid to rest when the captain, Declan Darcy, ever a man with a cool head in a crisis, nonchalantly slotted over the winning point from a forty-five in the dying moments of yet another close game to win by 1-10 to 0-12. Now for Galway in Carrick!

Here again Galway edged ahead in the second half and looked like winners until another long-range pointed free by Declan Darcy, again in the final minute, forced a draw of 1-6 to 0-9 for Leitrim after a poor game saved only by the close exchanges. The replay in Tuam was much better, and again Leitrim came from behind to force a deserved win by 0-11 to 0-10, with Pádraig Kenny this time scoring the winning point after Séamus Quinn gave a superlative exhibition of full-back play. Leitrim were doing it the hard way. Mayo in Hyde Park lay ahead in the final.

The Connacht final on 24 July was a marvellous occasion for Leitrim's army of fans, but they suffered heartaches galore before emerging victorious, very deservedly, 0-12 to 2-4, despite the setback of having to concede a ridiculously soft goal in the early seconds of the match. It wasn't a great game. Leitrim were clearly on top but played edgily and allowed an inferior Mayo team to come too close to them in the end. But when the final whistle sounded those of us present witnessed the most emotive scenes ever seen in a Connacht sports-field. It was my fiftieth Connacht senior final occasion in different capacities—player, official, spectator, and sports writer—but nothing ever surpassed the after-match scenes at Leitrim's second Connacht senior success, their first since 1927. When Tom Gannon, captain and lone survivor of 1927, went onto the presentation podium to embrace the winning captain, Declan Darcy, and the long-serving hero Mickey Quinn, who had a capital game, not a Leitrim eye was dry, and even those of us with no attachment were affected.

The homecoming with the J. J. Nestor Cup was something to savour, and every corner of Lovely Leitrim was visited. John O'Mahony had done it again, a quiet man of steel with the winning touch.

Like Clare two years before, Leitrim now had to face Dublin in Croke Park in the semi-final on 21 August.

Though Leitrim suffered the same fate as Clare, losing to Dublin by 3-15 to 1-9, they lost no honour and gave their marvellous following among an attendance of 53,000 an occasion to savour. Every house in County Leitrim must have been represented in Croke Park for Leitrim's first senior football championship game in the national venue. When Declan Darcy raced ahead of his team onto Croke Park, every Connacht person present rose to salute the underdog. What a moment of pride it must have been for the legion of Leitrim people present or at home watching and their many exiles throughout the globe! The names McHugh, Honeyman, Quinn, Reynolds, Moran, Darcy, Flanagan, Quinn (Mickey), Donohue, Rooney, Dugdale, Kieran, McGlynn, Kenny, Conlon, Ward and Breen are etched for ever in Leitrim folklore. They will be spoken about for ever in all the villages of Lovely Leitrim.

38

GREAT EXPONENTS AND SPECIAL SELECTIONS

This chapter is not an exercise in nominating the great exponents of Gaelic football since the game came into being. Styles have changed too much; facilities are vastly better than those available even half a century ago; training and tactical approaches have changed utterly; even the rules are different. Who am I to compare the giants of earlier years, such as Dick Fitzgerald (Kerry), 'Sandman' Jack Carvin (Louth), Jack Grace (Dublin), Seán O'Kennedy (Wexford), Larry Stanley (Kildare), the McDonnells and Joe Norris (Dublin), Michael 'Knacker' Walsh (Galway) and all those wonderful Kerrymen from the era of Joe Barrett and John Joe Sheehy with the players of today? Few in fact are alive who can remember the stars of the nineteen-thirties or forties; but the memories of John Joe O'Reilly (Cavan) and his brother Big Tom, Jim McCullagh (Armagh), Purty Kelly (Mayo), Tommy Murphy (Laois), Paddy Kennedy, Bob Stack and Paddy Bawn Brosnan (Kerry), Dinny O'Sullivan (Galway), Tadhg Crowley (Cork) and Bill Carlos (Roscommon) live on.

To commemorate the centenary of the birth of the GAA, the *Sunday Independent,* in conjunction with the Irish Nationwide Building Society, selected a Team of the Century in 1984. The final fifteen were chosen by a panel of GAA cognoscenti guided by the choices of people who took part in a survey organised by the paper. It wasn't a foolproof method, being grossly unfair to the stars of the GAA's early days, but it generated much excitement at the time. It reads as follows:

Dan O'Keeffe
(Kerry)

Enda Colleran   Paddy O'Brien   Seán Flanagan
(Galway)   (Meath)   (Mayo)

Seán Murphy	John Joe O'Reilly	Stephen White
(Kerry)	(Cavan)	(Louth)

Mick O'Connell	Jack O'Shea
(Kerry)	(Kerry)

Seán O'Neill	Seán Purcell	Pat Spillane
(Down)	(Galway)	(Kerry)
Mikey Sheehy	Tom Langan	Kevin Heffernan
(Kerry)	(Mayo)	(Dublin)

It was a fine team, of course, and a wonderful distinction for those selected, who were suitably honoured at a presentation banquet in Dublin. Subsequently a Centenary Team comprising players who had never won an all-Ireland senior football championship medal was chosen by a similar panel; and though this did not generate as much excitement, it was due recognition for the stars who made it to the top with skill and effort but never had the honour of winning a Celtic cross—all great players, some of whom had never even won a senior provincial medal. At the presentation banquet in Dublin each one received as a memento a replica of an all-Ireland medal.

The chosen team was:

Aidan Brady
(Roscommon)

Willie Casey	Eddie Boyle	John McKnight
(Mayo)	(Louth)	(Armagh)
Gerry O'Reilly	Gerry O'Malley	Seán Quinn
(Wicklow)	(Roscommon)	(Armagh)

Jim McKeever	Tommy Murphy
(Derry)	(Laois)

Seán O'Connell	Packy McGarty	Mickey Kearins
(Derry)	(Leitrim)	(Sligo)
Charlie Gallagher	Willie McGee	Dinny Allen
(Cavan)	(Mayo)	(Cork)

Both selections generated any amount of controversy. Of course no such representative selection spanning the years will please everybody. These selections led to a spate of similar selections for counties and clubs; but then the GAA has an extraordinary capacity for looking back and revering its heroes, many of whom are remembered long after their death in song and story.

An Post, in conjunction with the GAA, chose a Gaelic Football Team of the Millennium, again using a panel of experts comprising former footballers, retired GAA presidents and former GAA writers to select their own personal teams. This was whittled down to a smaller panel, who made the final choice. An Post honoured the chosen fifteen by producing a stamp sheet showing paintings of the fifteen selected players in their county colours. The stamps were very well received and are now treasured collectors' items. Eight of the nine chosen are alive and well and were present in the Panoramic Restaurant in the New Stand at Croke Park when the selection was announced in August 1999.

The GAA Museum in Croke Park plans to establish its own Hall of Fame. The first to join it is the Millennium Gaelic Football team, to be followed by the Millennium Hurling Team selected in the summer of 2000. These teams will be added to each year, the plan being to spread the continuing display of the Hall of Fame throughout the reconstructed stadium so that the fans who throng Croke Park will see the men and women who sowed the seeds of GAA history.

The Millennium Gaelic Football Team differed little from the Centenary Year Selection. Here it is:

Dan O'Keeffe

| Enda Colleran | Joe Keohane (Kerry) | Seán Flanagan |
| Seán Murphy | John Joe O'Reilly | Martin O'Connell (Meath) |

Mick O'Connell   Tommy Murphy (Laois)

| Seán O'Neill | Seán Purcell | Pat Spillane |
| Mikey Sheehy | Tom Langan | Kevin Heffernan |

The selection was well received; but the omission of Jack O'Shea was greeted with disbelief—not indeed that any offence was offered to the memory of Tommy Murphy, the Boy Wonder from County Laois, or indeed Mick O'Connell, one of the truly greats of all time; but Jack O'Shea is generally regarded as the greatest player to emerge in the past twenty-five years.

This selection generated much discussion, and the commemorative stamps became an instant success. The Stamp Design and Production Manager of An Post, Declan O'Leary, described the issue as 'the most successful stamp issue ever by An Post, generating interest at home and abroad in the strangest and most far-flung areas, surpassing the previous top launches commemorating the papal visit to Ireland and Ireland's involvement in the World Cup.' The idea created maximum publicity for the GAA and, as in 1984, started a plethora of county, club and provincial commemorative selections. And no doubt men like Jack O'Shea, Paddy O'Brien, Stephen White and many others will in time be added to the GAA Hall of Fame.

39

MEATH'S ALL-IRELAND
DOMINANCE

D ublin had been champing at the bit for a number of years
before 1995. There was that epic four-game saga of 1991
against Meath; and in 1992 very few outside County Donegal
gave much for their chances of beating the experienced Dubs in
Donegal's first final in Croke Park. Derry were Dublin's conquerors in
a very close semi-final in 1993. But Dublin kept coming back, now
under Dr Pat O'Neill as manager and his fellow-selectors Jim Brogan,
Fran Ryder, and Bobby Doyle, all former Dublin stars. But Down
proved too good for them in the all-Ireland final of 1994.

Still, for all the close encounters, Dublin were itching to go for the
all-Ireland crown of 1995. With the long-serving goalkeeper John
O'Leary as captain, Dublin set off in quest of a fourth successive
Leinster crown by defeating Louth in Navan on 18 June by 0-19 to 2-
5. Charlie Redmond was the star, while Jason Sherlock, an exciting
nineteen-year-old, got a rousing reception when he came on as a
substitute for Seán Cahill in the first half and scored a point from a
free on his debut. On Sunday 9 July, at Navan again, Laois were beaten
1-13 to 0-9. Jason Sherlock was on from the start this time, and the
'Jayo' phenomenon grew when the youngster pounced in the second
half for the only goal of the game and was unlucky not to have scored
another.

Jayo was now the talk of Ireland; but Dublin wasn't a one-man
band. Dessie Farrell was beginning to stamp his authority in attack,
and Charlie Redmond was still popping over points; but Jayo's goal
was the flavour of the time, and the fact that he lost a boot before
scoring added to the allure of Gaelic football's new-found hero.

In the Leinster final at Croke Park on 30 July, Dublin easily beat a
fading Meath team—a mix of the old and the new—by 1-18 to 1-8,

for their fourth successive Leinster crown, with the style of champions, none better than Dessie Farrell, Paul Clarke, that consummate ball-player Paul Curran, Jayo, and the sharpshooter Charlie Redmond.

In the all-Ireland semi-final on 20 August, Cork were beaten 1-12 to 0-12 when Brian Stynes had a stormer at midfield and Jason Sherlock left the Cork full-back Mark O'Connor flatfooted for a decisive first-half goal. Jayo couldn't do anything wrong after this. In the other semi-final Tyrone edged out a resurgent Galway in a close one, mainly through the brilliance of Peter Canavan. Would Dublin's perseverance hold good, or would Tyrone continue the Ulster dominance?

Before a capacity crowd of 65,000, Dublin defeated Tyrone by 1-10 to 0-12 on Sunday 17 September. It was ever so close. Peter Canavan scored 0-11 in total and was unlucky to be blown up for passing the ball along the ground, after falling, for what would have been the equaliser. Still, Dublin deserved to win, as Tyrone tended to rely too much on the wonderful Canavan, while Dublin by contrast had Jayo, who laid on the pass for Charlie Redmond's goal. Dublin were well on top in the second half but failed to put Tyrone away, then had to endure hanging on after Charlie Redmond received his walking papers for retaliation fourteen minutes into the second half. The real Dublin heroes, however, were Paul Curran and Dessie Farrell, with John O'Leary a commanding captain in goal.

Sam Maguire was back in the capital for the first time in twelve years, and Jayo walked tall as the idol of an army of young fans. The Dublin team was:

John O'Leary

Ciarán Walsh	Paddy Moran	Keith Galvin
Paul Curran	Keith Barr	Mick Deegan

Paul Bealin   Brian Stynes

Jim Gavin	Paul Clarke	Dessie Farrell
Charlie Redmond	Jason Sherlock	Mick Galvin

Substitutes: Pat Kilroy for Keith Galvin, Robbie Boyle for Mick Galvin, Vinnie Murphy for Dessie Farrell.

Little was expected of Meath in 1996, but that man Seán Boylan was still in charge of affairs, and when the 1996 senior football championship began for them against Carlow on 16 June 1996 a Carlow surprise win after some encouraging earlier displays wasn't ruled out. But there was a gulf in class between the sides, and Meath won easily by 0-24 to 0-6 with an impressive young team that included only Martin O'Connell, Colm Coyle and Tommy Dowd of the old brigade. Boylan's Babes were on the move, with the former minor stars Trevor Giles, Darren Fay, Barry Callaghan, Paddy Reynolds, Graham Geraghty, Enda McManus and Conor Martin cutting their senior teeth in style.

Next Laois were conquered in Croke Park on 7 July by 2-14 to 1-9, with Graham Geraghty the star and great help from his half-forward colleagues Trevor Giles and Tommy Down. It was the traditional Meath v. Dublin Leinster final again on 28 July, and before a huge crowd of 55,000 Meath defeated the all-Ireland champions with the score 0-10 to 0-8. John McDermott was magnificent at midfield on a day of torrential rain, and in the final ten minutes Meath's mental toughness wore down a two-point deficit with four points in the last seven minutes from Brendan Reilly, Trevor Giles, Barry Callaghan, and Tommy Dowd. Seán Boylan, always affable in defeat or victory, carried the broadest of smiles at the press reception afterwards.

In the semi-final Tyrone were well beaten by 2-15 to 0-12, with John McDermott and Jimmy McGuinness dominating midfield and Graham Geraghty again the star of the attack. Meath were much criticised after the game for a perceived over-physical approach, which resulted in injuries to Brian Dooher, Peter Canavan, and Brian McBride, but these injuries came in the heat of battle and were more accidental than contrived—apart perhaps from a late tackle on Peter Canavan. Tyrone supporters afterwards tended to overplay it; on the day they were not the force they were in 1995 and were well beaten.

Meanwhile Mayo, with a new momentum and buzz, created largely by the new manager, John Maughan, so successful with Clare in 1992, had come storming out of Connacht, defeating London by 1-11 to 1-5, Roscommon by 0-14 to 0-11, and Galway in a humdinger Connacht final in Castlebar by 3-9 to 1-11. Then followed a superb semi-final defeat of Kerry by 2-13 to 1-10, in which John Casey excelled at full-forward and names like James Nallen, Pat Fallon, Colm McManamon and Liam McHale were on everybody's lips. The west was truly awake, and the former Mayo star John Maughan became the darling of the public as the green-and-red brigade trained assiduously in Castlebar and elsewhere for the big day. Not since 1951 had the Sam Maguire Cup come to Mayo, a county whose love for Gaelic football is second to none. A wonderful spirit enveloped the county, and the green and red was to be seen on every telephone or electricity pole and flying from every vantage point.

Mayo did everything but win the 1996 final, dominating the game, mainly through the brilliance of Liam McHale, always a hero in County Mayo, whose basketball skills were employed to perfection as he shot the ball accurately all over the place on his greatest day. The westerners deservedly led at half time by 0-7 to 0-4, mainly through the accuracy of Maurice Sheridan's frees and James Horan's point-popping skill from play. Ten minutes into the second half came the moment when green-and-red flags flew high, as Ray Dempsey goaled to put Mayo six points ahead. One thought of Tyrone in 1986.

It was here that Meath's great never-say-die spirit surfaced in the midfield artistry of John McDermott, in the forward skill of Trevor Giles and Brendan Reilly and in the defensive play of Darren Fay as Meath gnawed away at Mayo's lead, point by point. Instead of coasting home, Mayo suddenly were tactically bereft as the inevitability of a draw loomed. It came in the shape of a speculative lob by Colm Coyle, which hopped over the bar and might have been a goal. Meath gave a gasp of relief, and in a sense Mayo were glad that the referee, Pat McEnaney, blew some two or three minutes early, allowing a bare fifteen seconds of extra time. Mayo had clearly lost all their shape. Meath were not going to give their opponents a second bite at the cherry. The score, 1-9 to 0-12, put Colm Coyle into folklore status in the annals of Meath football.

Two weeks later, on Sunday 29 September, 66,000 spectators were back in Croke Park for the replay, a game remembered for all the wrong reasons: the day of 'the big fight and the big wind,' as Brian Carthy described it in The Championship (1996). The game was under way little more than five minutes when a vicious brawl broke out near the Meath goal, involving numerous players from both sides. After the first flare-up players arrived from all directions to lend a hand. The 'one in, all in' policy adopted by both teams was a huge embarrassment to both counties and to the GAA, and the television film is often shown to this day as a deterrent to such a disgrace happening again in any game, least of all in the showcase of the GAA. Players seemed intent on settling any old scores from the drawn game; and for a county like Mayo, whose open style of football has always been their forte, it was anathema. Meath clearly won the fisticuffs battle—an honour, I'm sure, from which they derive little pride. Both team managements deserve censure for not killing any grudge element beforehand.

Pat McEnaney had a tough time sorting out the mess. He sent Liam McHale of Mayo and Colm Coyle of Meath packing; he could well have sent a few more from both sides to the line. It was tough on

McHale, who was more sinned against than sinning; but, like all the rest, he became embroiled and had run a distance to get involved. Thankfully we were spared any more brawls.

Mayo, with wind advantage, led at half time by 1-6 to 1-2, with James Horan again their best forward and a fine goal by the substitute P. J. Loftus, negatived shortly afterwards by a penalty goal from Trevor Giles for a foul on Tommy Dowd. Was the lead enough?

Meath shot back, with three points in five minutes, but Mayo really fought now, none better than Pat Fallon, Colm McManamon, and James Horan; and the green-and-red were still in front by two points entering the final ten minutes. Now Tommy Dowd availed of a quick free from Graham Geraghty to snatch a goal while falling, the kind of score that wins all-Irelands, to put Meath ahead for the first time. James Horan—that man again—levelled it with less than five minutes left. It was now or never for both teams; and yet one sensed that Meath had the greater passion. Then it happened. Brendan Reilly got possession in the right corner, worked his way in and, cool as a cucumber, popped over the winner with his left foot. The final whistle sounded, and Meath had won their fifth all-Ireland, by 2-9 to 1-11, with a team of mostly new heroes.

Meath's team in the replay was:

Conor Martin

| Mark O'Reilly | Darren Fay | Martin O'Connell |
| Colm Coyle | Enda McManus | Paddy Reynolds |

Jimmy McGuinness   John McDermott

| Trevor Giles | Tommy Dowd | Graham Geraghty |
| Colm Brady | Brendan Reilly | Barry Callaghan |

Substitutes: Jody Devine for Barry Callaghan, Ollie Murphy for Brendan Reilly.

Mayo had fought hard, but Meath's great spirit prevailed, and Boylan's Babes were the toast of County Meath. The long journey home to County Mayo was a painful one. In the national and local radio phone-ins that have become so much a part of the sporting scene there was much discussion of the infamous brawl.

Kerry's absence from the all-Ireland scene was beginning to be felt in the county. Where once the Sam Maguire Cup made a few visits per decade, the new cup had never gone to County Kerry; and despite the fact that all-Ireland titles were coming Kerry's way in other grades, the flagship senior title hadn't been won since 1986. The former Kerry star Páidí Ó Sé, one of the greats of the Mick O'Dwyer era, was now in charge; and, having groomed many of the senior squad to under-21 all-Ireland success in 1995 and 1996, he was reasonably optimistic in 1997 and was buoyed up after Kerry won the national football league of 1996/7 with good wins over Laois (2-13 to 1-10) and Cork (3-7 to 1-8) in the semi-final and final, respectively.

They began their return to glory with a 2-12 to 1-10 win over Tipperary at Tralee on 29 June. At one point Tipperary seemed set to shock Kerry, as Clare had done the previous Sunday when disposing of Cork in Ennis; but Kerry survived through a late goal by Denis O'Dwyer. They went on to defeat Clare in the Munster final by 1-13 to 0-11 when the goal-scoring hero Pa Laide (son of the former Galway all-Ireland player Mick Laide) emerged as Man of the Match. Maurice Fitzgerald was another to display his silken skill. Kerry were now in the all-Ireland semi-final against their old rivals Cavan, who, coached by the former Donegal star Martin McHugh, had come though in Ulster in flying style with new stars like the Reillys (Peter, Larry, and Damien), Ronan Carolan of the magic feet, young Dermot McCabe, and the experienced captain, Stephen King.

The return of Cavan as Ulster champions after a long lapse of twenty-eight years produced emotive scenes in Clones on Ulster final day as the former heroes Mick Higgins, P. J. Duke, the great John Joe and Big Tom O'Reilly, Simon Deignan and Tony Tighe were recalled in song and story for the triumphant return of the Anglo-Celt Cup to Bréifne. That Ulster final, won by Cavan over Derry by 1-14 to 0-16, is remembered as a classic game in which the score was level no fewer than eight times in the first half alone.

Memories of the New York all-Ireland final of fifty years previously came flooding back as the royal blue of Cavan raced onto Croke Park in a nostalgic return before a wonderful attendance reminiscent of Clare and Leitrim in 1992 and 1994. Kerry proved too good in the end by 1-17 to 1-10, though Cavan led at half time, 1-7 to 0-9, after a wonderful goal by Fintan Cahill. Kerry took over in the last quarter, thanks to a fine goal by Michael Francis Russell and some classic points by Maurice Fitzgerald. Séamus Moynihan was another to star, while Declan O'Keeffe in goal brought off one classic save reminiscent of his namesake, the great Danno. Kerry were in another final at last.

Meantime Mayo had come through in the west after a thrill-a-minute win over Galway in Tuam, ending a 46-year championship jinx at the venue, and a less than convincing and rather lucky escape against Sligo in the Connacht final by 0-11 to 1-7, with the referee,

Mick Curley, blowing full time after twenty seconds of injury time. In between Mayo had also beaten Leitrim at Castlebar.

But there was no doubting Mayo's superiority over Offaly at Croke Park in the semi-final, 0-13 to 0-7, on a very wet surface, with Pat Fallon in stellar form and Noel Connelly, the captain, marshalling an excellent defence. Kieran McDonald impressed in attack, while Offaly, who had defeated Meath in an epic Leinster final, were a huge disappointment. Would Mayo, with the experience gained in 1996, come good at last?

Some all-Ireland finals throw up a real star; other finals give a real star a chance to display his repertoire of skills. This is what happened in 1997 when Maurice Fitzgerald of Kerry, long considered by many to be the most skilful footballer in the land, demonstrated to all and sundry his real genius with a football. It was as good a display of kicking skill as has ever been seen in a final, and Fitzgerald inspired Kerry to defeat Mayo by 0-13 to 1-7. He scored no less than nine points from frees and from play, and the final point from his hands from a free out on the New Stand sideline climaxed a wondrous display.

Early in the game Maurice had accidentally collided with his colleague Billy O'Shea, who suffered a compound fracture of his ankle; but this didn't faze the Cahersiveen man, son of the former Kerry player Ned Fitzgerald and great friend of Kerry's nonpareil Mick O'Connell.

Mayo again erred tactically by selecting the veteran Dermot Flanagan, who had to retire early on. They were dreadful in the first twenty minutes, didn't raise a flag until the twenty-third minute, and were led by 0-8 to 0-3 at half time. But they did improve in the second half, inspired by Peter Burke in goal, Ken Mortimer and Pat Fallon, and a well-struck penalty by Kieran McDonald. James Horan, who seems to thrive on Croke Park soil, scored two points, and the game was up for grabs. But Kerry weathered the storm when Mayo had some pathetic misses. Maurice Fitzgerald, inspired by the old-style centre-half-back Liam O'Flaherty, scored some spectacular late points; and that was that.

It was nostalgic to see the stars of the New York final of 1947 parading onto the field during one of the intervals and to meet Peter Donoghoe, the 'Babe Ruth' of Gaelic football, as well as Mick Higgins, Tony Tighe, and those greats of Kerry, Eddie Dowling, Batt Garvey, and Eddie Walsh of Knocknagoshel.

The winning Kerry team of 1997 was:

Declan O'Keeffe

Killian Burns   Barry O'Shea   Stephen Stack

Séamus Moynihan   Liam O'Flaherty   Éamonn Breen

Dara Ó Sé   William Kirby

Pa Laide   Liam Hassett (*captain*)   Denis O'Dwyer

Billy O'Shea   Dara Ó Cinnéide   Maurice Fitzgerald

Substitutes: John Crowley for Barry O'Shea, Dónal Daly for William Kirby, Michael Francis Russell for Dara Ó Cinnéide.

It wasn't one of the great Kerry teams; but you'd swear it was the first time the Sam Maguire Cup went to County Kerry, such was the welcome for the green-and-gold heroes on their return home. Páidí Ó Sé received more plaudits than he ever did as a player; but then manager mania had gripped the GAA scene long before 1997.

If Kerry craved the Sam Maguire, just imagine what the desire to lift the cup was like in County Galway, where no-one under thirty-five could remember the euphoria and the bonfires for the end of the three-in-a-row era of 1966. Good teams had come and gone since— some at the first hurdle, as in 1997, some at the last hurdle, as in 1971, 1973, 1974, and 1983. Galwegians had almost given up hope of ever seeing Sam being toasted in Ballinasloe, Tuam, Galway, or Clifden.

The craving was even worse in County Kildare, another county steeped in tradition since the days of Larry Stanley and earlier and that had always remained true to the code, despite many more reverses than Galway. The Lily-Whites hadn't won a Leinster senior football championship since 1956; but in 1990 Mick O'Dwyer was persuaded to take over as manager, and he immediately elevated the whole profile of Kildare football. He led Kildare into a national football league final almost immediately and guided them into a serious challenging position in Leinster. The same happened with Galway when much later, in the autumn of 1997, John O'Mahony of Mayo, former manager of the successful Mayo and Leitrim teams, was invited to take over as manager. With his thorough and perfectionist approach to detail he got Galway moving and reawakened a long-dormant support, and by the time the 1998 all-Ireland championship was upon us, both Galway and Kildare were quietly fancied, certainly within their own counties and by a few knowing ones without. Galway's football odyssey of 1998 was about to begin.

McHale Park in Castlebar was the venue for the beginning of the Galway surge against the old rivals, Mayo, on Sunday 24 May in glorious weather. The first half of this game was as good a half as I've ever seen in Connacht—drama, great scores, non-stop up-and-down action before a capacity shirt-sleeved gathering, and the sides level at the break: Galway 1-8, Mayo 2-5. The first thirty-five minutes seemed like ten. It took Galway a long time to take over in the second half, and Mayo were not mastered until the final minutes, before Galway won by 1-13 to 2-6.

Connacht football was taken seriously now. Live television coverage, very much the norm now, had beamed this game throughout the country, and there was much praise for Galway's style of play, a very good mix of the old and the new, fashioned by John O'Mahony. John Divilly's direct play at centre-half-back was a revelation. Kevin Walsh caught like a champion at midfield and seemed to have plenty of time on the ball; but it was the slick combined play of the forwards that really stamped Galway as a team to be watched.

Galway's growing army of supporters invaded Carrick-on-Shannon for the Connacht semi-final on 14 June, when Derek Savage had a field day in Galway's easy win by 1-16 to 0-5. Would anybody halt the Galway machine?

On 19 July, however, Roscommon put a stop to the Galway gallop in Tuam on a very wet day, and a late and lucky pointed free from the old reliable Niall Finnegan saved Galway blushes. It had been very close, and the ever-increasing confidence of supporters had crept unconsciously into the team. Roscommon, managed by the former star goalkeeper Gay Sheeran, had had the benefit of a draw and replay with Sligo and, as always, played with passion and pride. In the end Galway hung on for a draw, 0-11 each.

Martin McNamara had made some brilliant stops in goal. Galway were subsequently dubbed by one newspaper 'Fancy Dans' and a 'nice team'; and they certainly deserved to be censured. The 'Fancy Dans' appellation was used to good effect by John O'Mahony many times subsequently.

Galway's growing army of support was deflated, yes, but it was out in force for the replay on a glorious Saturday evening in Hyde Park, Roscommon, on 1 August. A Mardi Gras atmosphere surrounded Roscommon that evening, and the game that ensued was one of the most thrilling of all Connacht finals, certainly the best since those epic duels between Mayo and Galway in 1948.

Again it was 0-11 apiece at the end of normal time in a game that saw Kevin Walsh lord of midfield and Eddie Lohan of Roscommon ever so accurate with frees from all angles and distances. In extra time

Jarlath Fallon opened up as only he can with three capital points from play, to leave Galway in front, 0-16 to 0-14, at half time of extra time. The game had just resumed when Michael Donnellan scored the all-important goal after an untypical handling error from the Roscommon goalkeeper, Derek Thompson; and even though Roscommon continued to fight bravely, Galway had done enough to win by 1-17 to 0-17. Lucky again perhaps; but a good team makes its own luck. Roscommon had contributed handsomely to a wonderful occasion, and Galway's 'Fancy Dans' had moved on. It was a name never applied to that team again in 1998.

In the semi-final on 23 August, before 39,000 supporters, Galway easily accounted for Derry, the forwards scintillatingly led by Ja Fallon, Pádhraic Joyce, and Michael Donnellan, who showed rare pace, and the brilliant Tomás Mannion at left-corner-back. The score: 0-16 to 1-8. Derry's goal from a penalty came in the thirty-fourth minute of the second half.

Galway were back in a final at last. Their opponents, the Lily-Whites of Kildare, after a replayed win over Dublin, defeated Laois, Meath and Kerry in turn, gathering momentum along the way, with Glen Ryan, Anthony Rainbow, Niall Buckley, Martin Lynch and Karl O'Dwyer (son of Micko) inspiring a football-mad county.

When all-Ireland day, 27 September, dawned, Kildare were raging-hot favourites with all neutrals. But Galway's 32-year wait couldn't be denied—though at half time, as Kildare led by 1-5 to 0-5, many Galway followers were beginning to lose faith. Galway's second-half performance of old-style football, coupled with wonderful forward power and some stellar performances from Ja Fallon, Michael Donnellan, Kevin Walsh, Tomás Mannion, Pádhraic Joyce, and Martin McNamara, raised the standard of Gaelic football and reminded dyed-in-the-wool supporters of what the game could be like when played by two skilful and sporting teams, with the ball doing the work and no opportunism or gamesmanship displayed.

Galway went on to win by 1-14 to 1-10; and when Seán Óg de Paor raced through for the insurance point I felt relaxed at last, and tears of joy weren't too far away. When Ray Silke raised Sam high he raised also the pent-up emotions of thousands of Galway fans at home and abroad who had almost given up hope of seeing the maroon-and-white triumphant on all-Ireland senior final day again.

The celebrations afterwards were unbelievable. Kildare supporters were as dignified in defeat as their team was on the field of play. The joy of every Galwegian that night was palpable.

> Then on Monday evening
> We'd bring the cup back home;
> The bonfires would be blazing
> All along the road.
> 'Cos me heart is in maroon and white,
> I'll stick with what I know:
> It's maroon and white for ever,
> No matter where I go.

And the homecoming to Tuam especially was just like that. There were plaudits from all sides for the quality of football served up. One point kick from the hands by Ja Fallon from the sideline near the Hogan Stand was just as spectacular as Maurice Fitzgerald's a year before. Pádhraic Joyce's goal, after a wonderful run by Michael Donnellan, was magic.

Some months later Pádhraic Stevens and Leo Moran composed a follow-up to their 'Maroon and White for Ever', entitled 'The Night We Brought the Cup to Tuam'.

> Forty thousand people
> Came from near and far,
> Waiting in the darkness
> For our heroes to appear,
> Forty thousand people
> United now as one,
> Our differences forgotten:
> The championship was won.
>
> Me heart is in maroon and white,
> That's what I always say:
> Maroon and white of Galway
> For ever and a day.

The greatest tributes of all came from Eugene McGee in the *Irish Independent* ('Yesterday in Croke Park, Galway re-invented the great game of Gaelic football') and from the former Kerry maestro Mick O'Connell ('Congrats and thanks to Galway for halting the ruination of Gaelic football').

The winning team was:

Martin McNamara

Tomás Meehan   Gary Fahy   Tomás Mannion

Ray Silke (*captain*)   John Divilly   Seán Óg de Paor

Kevin Walsh   Seán Ó Domhnaill
Shay Walsh   Jarlath Fallon   Michael Donnellan
Derek Savage   Pádhraic Joyce   Niall Finnegan
Substitute: Paul Clancy for Shay Walsh.

From the beginning of the year, Meath were being spoken of as potential champions for 1999. True to expectations, their young lions, still under Seán Boylan's management, started off by defeating Wicklow in Croke Park on 6 June by 2-10 to 0-6, with Trevor Giles back after an injury under the new captain, Graham Geraghty. Then followed a fine win over Offaly in Croke Park on 4 July, 1-13 to 0-9, the goal coming from Ollie Murphy from a pass by Graham Geraghty. In the Leinster final Meath beat Dublin well in the end by 1-14 to 0-12, Ollie Murphy again scoring the goal that mattered and finishing with a fine personal tally of 1-5.

Galway lost their all-Ireland crown limply enough to Mayo, who subsequently went down to Cork, conquerors of Kerry in Munster. Armagh came storming out of Ulster with their first provincial title since 1982, defeating Down by 3-12 to 0-10, with Diarmuid Marsden and Oisín McConville outstanding. But in a dreadful all-Ireland semi-final on 19 August, before a huge attendance of 61,000, the Armagh men, after starting well, succumbed on the score 0-15 to 2-5, Meath pulling away in the end.

A new tactic of 'getting bodies behind the ball' threatened to ruin the game as a spectacle. It became very much a case of the survival of the fittest in midfield, especially after kick-outs from goal. No-one raved about the quality of play. Meath's young team, however, were very impressive at the end and were the favourites to beat Cork, now managed by Larry Tompkins, in the all-Ireland final.

In the final on 26 September, Meath defeated Cork by 1-11 to 1-8, taking over again in fine style nearing the end to claim their seventh all-Ireland crown on the fiftieth anniversary of their first win in 1949. In wet conditions, Meath led at half time by 1-5 to 0-5, the goal again coming from Ollie Murphy. The second half started with Kevin O'Dwyer saving a penalty from Trevor Giles. Cork took heart and went into the lead for the first time with a smashing goal from Joe Kavanagh. It was now Meath who dug deep, inspired by Graham Geraghty, Trevor Giles and John McDermott, Evan Kelly and Mark O'Reilly; and when it really mattered they had the reserves of determination, passion and will to win that saw them climb the final hurdle. Cork overdid the short passing game, while Seán Boylan's Babes often used the direct long ball to huge advantage.

Boylan was rightly heralded as the messiah of Meath football. A truly remarkable gentleman of sport, he had taken over in 1982 yet seventeen campaigns later was still at the helm after guiding Meath to four all-Ireland and seven Leinster senior football successes. No matter what, he stayed loyal to his beloved Meath, delivering two very successful teams in successive decades and remaining the unspoilt smiling face of Meath football. Meath and the GAA can be proud of this marvellous ambassador of sport.

The winning team was:

Cormac Sullivan

Mark O'Reilly   Darren Fay   Cormac Murphy

Paddy Reynolds   Enda McManus   Hank Traynor

Nigel Crawford   John McDermott

Evan Kelly   Trevor Giles   Nigel Nestor

Ollie Murphy   Graham Geraghty (*captain*)   Dónal Curtis

Substitutes: Richie Kealy for Nigel Nestor, Barry Callaghan for Hank Traynor, Tommy Dowd for Evan Kelly.

Typical of Seán Boylan, he made sure to introduce Tommy Dowd into the fray before the end, loyal as always to the old guard.

40

RULE CHANGES AND OTHER DEVELOPMENTS, 1934–2000

I n 1935 the GAA Congress decided, in its wisdom, that the playing rules for games could be reviewed only in years divisible by five. This decision gave some breathing-space to the games and cut out unnecessary tinkering with the rules. In the same year Kerry refused to participate in the inter-county championships because of political tensions, but happily they were back in the fold again in 1936.

Work began on the building of the old Cusack Stand in February 1936, though completion was delayed by a builders' strike in 1937, as was to happen again in 1999 with the reconstruction of the Canal End Stand. Mícheál O'Hehir as a youngster made his debut as a commentator on 14 August 1938 for the all-Ireland senior football semi-final between Galway and Monaghan in Mullingar; and just a week later the Cusack Stand was formally opened by Pádraig McNamee, Ulster's first president of the GAA.

Mícheál O'Hehir made an instant impact. He had the voice and the enthusiasm and that boyish charm that was to last a lifetime—a lifetime in which he, more than anyone else, helped to make the GAA and its games more popular than ever dreamt of by the association's founders. His contribution to the evolution of Gaelic football to being the most popular game in Ireland has never been given the acknowledgment it deserves. As a game, he loved hurling even more than football, and his contribution to its continued popularity was no less significant. But who can forget his vivid descriptions of goals and points, of catches and solo runs, of the feats of men like Joe Keohane and Dan O'Keeffe, Dinny Sullivan and Bobby Beggs, Paddy Prendergast and Paddy 'Bawn' Brosnan, of the wondrous fielding of Paddy Kennedy, Mick O'Connell, Jack O'Shea, Éamonn Boland, and Tommy Murphy, the Boy Wonder! He electrified the listener as he recorded the wondrous attacking flair of men like Seán Purcell, Seán O'Neill, Tadhgy Lyne, Iggy Jones, Pat Spillane, Peter McDermott, Kevin Heffernan ... O'Hehir inspired countless waves of youngsters to emulate the heroes he largely created among those who were entranced by his magic wand. We all dreamed dreams of wearing the county jersey and having Mícheál O'Hehir speak our name.

This history is dedicated to the memory of Mícheál O'Hehir, a small tribute to the youngster who began broadcasting in 1938 and continued to enthral right up to 1985, when illness put an end to his career.

In 1940 the Congress defeated motions calling for a penalty kick and for the abolition of the palmed pass, then very much in vogue. The throw-in for a sideline ball was still in operation. Some of the wording of the throw-in rule makes comic reading now:

> The ball may be thrown in any direction, and the player throwing in the ball must have one foot outside the line at the time of throwing, and must not hold the ball by the lace or thong.

The ball then was the one with bladder and nozzle and lace and was not as sophisticated as it is today. The player taking the throw-in wasn't permitted to score directly, though of course these throw-ins often led indirectly to a score. The player throwing in the ball was not allowed to play the ball himself before it was played by another player.

The Second World War was now affecting life in general. Travelling was restricted because of the rationing of petrol. The National League and junior all-Ireland championships were cancelled; the minor all-Irelands were cancelled for three years, 1942–4. Times were tough. Petrol rations were withdrawn, and Sunday bus services ceased; this was the era of the bicycle. But interest in Gaelic football never waned; in fact the general secretary of the GAA, Pádraig Ó Caoimh, told the Congress in 1945 that the previous year was one of 'peak achievement', with a record total of 1,944 clubs affiliated to the GAA.

In the same year Congress defeated a motion from Kerry to outlaw the hand-pass; but subsequently the Central Council, acting on the advice of referees, interpreted the rule as meaning that in the hand-pass the ball must be struck with the fist. The fisted pass was in, but it didn't last long, as the open hand-pass as it existed before 1945 was restored. The year 1945 also saw the introduction of the sideline kick off the ground, to replace the old throw-in.

The ball to be kicked off the ground where it crossed the sideline (as indicated by the linesman) by a player of the opposing team to that which touched it last before crossing. A score made from such kick is allowed.

We had seen the end of a well-known skill. In Galway the two greatest exponents of the throw-in were Frank Fox in the thirties and Tom Sullivan in the forties; but every county had its own specialist throwers.

In 1950 the open-hand pass was abolished and replaced by the fisted pass, a situation that was to obtain for some time. Congress accepted an application from New York to play in the national football league, entering the competition at the final stage to play the champions at home, and in that initial year they became national football league champions, defeating Cavan in Croke Park by 2-8 to 0-12. In the 1951 final Meath reversed the trend, defeating New York in John Kerry O'Donnell's Gaelic Park by 1-10 to 0-10. In 1951 also Congress voted against the use of the Bogue block as a timing device for ending games, which had been experimented with in certain games for the previous two years.

Full-time or collective training at all-Ireland final, semi-final and provincial final levels was all the rage in the thirties and forties but was prohibited by Congress of 1954, on a vote of ninety-five to fifty-six, the report of a sub-committee concluding that the practice infringed the amateur status of the association. Innocent times!

In 1955, a rule change year, Congress voted to limit the number of substitutes allowed in a game to three and introduced a no-stoppage rule to ensure continuity of play. Before this it had been the custom for players who were being replaced, because of loss of form or any other reason, to feign injury and then generally hobble off after being attended to. There was no need and no place for such sham after this. People will smile on reading this, but it did happen!

In 1956 Pádraig Ó Caoimh reported on the planning of the new Hogan Stand to cater for the ever-increasing crowds in a year in which 2,603 clubs were affiliated. Then, in 1958, Congress turned down a proposal seeking an 'open draw' for the all-Irelands. The first ten-year ticket scheme for all-Ireland finals was introduced to defray the cost of the new Hogan Stand, which was officially opened on Sunday 7 June 1959, the seventy-fifth anniversary of the foundation of the GAA.

In 1960 goalkeepers were allowed to pick the ball off the ground without having to toe it up in the accepted fashion. The rule that stipulates this pick-up is still there, though nowadays not much observed. The skill popularly known as 'selling a dummy'—changing the ball from one hand to the other—was legalised also. The referee was given the power to place the ball for a free kick or to indicate the position from which it should be taken. If a free rebounded off the upright or post, the player who took the kick was allowed to touch the ball again before an opponent had played it first.

In 1965 came a huge change affecting the start of all games. Only two players from each side were to line up at the centre of the field for the throw-in. Hitherto it had been eight from each side (the two midfielders and the six forwards), with the backs holding their own positions for the start of the game; now the six forwards took up their own forward positions alongside the opposing backs marking them. A fair shoulder charge, very much the accepted tackling device in Gaelic football, was re-defined as shoulder to shoulder.

In 1970 the duration of senior championship games was extended to eighty minutes (forty minutes per half) for provincial finals and all-Ireland semi-finals and finals, a move generally well received but after a time considered too big a leap and one that should have included all senior inter-county championship games. Players had to learn to pace themselves. Some huge totals were amassed: scoring records were set, and these have to be viewed separately from records achieved in sixty-minute or seventy-minute games, as obtained later. Players were allowed to take a quick free kick without having to wait for the referee's whistle—the first influence generated by Ron Barassi's Australian team, which visited Ireland first in 1967, and the other tours in the interim.

A Handbook for Referees and Players was prepared in 1973, incorporating one first printed in 1966, including the amendments of the 1973 Congress. Potential changes in the rule were given a trial run for a year before being ratified in a rule-changing year and incorporated in the rule book. This obtained in 1974, with many such changes being accepted in 1975.

New rectangles were drawn up in front of the goal, one 15 yards wide and 5 yards deep, the other 21 yards wide and 14 yards deep. In future the goalkeeper could not be charged within the smaller rectangle. This was a welcome move, as goalkeepers in the past were fair game and at times subjected to dog's abuse under the dropping ball. Men like Dan O'Keeffe, Johnny Geraghty and Tom Bourke never got such protection, and some of the elder statesmen of the GAA at the time felt they were overprotected by the new rule. The third-man tackle, as obtained in the past, was banned for ever more.

Another welcome addition was the leverage given to the referee to apply a ten-yard penalty for dissent against an offending player after a free was awarded. The palmed pass was back again, as well as the fisted pass, a gambit Mick O'Dwyer used to great success with his great teams of the seventies and later.

Goalkeepers were required henceforth to wear a distinctive jersey, to help identify them and also to protect them. When a personal foul was committed by the defence on an attacking player within the larger rectangle, a penalty kick was to be awarded from the centre point on the 14-yard line. All players other than the defending goalkeeper and the player taking the kick had to be outside the 21-yard line for all penalties. For all other fouls committed by the defence within the 14-yard line but not within the smaller rectangle, a free was to be given on the 14-yard line opposite where the foul was committed.

The personal foul rule was introduced, whereby if a player tripped an opponent by hand or foot or pulled down an opponent he would be cautioned after the second such offence and sent to the line after the third such offence. After the referee had awarded a free and before it had been taken, if a player of the team awarded the free fouled an opponent by way of retaliation, the free awarded would be negatived and play restarted by the referee, who would throw in the ball over the heads of two players from each side where the foul occurred.

All these rules were adopted in 1975, and the seventy-minute duration was introduced for all senior county championship games, a situation that obtained until 2000, when Congress decided that all senior games, club and county, would be of seventy minutes' duration. Yet another gambit banned at that time was that of lifting the ball off the ground with the knees—not very often done but useful in a crisis.

There was quite a furore when the personal foul rule was implemented by decree, and quite a few footballers were dismissed, including Kerry's versatile full-back John O'Keeffe. A great sportsman all his life, he had, like all footballers, become used to using the personal foul as a ploy in defence. The GAA backed away from a strict implementation of the rule, which had been introduced to help clean up the game and rid us of much of the pull-and-drag mania that has tended to lessen Gaelic football as a spectator sport. With hindsight it can be seen as an unwise decision, and the game is still besmirched by the same negative personal fouling, which has tended to obstruct continuity of play and create a stop-start game; in this regard it is surpassed by hurling, where openness, continuity and thrills abound. So it was no surprise when the personal rule was removed in 1980. Players then were allowed to take a quick free, except when such a free was awarded inside the 13-metre line. Note the change also to the metric system; no longer would we talk of pointing fifties (or seventies in hurling): instead we talk of forty-fives and sixty-fives. We've become used to it now.

In 1985 players were allowed to place the ball themselves for a sideline kick, but from 1990 all sideline kicks had to be taken from the hands (another Australian influence). All free kicks are to be taken from the hands or from the ground, with the exception that kick-outs from goal must be taken from the ground.

It's surprising how quickly we have become used to the free-taking. With players like Jarlath Fallon, Trevor Giles, Maurice Fitzgerald and Peter Canavan, either option suits. Generally, players shoot from the hands nearer goal and place the ball further out, but it differs with individuals. 'Teeing up' the ball for a free kick was banned. Goalkeepers erred badly here and could be seen preparing tee-up areas for kick-outs from goal. The hand-pass was re-defined, being allowed when executed from one hand provided there was a distinct striking motion.

In recent years we have seen the re-introduction of the link with Australian rules, an international outlet that cannot but be good for the GAA. On the 1999 trip to Australia the Australians themselves for the first time turned up in huge numbers to see the games, and the hybrid game, marrying the two codes, seems to improve and to create a better spectacle. This international link should not be allowed to die.

During the past few years the Football Development Committee set up by the past president Joe McDonagh came forward with a set of radical proposals, which generated much worthwhile discussion but were rejected by the GAA at large. The committee suggested a whole new league-cum-championship structure to replace the tried-and-true knock-out senior football championship and national football league that had served us well over the years. The committee hoped their proposal would generate more games, more finance, and more exposure, but the proposals were too radical and were soundly defeated. In 2000 it was decided by Congress to form a committee representative of the pro and anti views to formulate new proposals that would be presented to a special congress in the autumn of 2000. There may be some changes to create more games and greater finance, but it is felt that the championship and league will continue as separate competitions in the future.

41

WHITHER GAELIC FOOTBALL?

This book has traced the path of Gaelic football from the origins of the rough-and-tumble game to all-Ireland glory, when the top clubs participated to represent their counties. It took some time for the movement to reach every corner of Ireland, but gradually the top clubs invited the best players from rival clubs to wear the county jersey. It was an unsophisticated time, a time of much turbulence, and one has to admire the patience, determination and persistence of the pioneers, from Cusack on, who created the game of Gaelic football and the attendant excitement and passion that so reflect our Irish personality.

Dublin clubs dominated the pioneering days until the arrival of Kerry, Louth, Cork and Antrim and the purchase of Croke Park. Wexford, known as the Yellow-Bellies, captured the first four-in-a-row. Kildare's Lily-Whites shot to fame and helped the game to evolve with their hand-passing techniques. Catching and kicking were at all times the great skills, and the rough-and-tumble gradually disappeared.

Nothing could halt the onward march of Gaelic football, not even 1916, Bloody Sunday, or the Civil War and its aftermath. Already the stars of the game were becoming household names: Dick Fitzgerald, Seán O'Kennedy, Larry Stanley, the McDonnells of Dublin. About this time Seán 'Baller' Lavan from Kiltimagh, County Mayo, set off in Croke Park on a solo run and presented the game with another unique skill. Galway won their first all-Ireland in a bizarre year, and Kerry's first golden era dawned, healing Civil War rivalries in green-and-gold jerseys. Cavan came marching out of Ulster in royal blue; Mayo and Galway rivalry reached its peak; and a youthful Mícheál O'Hehir began to enthral an adoring public with his magic voice.

Roscommon came like a bolt from the blue in the early forties, led by Jimmy Murray of Knockcroghery, with as fine a football team as ever graced an ever-developing Croke Park. There was now the huge

Cusack Stand to house the growing crowds under the vigilant eye of that wonderful administrator from Cork, Pádraig Ó Caoimh. These were the war years, the years of petrol rationing, and I remember well the hordes of cyclists passing through my native town of Dunmore en route to the Connacht final in Tuam in 1944, when home-made signs advertising 'Meat teas' were displayed on practically every house at the venue. Kerry always seemed to be the team to beat, but Meath under Brian Smyth and Mayo under Seán Flanagan came bursting through, while Cavan and the 'gallant John Joe' upheld the flag of Ulster, even on foreign fields, when the all-Ireland final was played outside Ireland for the first and only time in 1947 and all Ireland listened in to Mícheál O'Hehir's broadcast at the untimely hour of 9 p.m.

These were the days of collective training, and the accounts in the *Irish Press, Irish Independent* and, to a lesser extent, *Irish Times* were pasted into scrapbooks. Physical training consisted of sprints, long walks, and plenty of football, often two full training games a day. The days of the by-line in GAA reports were still to come; pen-names it was mostly then: Green Flag, Moltóir, Linesman, Andy Croke, Onlooker—does anyone remember? At all-Ireland finals an archbishop or bishop threw in the ball, the captains genuflecting to kiss the proffered ring, and all Croke Park stood and sang 'Faith of Our Fathers', just as lustily as they were to sing 'Amhrán na bhFiann' subsequently. Fans queued all through the night for seats on the sideline at Croke Park, and there was no wire round the field to prevent an invasion of the pitch—nor was there any need for it. You were close to the players; you could almost feel the shoulder charges.

About this time an over-indulgence in hand-passing led to its being banned. We never seemed to know where we stood with hand-passing. Kerry continued to come and conquer, defeating new teams like Carlow, Antrim, and Armagh. Standards were improving throughout the land, largely through the great work of primary school teachers, and priests, brothers and laymen too in the colleges, with the vocational schools beginning to make an impact. Gaelic football was never as popular as in the fifties and sixties, when teams from Dublin, Down, Offaly, Derry, Tyrone, Meath, Galway and, as always, Kerry hit the headlines. Cork too was becoming a football force; but it was the emergence of Down in their red-and-black strip and their promotion of the concept of total football that took the country by storm—that and the emergence of the Dublin team of native Dubliners in the fifties, who really got the capital city crazy on Gaelic football for the first time. Little wonder that over 90,000 crammed Croke Park to see Down win the Sam Maguire Cup for the second successive year, defeating Offaly in a thrill-packed final in 1961.

Television came in the early sixties. The GAA gave the live television rights of the all-Ireland finals and semi-finals to the fledgling RTE—then black-and-white only—for a nominal sum. It was feared that the live televising of games would denude the terraces, and for years, apart from all-Ireland finals, it did just that.

In the meantime the game was changing somewhat, evolving from a catch-and-kick game to a running game, with much more combination in attack and the hand-pass back in all its glory.

The seventies started with Offaly taking over at last. Tony McTague demonstrated the growing need for successful teams to have a top-class place-kicker to avail of the many opportunities being presented by a game that had now become riddled with pull-and-drag tactics, which often resulted in sixty frees being awarded in a game. The days of a free-flowing open game were gone for ever; Gaelic football was fast becoming a mishmash of soccer, rugby, basketball, and volleyball, with a resultant diminution in the basic skills of catching and kicking. Tactics were coming more into the game, and negative counter-moves, such as punching the ball away at midfield and marking closely, often to the point of clipping an opponent's heels or eyeballing him even before the throw-in, had come into being. Manager mania was about to take over at county and at club level.

The seventies were also the era of Heffo's Heroes of Dublin, who made Gaelic football fashionable; and then came Mick O'Dwyer's Dynamos to conquer Dublin and stride through a decade as no team had ever done before. Magical names: Spillane, Sheehy, Liston, and the greatest exponent of the running game, Jack O'Shea. Kerry could always produce super midfielders: Paddy Kennedy, Seán Brosnan, Mick O'Connell, and Jacko the great. After that Meath and Cork dominated, then the Ulster revival, and in more recent years Meath again and the return of Kerry and Galway.

All the time Croke Park grows apace. Sponsorship is well rooted now, and the public cannot get enough live television coverage, which tends to swell rather than diminish the crowds. We now have annual internationals with Australia, using compromise rules; and for years women's Gaelic football has been growing in popularity. Mícheál Ó Muircheartaigh rules the radio waves in much the same way that Mícheál O'Hehir did in the fifties and sixties. Past players write their own columns for the papers, and local radio has helped the continued popularity of Gaelic football. Teams train harder than ever before, and the game, though riddled still with frees, is much faster than it was in the old days, when players had so much more time on the ball. Managers still remain centre stage, but they are now joined by coaches, trainers, psychologists, dieticians and physiotherapists as necessary contributions to the wider managerial scene. Manners are gone out of the game, and you tend to be surprised if a player ever hands the ball back to an opponent or doesn't in some way take an advantage.

The growth in Gaelic football and its attendant popularity was not due to the all-Ireland senior football championship alone. Along the way its success was in no small measure helped by the well-ordered and democratic structure of the GAA, from club to county board, provincial council, and Central Council. This broad structure created the need for development in many ways, including the creation of more competitions to embrace different age groups, including the universities, colleges, and vocational schools, as well as the introduction of different grades in the all-Ireland series.

The Sigerson Cup for universities came into being in 1911. This was and is a wonderful competition, which at the start catered only for UCD, UCC, and UCG. It was broadened to include Queen's University, Belfast, in 1923, Trinity College in 1963, and St Patrick's College, Maynooth, in 1972, then mushroomed to include all the regional technical colleges, the new universities, the teacher training colleges, Thomond College, Limerick, and the Garda Training College, Templemore. Nowadays a whole series of play-offs is necessary to determine the final eight for Sigerson Cup weekend, which is still a tough knock-out competition in which the fittest survive and committed championship football is seen at its best.

The development of a competitive structure began in the secondary schools (diocesan colleges mainly from 1918 onwards), and this had a huge effect in popularising the game. It began in Ulster from 1919 and in Leinster from 1920. In Leinster, St Mel's College, Longford, developed a fine tradition; then came Munster in 1928, where the Kerry and Cork colleges tended to dominate, and finally Connacht in 1929, with St Jarlath's College, Tuam, carving out a special niche for itself, having won more all-Ireland and provincial senior titles than any other college. Colleges football has always been the *crème de la crème* of Gaelic football, the purest of the code. Nowadays the power of the diocesan boarding-schools has dimmed, and new schools, such as St Patrick's College, Navan (2000), Good Counsel, New Ross (1999), Intermediate School, Killorglin (1996) and St Fachtna's, Skibbereen (1991), have all won all-Ireland senior football titles.

The first grade to be introduced after senior was the junior in 1912, and this served to give more adults the opportunity to wear a county jersey and in many instances provided a stepping-stone to senior inter-county status. It is a grade that has tended to diminish in status over the years, with lapses from 1917 to 1922, from 1942 to 1945, and again from 1974 to 1982. Some counties are allowed to select their second-best team, while others can select only from junior and intermediate grades within the county. Many counties do not participate nowadays, and it is a grade that, while still important in a club set-up, has tended to lose its appeal at inter-county level.

The introduction of the minor grade to cater for under-18s in 1929 was an imaginative and masterly stroke; and the practice of playing minor championship inter-county games before their senior counterparts immediately gave the grade a huge status. The minor grade became the breeding-ground for senior inter-county fulfilment, and practically all the top footballers of the last seventy years served their apprenticeship as minors, getting a feel for the big time.

Just browsing through the names of winning minor all-Ireland teams one sees names like Billy Myers, Bill Dillon, Seán Brosnan, Paddy Kennedy, Paddy Quinn, T. P. O'Reilly, Bill Doonan, Simon Deignan, Bill Carlos, Liam Gilmartin, Larry Cummins, Brendan Lynch, Nicky Maher, Ollie Freaney, Dan O'Mahony, Tom Moriarty, Paudie Sheehy, Colm Kennelly, Gerry Kirwan, Paddy Farnan, Lar Foley, Johnny Joyce, Des Foley, Bertie Cunningham, Paddy Holden, Mick Kissane, Brian McDonald, Noel Tierney, Enda Colleran, Christy Tyrrell, Séamus Leydon, Frank Cogan, Paud O'Donoghue, Martin Furlong, Eugene Mulligan, Willie Bryan ... all young minors who later won all-Ireland senior medals; and the trend has continued right up to the present day. Kerry top the list of all-Ireland minor football titles won, with eleven titles up to 1999, just ahead of Dublin (ten) and Cork (nine). In the history of the competition only one youngster had the honour of captaining two successive all-Ireland minor winning teams: Eddie Devlin of Tyrone, in 1947 and 1948. He later became a football legend, playing for Tyrone, Ulster, and Combined Universities.

In 1986 it was my pleasure to attend the English Football Association cup final in Wembley Stadium, London. I went to see Liverpool and Everton play, on a sunny day in May. No animosity existed between the rival fans, coming as they did from the same city, so different from the scene at other soccer games, where rival fans are caged and segregated in case of an eruption of naked aggression. I was keen to compare the top sporting event in England with our own, the all-Ireland senior final; so I arrived early and saw all the preliminaries before the big game. There were demonstrations of soccer skill from young performers who had qualified at regional venues; communal singing of well-known anthems such as 'Abide With Me' and 'You'll Never Walk Alone'; some games involving model aeroplanes in the rival colours operated by remote control to excite the fans; the appearance of the rival teams in their blazers or suits to greet the crowd. It was all very impressive, but nothing to compare with the all-Ireland final scene, when the minor final takes centre stage. I certainly enjoyed the Wembley experience greatly, but it helped me to appreciate our own all-Ireland showpiece all the more.

Nothing compares to an all-Ireland senior football final. When the teams march around the field (though nowadays their marching doesn't compare with that of teams of yore) behind the Artane Boys' Band and everybody stands for the national anthem, I always get a shiver of emotion in my spine, and I know why I'm so proud to be an Irishman on this day of days. After the game itself you have the sea of emotion erupting. The winning team and captain are mobbed. Last year, in the interests of safety, the whole presentation ceremony was altered, with fans kept off the pitch and the presentation being held on a podium in the centre of Croke Park instead of in the Hogan Stand, now being demolished and reconstructed. But don't be surprised if the old system returns at the completion of the entire Croke Park reconstruction.

Inter-provincial competition in Gaelic football took place spasmodically in the early years of the last century, the first inter-provincial competition involving all four football provinces taking place in 1905 for the Railway Shield. The competition was played three years in succession, 1905–7, then lapsed before being revived for the Tailteann Games of 1924. The competitions as we know them today were conceived at the GAA Congress of 1926, the brainchild of Pádraig Ó Caoimh, later to become general secretary of the GAA. He also suggested that the hurling and football finals be played annually on St Patrick's Day, so that the national holiday might be suitably honoured. So began the annual Railway Cup final, so called because the Great Southern and Western Railway stepped in and re-established the tradition it had begun with the Railway Shields in 1905 by presenting cups for both hurling and football, the first finals of which were played on 17 March 1927.

The Railway Cup competition became popular from the beginning, reaching its zenith in the forties and fifties with crowds of 40,000 and more, and Croke Park was the place to go on St Patrick's Day. Leinster tended to dominate at the start. Connacht won four Railway Cup titles in the thirties, Ulster their first in 1942. Ulster now top the list, with twenty-five titles. The competition has lost its appeal with the public, however, and the 17 March slot has for years been allotted to the all-Ireland inter-club senior finals, which now attract attendances comparable to the best Railway Cup ones. In the meantime the Railway Cup inter-provincial championship (football) has been kicked from pillar to post, sometimes in an autumn slot, now in January and February—not the best time for staging anything. While the GAA fixture list becomes more cluttered, it is past time that the authorities dispensed with both the Railway Cup and the all-Ireland junior competition, both of which have outlived their usefulness. As a former player in both competitions in their heyday I take no joy in the suggestion, for the Railway Cup especially gave a stage to the stars from the weaker counties and a place in the football sun to men like Mickey Kearins (Sligo), Packy McGarty (Leitrim), Mick Carley (Westmeath), Gerry O'Reilly and Andy Phillips (Wicklow), P. T. Treacy and Peter McGinnitty (Fermanagh).

The national football league, which came into being in 1925, has served Gaelic football well over the years, becoming the second premier competition and giving a regular series of games to all counties from October to May. It is a competition that has changed much in form over the years yet retains a basic thread of consistency, the final stages always decided by a knock-out system. As with the all-Ireland senior football championship, Kerry top the list, with sixteen titles, Mayo coming next with ten. Mayo became known as the league specialists in the thirties, winning six national football leagues in a row, 1933–8, and again in 1940 after a lapse of a year. Attendances at national football league games grew as the closing knock-out stages approached, and league finals had attendances of 50–60,000 and on one occasion 70,000 fans. In latter times interest in the league has dwindled, while the popularity of the senior football championship has grown. The media have tended to rubbish the national football league, mainly because many players who have played in the later rounds of the senior football championship have tended to take a rest for a time from inter-county activity. Also a factor is the importance of the inter-club all-Irelands, where the clubs involved want total allegiance from county players in their teams and put a veto on county representation. All this tends to lessen the status of the national football league. It would be a great pity if the stature of the competition was lessened any further. The inter-club all-Irelands have come to stay; there must be a place for both to survive and grow together.

The under-21 grade came into being in 1964, and while it has never established a true niche for itself at inter-club or inter-county level, it is taken very seriously. Many counties experience grave difficulties in running under-21 championships, while at inter-county level, weekday evenings are employed for fulfilling fixtures. That may be a trend for the future, but there is a high probability that the minor and under-21 grades will coalesce into one under-19 grade in the not-too-distant future. In the meantime Kerry and Cork head the list of all-Ireland under-21 titles, with nine apiece. One nice feature of the competition, as with the minor grade, is that counties that have still to win a senior all-Ireland have broken the barrier at under-21 level, such as Antrim, Tyrone, and Westmeath (in 1999). This has to be healthy. The under-21 grade may still survive, despite all the difficulties it faces.

The reconstruction of the facilities in Croke Park continues apace. Immediately the 1999 all-Ireland senior football final was over, the reconstruction of the Hogan Stand side of the stadium began. We had come to be proud of the new stand structure that had replaced the old Cusack Stand, then witnessed the construction of the canal end to tone in and continue the modern type New Stand style, which will also spread to the Hogan Stand side of the ground. It was with much nostalgia that many of us viewed the demolition of the Hogan Stand. This was where we saw many great games, met many friends, witnessed many feats of splendour—happy and sad occasions, but many moments to cherish for ever. Eugene McGee wrote in the *Irish Independent* on Monday 4 October 1999:

> The Hogan Stand which opened in 1959 and which is now destined for the breaker's yard, holds many happy and sad memories for a great number of Irish people.

GAA fans remember where they were in 'the Hogan' when great acts of drama involving their team were enacted out on the pitch. All-Irelands won and lost and forever etched in the memory. Inevitably, there will be some sadness at the Hogan's departure. However, the main emotion will be one of pride as people look forward to the building of the new stand, presumably to be called the Hogan. It will rise from the debris of the old, a beacon symbolising the GAA's continuing vitality and its ability to harness the increased commercialism of today's world rather than be intimidated by it.

In February 1999, while attending a wonderful tribute to Kerry's legendary Mick O'Connell in the Great Southern Hotel, Killarney, one of the first people I encountered was Cathal O'Leary, the former

Dublin midfielder of the fifties. He told me:

> Your Galway team of 1998 played the best Gaelic football I have
> seen in twenty years. But for consistency the only pure Gaelic
> football now being played is the preserve of the ladies. They play
> attractive open football, move the ball around, and pulling and
> dragging is foreign to them. Reminds me of Gaelic football as it
> used to be.

Women's Gaelic football came into being in 1974. The women's
association was slow to develop but has built up steadily to a
membership of approximately 25,000. The rules are similar to those
of the men's game, with some modifications designed to speed up the
game and eliminate unnecessary bodily contact. The association
operates inter-county and other competitions similar to those of its
male counterpart, and it got a boost in 1986 when the all-Ireland
inter-county finals in junior and senior were played in Croke Park for
the first time. Now these occasions attract large attendances of about
20,000, and the game is spreading like wildfire inside Ireland and
among our exiles.

For some time the idea of women's Gaelic football was not taken
seriously. Old die-hards were heard to say, 'What's the world coming
to?' or 'Imagine them rising for the high ones, racing through to score,
or pulling on a ball on the ground.' I was one of those doubting
Thomases and could never imagine myself going to see such a game.
Not any more. Anyone who saw the television broadcast of the 1996
senior women's final between Monaghan and Laois (draw and replay)
had to become a fan. This was outstanding committed football, clean
and open and uncluttered, with wonderful scores, intelligent running
off the ball, no gamesmanship. Cathal O'Leary is right; let's hope the
women's game doesn't degenerate like the men's game over the years.
It's a growing sport and will become even bigger in the future.

Whither Gaelic football now? As we approach the twenty-first
century, Gaelic football is the most popular sport in Ireland, rooted in
every county, very strong still in the traditional strongholds, with a
closing in of standards throughout the country. The game itself, as we
have seen, is not without its difficulties. It is much faster now than
before, and the top county teams train as hard as any professionals
almost all year round, while the majority of club players, though in
less demand, are being given a regular quota of games over a slightly
shorter season. There is much competition from other sports for the
youngsters of today, but the GAA through its club structure and a very
imaginative Cumann na nBunscoil structure helps to guarantee its

slice of the young national cake, with the juvenile sections of each county board continuing the good work.

We need more and more live televising of games over the playing season, with more imaginative preview and review, to combat the over-indulgence in English soccer in particular being thrown at us almost every night. With four national channels we should be able to contribute more to our national games and approximate to the excellent coverage given to Gaelic games throughout the land on local radio. For our own part we should endeavour to improve the standard of our playing-fields, update our club premises, and continue to make our clubs and their premises the focal point of the communities they serve, be they rural or urban.

The game itself needs attention. The hand-pass is not clearly defined: any old thing goes with some referees. It would be so much easier if we reverted to the fisted pass only. The toe pick-up, once an art in itself, is ignored; the game nowadays is too fast to allow time for the legitimate pick-up, so in time we'll probably follow the women and allow the pick-up. The tackle is still loosely defined. In the past the shoulder charge sufficed; sadly today it has been replaced by much short-arm stuff, with the elbow to the face of an advancing forward one of the most dangerous ploys and not consistently frowned upon. The behind-the-ball incidents will hopefully be fully eradicated by the more consistent television coverage and video play-back.

The recent 'one in, all in' policy and the 'whole squad behind the ball' tactical ploys tend to demean the game. It is too much to ask for the return of some of the manners to the game? Surely team managers throughout the country can eradicate much of this, can select their teams on time, and stop duping the opposition and the public by selecting dud teams and then fielding them in completely different positions from those selected.

Yet for all its ills, Gaelic football is still Ireland's most popular sport. It is full of passion, commitment and determination and reflects much of ourselves. At present the greatest difficulty facing the game is a creeping professionalism, fuelled by the media, which is tending to vulgarise all sports. Hopefully it will come later rather than sooner and be controlled. I still want to read more about a player's worth as a footballer than the fee he receives for such a game or the price of the necklace he gives his girl-friend. The proposals of the Football Development Committee are a cause for concern: if carried they would have destroyed the all-Ireland as we know it, a competition that has served the game well. But they generated worthwhile discussion, irrespective of the outcome.

The GAA would do well to get the recently formed Gaelic Players' Association on its side and not treat them as hostile. Some of their spokesmen do not do their cause justice, but their administrator, Dónal O'Neill of County Down, is of proven and genuine GAA stock and won't sell the GAA's ideals or his own association cheaply. The majority of players don't want a pay-for-play policy to emerge: they just want better travelling expenses, better insurance cover, and adequate compensation for out-of-pocket expenses—all reasonable aspirations.

The refereeing of Gaelic football is a serious problem. Everybody realises that a referee's job grows more difficult and that as the game gets faster, physical contact tends to increase. The biggest bugbear seems to be the lack of a uniform standard of interpretation; but on this score the whole structure of assessment, grading and continuous updating of refereeing instruction has improved no end. One feels that county units could do more in the recruitment of younger referees. Paddy Collins of Westmeath has always been a great role model, but we need more of his type—a man of great common sense who allowed the game to flow and generally introduced a contagiously calm atmosphere into the greatest rivalries.

Any game that can throw up footballers of the quality of such present-day stars as Trevor Giles, Maurice Fitzgerald, Peter Canavan, Diarmuid Marsden, Paul Curran, Ciarán McManus, Jarlath Fallon, Paul Taylor and Anthony Tohill, just to name a few, has a lot going for it—in great need of repair in so many areas, yet always capable of producing the great game, the marvellous score, the high catch, the exciting solo run, and the unique all-Ireland final occasion to stir the soul and remind us of epics from the past. We must never let this game die.

Appendix 1

ALL-IRELAND SENIOR FOOTBALL CHAMPIONSHIP

1. Winning teams

Kerry (31)	1903,1904,1909, 1913, 1914, 1924,1926, 1929, 1930, 1931, 1932, 1937, 1939, 1940, 1941, 1946, 1953, 1955, 1959, 1962, 1969, 1970, 1975, 1978, 1979, 1980, 1981, 1984, 1985, 1986, 1997
Dublin (22)	1891, 1892, 1894, 1897, 1898, 1899, 1901, 1902, 1906, 1907, 1908, 1921, 1922, 1923, 1942, 1958, 1963, 1974, 1976. 1977, 1983, 1995
Galway (8)	1925, 1934, 1938, 1956, 1964, 1965, 1966, 1998
Meath (7)	1949, 1954, 1967, 1987, 1988, 1996, 1999
Cork (6)	1890, 1911, 1945, 1973, 1989, 1990
Wexford (5)	1893, 1915, 1916, 1917, 1918
Cavan (5)	1933, 1935, 1947, 1948, 1952
Down (5)	1960, 1961, 1968, 1991, 1994
Tipperary (4)	1889, 1895, 1900, 1920
Kildare (4)	1905, 1919, 1927, 1928
Louth (3)	1910, 1912, 1957
Mayo (3)	1936, 1950, 1951
Offaly (3)	1971, 1972, 1982
Limerick (2)	1887, 1896
Roscommon (2)	1943, 1944
Donegal (1)	1992
Derry (1)	1993

Note: There was no championship in 1888, the year of the 'American invasion'.

2. Results

1887	Clonskeagh	29 April 1888	Limerick (Commercials) 1-4, Louth (Dundalk Young Irelands) 0-3
1888	Championship unfinished		
1889	Inchicore	20 October	Tipperary (Bohercrowe) 3-6, Laois (Maryborough) 0-0
1890	Clonturk Park	26 June 1892	Cork (Midleton) 2-4, Wexford (Blues and Whites) 0-1
1891	Clonturk Park	28 February 1892	Dublin (Young Irelands) 2-1, Cork (Clondrohid) 1-9
1892	Clonturk Park	26 March 1893	Dublin (Young Irelands) 1-4, Kerry (Laune Rangers) 0-3
1893	Phoenix Park	24 June 1894	Wexford (Young Irelands) 1-1, Cork (Dromtariffe) 0-1
1894	Clonturk Park	24 March 1895	Dublin (Young Irelands) 0-6, Cork (Nils) 1-1 (draw)
	Thurles	21 April 1895	Cork 1-2, Dublin 0-5 (replay) Unfinished; Dublin awarded the title
1895	Jones's Road	15 March 1896	Tipperary (Arravale Rovers) 0-4, Meath (Pierce O'Mahonys) 0-3
1896	Jones's Road	6 February 1898	Limerick (Commercials) 1-5, Dublin (Young Irelands) 0-7
1897	Jones's Road	5 February 1899	Dublin (Kickhams) 2-6, Cork (Dunmanway) 0-2
1898	Tipperary	8 April 1900	Dublin (Geraldines) 2-8, Waterford (Erin's Hope) 0-4
1899	Jones's Road	10 February 1901	Dublin (Geraldines) 1-10, Cork (Nils) 0-6
1900	Jones's Road	26 October 1902	Tipperary (Clonmel Shamrocks) 3-7, London (Hibernians) 0-2
1901	Jones's Road	2 August 1903	Dublin 0-14, London (Hibernians) 0-2
1902	Cork	11 September 1904	Dublin (Bray Emmets) 2-8, London (Hibernians) 0-4
1903	Jones's Road	12 November 1905	Kerry (Tralee Mitchels) 0-11, London (Hibernians) 0-3
1904	Cork	1 July 1906	Kerry (Tralee Mitchels) 0-5, Dublin (Kickhams) 0-2

1905	Thurles	16 June 1907	Kildare (Roseberry) 1-7, Kerry 0-5
1906	Athy	20 October 1907	Dublin (Kickhams) 0-5, Cork (Fermoy) 0-4
1907	Tipperary	5 July 1908	Dublin (Kickhams) 0-6, Cork (Lees) 0-2
1908	Jones's Road	1 August 1909	Dublin (Geraldines) 1-10, London (Hibernians) 0-4
1909	Jones's Road	5 December	Kerry (Tralee Mitchels) 1-9, Louth (Tredaghs) 0-6
1910	Jones's Road		Louth (Tredaghs) walkover from Kerry (Tralee Mitchels)
1911	Jones's Road	14 January 1912	Cork (Lees) 6-6, Antrim (Shauns) 1-2
1912	Jones's Road	3 November	Louth (Tredaghs) 1-7, Antrim (Mitchels) 1-2
1913	Croke Park	14 December 1913	Kerry (Killarney) 2-2, Wexford (Raparees) 0-3
1914	Croke Park	1 November 1914	Kerry 1-3, Wexford 2-0 (draw)
	Croke Park	29 November 1914	Kerry (Killarney) 2-3, Wexford (Blues and Whites) 0-6 (replay)
1915	Croke Park	7 November 1915	Wexford (Blues and Whites) 2-4, Kerry (selection) 2-1
1916	Croke Park	17 December 1916	Wexford (Blues and Whites) 3-4, Mayo (Stephenites, Ballina) 1-2
1917	Croke Park	9 December 1917	Wexford (Blues and Whites) 0-9, Clare (selection) 0-5
1918	Croke Park	16 February 1919	Wexford (Blues and Whites) 0-5, Tipperary (Fethard) 0-4
1919	Croke Park	28 September 1919	Kildare (Caragh) 2-5, Galway (selection) 0-1
1920	Croke Park	11 June 1922	Tipperary 1-6, Dublin (O'Tooles) 1-2
1921	Croke Park	17 June 1923	Dublin (St Mary's) 1-9, Mayo (Stephenites, Ballina) 0-2
1922	Croke Park	7 October 1923	Dublin (O'Tooles) 0-6, Galway (Ballinasloe) 0-4
1923	Croke Park	28 September 1924	Dublin 1-5, Kerry 1-3
1924	Croke Park	26 April 1925	Kerry 0-4, Dublin 0-3
1925	Galway declared champions		

1926	Croke Park	5 September	Kerry 1-3, Kildare 0-6 (draw)
	Croke Park	17 October	Kerry 1-4, Kildare 0-4 (replay)
1927	Croke Park	25 September	Kildare 0-5, Kerry 0-3
1928	Croke Park	30 September	Kildare 2-6, Cavan 2-5
1929	Croke Park	22 September	Kerry 1-8, Kildare 1-5
1930	Croke Park	28 September	Kerry 3-11, Monaghan 0-2
1931	Croke Park	27 September	Kerry 1-11, Kildare 0-8
1932	Croke Park	25 September	Kerry 2-7, Mayo 2-4
1933	Croke Park	24 September	Cavan 2-5, Galway 1-4
1934	Croke Park	23 September	Galway 3-5, Dublin 1-9
1935	Croke Park	22 September	Cavan 3-6, Kildare 2-5
1936	Croke Park	27 September	Mayo 4-11, Laois 0-5
1937	Croke Park	26 September	Kerry 2-5, Cavan 1-8 (draw)
	Croke Park	17 October	Kerry 4-4, Cavan 1-7 (replay)
1938	Croke Park	25 September	Galway 3-3, Kerry 2-6 (draw)
	Croke Park	23 October	Galway 2-4, Kerry 0-7 (replay)
1939	Croke Park	24 September	2-5, Meath 2-3
1940	Croke Park	22 September	Kerry 0-7, Galway 1-3
1941	Croke Park	7 September	Kerry 1-8, Galway 0-7
1942	Croke Park	20 September	Dublin 1-10, Galway 1-8
1943	Croke Park	26 September	Roscommon 1-6, Cavan 1-6 (draw)
	Croke Park	10 October	Roscommon 2-7, Cavan 2-2 (replay)
1944	Croke Park	24 September	Roscommon 1-9, Kerry 2-4
1945	Croke Park	23 September	Cork 2-5, Cavan 0-7
1946	Croke Park	6 October	Kerry 2-4, Roscommon 1-7 (draw)
	Croke Park	27 October	Kerry 2-8, Roscommon 0-10 (replay)
1947	Polo Grounds, New York	14 September	Cavan 2-11, Kerry 2-7
1948	Croke Park	26 September	Cavan 4-5, Mayo 4-4
1949	Croke Park	25 September	Meath 1-10, Cavan 1-6
1950	Croke Park	24 September	Mayo 2-5, Louth 1-6
1951	Croke Park	23 September	Mayo 2-8, Meath 0-9
1952	Croke Park	28 September	Cavan 2-4, Meath 1-7 (draw)
	Croke Park	12 October	Cavan 0-9, Meath 0-5 (replay)

1953	Croke Park	27 September	Kerry 0-13, Armagh 1-6
1954	Croke Park	26 September	Meath 1-13, Kerry 1-7
1955	Croke Park	25 September	Kerry 0-12, Dublin 1-6
1956	Croke Park	7 October	Galway 2-13, Cork 3-7
1957	Croke Park	22 September	Louth 1-9, Cork 1-7
1958	Croke Park	28 September	Dublin 2-12, Derry 1-9
1959	Croke Park	27 September	Kerry 3-7, Galway 1-4
1960	Croke Park	25 September	Down 2-10, Kerry 0-8
1961	Croke Park	24 September	Down 3-6, Offaly 2-8
1962	Croke Park	23 September	Kerry 1-12, Roscommon 1-6
1963	Croke Park	22 September	Dublin 1-9, Galway 0-10
1964	Croke Park	27 September	Galway 0-15, Kerry 0-10
1965	Croke Park	26 September	Galway 0-12, Kerry 0-9
1966	Croke Park	25 September	Galway 1-10, Meath 0-7
1967	Croke Park	24 September	Meath 1-9, Cork 0-9
1968	Croke Park	22 September	Down 2-12, Kerry 1-13
1969	Croke Park	28 September	Kerry 0-10, Offaly 0-7
1970	Croke Park	27 September	Kerry 2-19, Meath 0-18
1971	Croke Park	26 September	Offaly 1-14, Galway 2-8
1972	Croke Park	24 September	Offaly 1-13, Kerry 1-13 (draw)
	Croke Park	15 October	Offaly 1-19, Kerry 0-13 (replay)
1973	Croke Park	23 September	Cork 3-17, Galway 2-13
1974	Croke Park	22 September	Dublin 0-14, Galway 1-6
1975	Croke Park	28 September	Kerry 2-12, Dublin 0-11
1976	Croke Park	26 September	Dublin 3-8, Kerry 0-10
1977	Croke Park	25 September	Dublin 5-12, Armagh 3-6
1978	Croke Park	24 September	Kerry 5-11, Dublin 0-9
1979	Croke Park	16 September	Kerry 3-13, Dublin 1-8
1980	Croke Park	21 September	Kerry 1-9, Roscommon 1-6
1981	Croke Park	20 September	Kerry 1-12, Offaly 0-8
1982	Croke Park	19 September	Offaly 1-15, Kerry 0-17
1983	Croke Park	18 September	Dublin 1-10, Galway 1-8
1984	Croke Park	23 September	Kerry 0-14, Dublin 1-6
1985	Croke Park	22 September	Kerry 2-12, Dublin 2-8
1986	Croke Park	21 September	Kerry 2-15, Tyrone 1-10
1987	Croke Park	20 September	Meath 1-14, Cork 0-11
1988	Croke Park	18 September	Meath 0-12, Cork 1-9 (draw)
	Croke Park	9 October	Meath 0-13, Cork 0-12 (replay)

1989	Croke Park	17 September	Cork 0-17, Mayo 1-11
1990	Croke Park	16 September	Cork 0-11, Meath 0-9
1991	Croke Park	15 September	Down 1-16, Meath 1-14
1992	Croke Park	20 September	Donegal 0-18, Dublin 0-14
1993	Croke Park	19 September	Derry 1-14, Cork 2-8
1994	Croke Park	18 September	Down 1-12, Dublin 0-13
1995	Croke Park	17 September	Dublin 1-10, Tyrone 0-12
1996	Croke Park	15 September	Meath 0-12, Mayo 1-9 (draw)
	Croke Park	29 September	Meath 2-9, Mayo 1-11 (replay)
1997	Croke Park	28 September	Kerry 0-13, Mayo 1-7
1998	Croke Park	27 September	Galway 1-14, Kildare 1-10
1999	Croke Park	26 September	Meath 1-11, Cork 1-8

Appendix 2

All-Ireland Minor Football Championship, 1929–99

1. Winning teams

Kerry (11)	1931, 1932, 1933, 1946, 1950, 1962, 1963, 1975, 1980, 1988, 1994
Dublin (10)	1930, 1945, 1954, 1955, 1956, 1958, 1959, 1979, 1982, 1984
Cork (9)	1961, 1967, 1968, 1969, 1972, 1974, 1981, 1991, 1993
Mayo (6)	1935, 1953, 1966, 1971, 1978, 1985
Galway (5)	1952, 1960, 1970, 1976, 1986
Tyrone (4)	1947, 1948, 1973, 1998
Derry (3)	1965, 1983, 1989
Roscommon (3)	1939, 1941, 1951
Meath (3)	1957, 1990, 1992
Down (3)	1977, 1987, 1999
Cavan (2)	1937, 1938
Laois (2)	1996, 1997
Louth (2)	1936, 1940
Armagh (1)	1949
Clare (1)	1929
Offaly (1)	1964
Tipperary (1)	1934
Westmeath (1)	1995

Note: The competition was suspended between 1942 and 1944 (inclusive).

2. Results

1929	Clare 5-3, Longford 3-5
1930	Dublin 1-3, Mayo 0-5
1931	Kerry 3-4, Louth 0-4
1932	Kerry 3-8, Laois 1-3
1933	Kerry 4-1, Mayo 0-9
1934	Tipperary awarded title

1935	Mayo 1-6, Tipperary 1-1
1936	Louth 5-1, Kerry 1-8
1937	Cavan 1-11, Wexford 1-5
1938	Cavan 3-3, Kerry 0-8
1939	Roscommon 1-9, Monaghan 1-7
1940	Louth 5-5, Mayo 2-7
1941	Roscommon 3-6, Louth 0-7
1942	No competition
1943	No competition
1944	No competition
1945	Dublin 4-7, Leitrim 0-4
1946	Kerry 3-7, Dublin 2-3
1947	Tyrone 4-4, Mayo 4-3
1948	Tyrone 0-11, Dublin 1-5
1949	Armagh 1-7, Kerry 1-5
1950	Kerry 3-6, Wexford 1-4
1951	Roscommon 2-7, Armagh 1-5
1952	Galway 2-9, Cavan 1-6
1953	Mayo 2-11, Clare 1-6
1954	Dublin 3-3, Kerry 1-8
1955	Dublin 5-4, Tipperary 2-7
1956	Dublin 5-14, Leitrim 2-2
1957	Meath 3-9, Armagh 0-4
1958	Dublin 2-10, Mayo 0-8
1959	Dublin 0-11, Cavan 1-4
1960	Galway 4-9, Cork 1-5
1961	Cork 3-7, Mayo 0-5
1962	Kerry 6-5, Mayo 0-7
1963	Kerry 1-10, Westmeath 0-2
1964	Offaly 0-15, Cork 1-11
1965	Derry 2-8, Kerry 2-4
1966	Mayo 1-12, Down 1-8
1967	Cork 5-14, Laois 2-3
1968	Cork 3-5, Sligo 1-10
1969	Cork 2-7, Derry 0-11
1970	Galway 1-8, Kerry 2-5 (draw)
	Galway 1-11, Kerry 1-10 (replay)
1971	Mayo 2-15, Cork 2-7
1972	Cork 3-11, Tyrone 2-11
1973	Tyrone 2-11, Kildare 1-6
1974	Cork 1-10, Mayo 1-6
1975	Kerry 1-10, Tyrone 0-4

1976	Galway 1-10, Cork 0-6
1977	Down 2-6, Meath 0-4
1978	Mayo 4-9, Dublin 3-8
1979	Dublin 0-10, Kerry 1-6
1980	Kerry 3-12, Derry 0-11
1981	Cork 4-9, Derry 2-7
1982	Dublin 1-11, Kerry 1-5
1983	Derry 0-8, Cork 1-3
1984	Dublin 1-9, Tipperary 0-4
1985	Mayo 3-3, Cork 0-9
1986	Galway 3-8, Cork 2-7
1987	Down 1-12, Cork 1-5
1988	Kerry 2-5, Dublin 0-5
1989	Derry 3-9, Offaly 1-6
1990	Meath 2-11, Kerry 2-9
1991	Cork 1-9, Mayo 1-7
1992	Meath 2-5, Armagh 0-10
1993	Cork 2-7, Meath 0-9
1994	Kerry 0-16, Galway 1-7
1995	Westmeath 1-10, Derry 0-11
1996	Laois 2-11, Kerry 1-11
1997	Laois 3-11, Tyrone 1-14
1998	Tyrone 2-11, Laois 0-11
1999	Down 1-14, Mayo 0-14

Appendix 3

RAILWAY CUP FOOTBALL INTER-PROVINCIAL CHAMPIONSHIP, 1927–2000

1. Winning teams

Ulster (25)	1942, 1943, 1947, 1950, 1956, 1960, 1963, 1964, 1965, 1966, 1968, 1970, 1971, 1979, 1980, 1983, 1984, 1989, 1991, 1992, 1993, 1994, 1995, 1998, 2000
Leinster (24)	1928, 1929, 1930, 1932, 1933, 1935, 1939, 1940, 1944, 1945, 1952, 1953,1954, 1955, 1959, 1961, 1962, 1974, 1985, 1986, 1987, 1988, 1996, 1997
Munster (14)	1927, 1931, 1941, 1946, 1948, 1949, 1972, 1975, 1976, 1977, 1978, 1981, 1982, 1999
Connacht (9)	1934, 1936, 1937, 1938, 1951, 1957, 1958, 1967, 1969
Universities (1)	1973

2. Results

1927	Croke Park	17 March	Munster 2-3, Connacht 0-5
1928	Croke Park	17 March	Leinster 1-8, Ulster 2-4
1929	Croke Park	17 March	Leinster 1-7, Munster 1-3
1930	Croke Park	17 March	Leinster 2-3, Munster 0-6
1931	Croke Park	17 March	Munster 2-2, Leinster 0-6
1932	Croke Park	17 March	Leinster 2-10, Munster 3-5
1933	Croke Park	17 March	Leinster 0-12, Connacht 2-5
1934	Croke Park	17 March	Connacht 2-9, Leinster 2-8
1935	Croke Park	17 March	Leinster 2-9, Munster 0-7
1936	Croke Park	17 March	Connacht 3-11, Ulster 2-3
1937	Croke Park	17 March	Connacht 2-4, Munster 0-5
1938	Croke Park	17 March	Connacht 2-6, Munster 1-5
1939	Croke Park	17 March	Leinster 3-8, Ulster 3-3
1940	Croke Park	17 March	Leinster 3-7, Munster 0-2
1941	Croke Park	16 March	Munster 1-8, Ulster 1-8 (draw)

	Croke Park	14 April	Munster 2-6, Ulster 1-6 (replay)
1942	Croke Park	17 March	Ulster 1-10, Munster 1-5
1943	Croke Park	17 March	Ulster 3-7, Leinster 2-9
1944	Croke Park	17 March	Leinster 1-10, Ulster 1-3
1945	Croke Park	17 March	Leinster 2-5, Connacht 0-6
1946	Croke Park	17 March	Munster 3-5, Leinster 1-9
1947	Croke Park	17 March	Ulster 1-6, Leinster 0-3
1948	Croke Park	17 March	Munster 4-5, Ulster 2-6
1949	Croke Park	17 March	Munster 2-7, Leinster 2-7 (draw)
	Croke Park	20 March	Munster 4-9, Leinster 1-4 (replay)
1950	Croke Park	17 March	Ulster 4-11, Leinster 1-7
1951	Croke Park	17 March	Connacht 1-9, Munster 1-8
1952	Croke Park	17 March	Leinster 0-5, Munster 0-3
1953	Croke Park	17 March	Leinster 2-9, Munster 0-6
1954	Croke Park	17 March	Leinster 1-7, Connacht 1-5
1955	Croke Park	17 March	Leinster 1-14, Connacht 1-10
1956	Croke Park	17 March	Ulster 0-12, Munster 0-4
1957	Croke Park	17 March	Connacht 2-9, Munster 1-6
1958	Croke Park	17 March	Connacht 2-7, Munster 0-8
1959	Croke Park	17 March	Leinster 2-7, Munster 0-7
1960	Croke Park	17 March	Ulster 2-12, Munster 3-8
1961	Croke Park	17 March	Leinster 4-5, Munster 0-4
1962	Croke Park	17 March	Leinster 1-11, Ulster 0-11
1963	Croke Park	17 March	Ulster 2-8, Leinster 1-9
1964	Croke Park	17 March	Ulster 0-12, Leinster 1-6
1965	Croke Park	17 March	Ulster 0-19, Connacht 0-15
1966	Croke Park	17 March	Ulster 2-5, Munster 1-5
1967	Croke Park	17 March	Connacht 1-9, Ulster 0-11
1968	Croke Park	17 March	Ulster 1-10, Leinster 0-8
1969	Croke Park	17 March	Connacht 1-12, Munster 0-6
1970	Croke Park	17 March	Ulster 2-11, Connacht 0-10
1971	Croke Park	17 March	Ulster 3-11, Connacht 2-11
1972	Croke Park	17 March	Munster 1-15, Leinster 1-15 (draw)
	Cork	23 April	Munster 2-14, Leinster 0-10 (replay)
1973	Croke Park	17 March	Universities 2-12, Connacht 0-18 (draw)
	Athlone	23 April	Universities 4-9, Connacht 1-11 (replay)

1974	Croke Park	17 March	Leinster 2-10, Connacht 1-7
1975	Croke Park	17 March	Munster 6-7, Ulster 0-15
1976	Croke Park	17 March	Munster 2-15, Leinster 2-8
1977	Croke Park	17 March	Munster 1-14, Connacht 1-9
1978	Croke Park	27 March	Munster 2-7, Ulster 2-7 (draw)
	Croke Park	16 April	Munster 4-12, Ulster 0-19 (replay)
1979	Croke Park	18 March	Ulster 1-7, Munster 0-6
1980	Croke Park	17 March	Ulster 2-10, Munster 1-9
1981	Ennis	17 March	Munster 3-10, Connacht 1-9
1982	Tullamore	17 March	Munster 1-8, Connacht 0-10
1983	Cavan	17 March	Ulster 0-24, Leinster 2-10
1984	Ennis	18 March	Ulster 1-12, Connacht 1-7
1985	Croke Park	17 March	Leinster 0-9, Munster 0-5
1986	Ballinasloe	17 March	Leinster 2-8, Connacht 2-5
1987	Droichead Nua	4 October	Leinster 1-13, Munster 0-9
1988	Ballina	16 October	Leinster 2-9, Ulster 0-12
1989	Páirc Uí Chaoimh	8 October	Ulster 1-11, Munster 1-8
1990	No competition		
1991	Croke Park	7 April	Ulster 1-11, Munster 1-8
1992	Newry	15 March	Ulster 2-7, Munster 0-8
1993	Longford	31 October	Ulster 1-12, Leinster 0-12
1994	Ennis	6 March	Ulster 1-6, Munster 1-4
1995	Clones	26 February	Ulster 1-9, Leinster 0-8
1996	Droichead Nua	14 April	Leinster 1-13, Munster 0-9
1997	Castlebar	9 February	Leinster 2-14, Connacht 0-12
1998	Clones	8 February	Ulster 0-20, Leinster 0-17
1999	Tuam	2 May	Munster 0-10, Connacht 0-6
2000	Sligo	6 February	Ulster 1-9, Connacht 0-3

Appendix 4

National Football League, 1927–2000

1. Winning teams

Kerry (16)	1928, 1929, 1931, 1932, 1959, 1961, 1963, 1969, 1971, 1972, 1973, 1974, 1977, 1982, 1984, 1997
Mayo (10)	1934, 1935, 1936, 1937, 1938, 1939, 1941, 1949, 1954, 1970
Dublin (8)	1953, 1955, 1958, 1976, 1978, 1987, 1991, 1993
Meath (7)	1933, 1946, 1951, 1975, 1988, 1990, 1994
Cork (5)	1952, 1956, 1980, 1989, 1999
Derry (5)	1947, 1992, 1995, 1996, 2000
Down (4)	1960, 1962, 1968, 1983
Galway (4)	1940, 1957, 1965, 1981
New York (3)	1950, 1964, 1967
Laois (2)	1927, 1986
Cavan (1)	1948
Longford (1)	1966
Monaghan (1)	1985
Roscommon (1)	1979
Offaly (1)	1998

Appendix 5

ALL-IRELAND UNDER-21 CHAMPIONSHIP, 1964–2000

Winning teams

Cork (9)	1970, 1971, 1980, 1981, 1984, 1985, 1986, 1989, 1994
Kerry (9)	1964, 1973, 1975, 1976, 1977, 1990, 1995, 1996, 1998
Mayo (3)	1967, 1974, 1983
Tyrone (3)	1991, 1992, 2000
Roscommon (2)	1966, 1978
Donegal (2)	1982, 1987
Derry (2)	1968, 1997
Antrim (1)	1969
Down (1)	1979
Galway (1)	1972
Kildare (1)	1965
Meath (1)	1993
Offaly (1)	1988
Westmeath (1)	1999

Appendix 6

ALL-IRELAND SENIOR FOOTBALL CLUB CHAMPIONSHIP, 1970/71– 1999/2000

1. Winning teams

Nemo Rangers (Cork) (6)	1973, 1979, 1982, 1984, 1989, 1994
St Finbarr's (Cork) (3)	1980, 1981, 1987
Crossmaglen Rangers (Armagh) (3)	1997, 1999, 2000
UCD (Dublin) (2)	1974, 1975
Burren (Down) (2)	1986, 1988
East Kerry (1)	1971
Bellaghy (Derry) (1)	1972
St Vincent's (Dublin) (1)	1976
Austin Stacks (Tralee) (1)	1977
Thomond College (Limerick) (1)	1978
Port Laoise (Laois) (1)	1983
Castleisland Desmonds (Kerry) (1)	1985
Baltinglass (Wicklow) (1)	1990
Lavey (Derry) (1)	1991
Dr Crokes (Killarney) (1)	1992
O'Donovan Rossa (Skibbereen) (1)	1993
Kilmacud Crokes (Dublin) (1)	1995
Laune Rangers (Kerry) (1)	1996
Corrofin (Galway) (1)	1998

2. Results

1971	Croke Park	21 November	East Kerry 5-9, Bryansford 2-7
1972	Croke Park	12 May	Bellaghy 0-15, UCC 1-11
1973	Port Laoise	4 June	Nemo Rangers 2-11, St Vincent's 2-11 (draw)
	Thurles	24 June	Nemo Rangers 4-6, St Vincent's 0-10 (replay)
1974	Croke Park	18 March	UCD 1-6, Clan na Gael (Armagh) 1-6 (draw)
	Croke Park	28 April	UCD 0-14, Clan na Gael 1-4 (replay)

1975	Croke Park	16 March	UCD 1-11, Nemo Rangers 0-12
1976	Port Laoise	14 March	St Vincent's 4-10, Roscommon Gaels 0-5
1977	Croke Park	13 March	Austin Stacks 1-13, Ballerin 2-7
1978	Croke Park	26 March	Thomond College 2-14, St John's 1-3
1979	Croke Park	17 March	Nemo Rangers 2-9, Scotstown 1-3
1980	Tipperary	25 May	St Finbarr's 3-9, St Grellan's, Ballinasloe 0-8
1981	Croke Park	31 May	St Finbarr's 1-8, Walters Town 0-6
1982	Ennis	16 May	Nemo Rangers 6-11, Garrymore 1-8
1983	Cloughjordan	20 March	Port Laoise 0-12, Clann na nGael 2-0
1984	Athlone	12 February	Nemo Rangers 2-10, Walterstown 0-5
1985	Tipperary	24 March	Castleisland Desmonds 2-2, St Vincent's 0-7
1986	Croke Park	16 March	Burren 1-10, Castleisland Desmonds 1-6
1987	Croke Park	17 March	St Finbarr's 0-10, Clann na nGael 0-7
1988	Croke Park	17 March	Burren 1-9, Clann na nGael 0-8
1989	Croke Park	17 March	Nemo Rangers 1-13, Clann na nGael 1-3
1990	Croke Park	17 March	Baltinglass 2-7, Clann na nGael 0-7
1991	Croke Park	17 March	Lavey 2-9, Salthill 0-10
1992	Croke Park	17 March	Dr Crokes 1-11, Thomas Davis 0-13
1993	Croke Park	17 March	O'Donovan Rossa 1-12, Éire Óg 3-6 (draw)
	Limerick	28 March	O'Donovan Rossa 1-7, Éire Óg 0-8 (replay)
1994	Croke Park	17 March	Nemo Rangers 3-11, Castlebar Mitchels 0-8
1995	Croke Park	17 March	Kilmacud Crokes 0-8, Bellaghy 0-5
1996	Croke Park	17 March	Laune Rangers 4-5, Éire Óg 0-11
1997	Croke Park	17 March	Crossmaglen Rangers 2-13, Knockmore 0-11
1998	Croke Park	17 March	Corrofin 0-15, Erin's Isle 0-10
1999	Croke Park	17 March	Crossmaglen Rangers 0-9, Ballina Stephenites 0-8
2000	Croke Park	17 March	Crossmaglen Rangers 1-14, Na Fianna 0-12

Appendix 7

ALL-IRELAND B FOOTBALL, 1990–99

Leitrim (1)	1990
Clare (1)	1991
Wicklow (1)	1992
Laois (1)	1993
Carlow (1)	1994
Tipperary (1)	1995
Fermanagh (1)	1996
Louth (1)	1997
Monaghan (1)	1998
Antrim (1)	1999

Appendix 8

ALL-IRELAND SENIOR FOOTBALL (A) COLLEGES CHAMPIONSHIP, 1946–99

Winning teams

St Jarlath's College, Tuam (11)	1947, 1958, 1960, 1961, 1964, 1966, 1974, 1978, 1982, 1984, 1994
St Colman's College, Newry (6)	1967, 1975, 1986, 1988, 1993, 1998
St Mel's College, Longford (4)	1948, 1962, 1963, 1987
Coláiste Chríost Rí, Cork (4)	1968, 1970, 1983, 1985
Carmelite College, Moate (3)	1976, 1980, 1981
St Patrick's College, Maghera (3)	1989, 1990. 1995
St Brendan's College, Killarney (2)	1969, 1992
Ardscoil Rís, Dublin (1)	1979
Franciscan College, Gormanston (1)	1973
St Columb's College, Derry (1)	1965
St Colman's College, Claremorris (1)	1977
St Joseph's College, Fairview (1)	1959
St Mary's CBS, Belfast (1)	1971
St Patrick's College, Armagh (1)	1946
St Patrick's College, Cavan (1)	1972
St Nathy's College, Ballaghaderreen (1)	1957
St Fachtna's, Skibbereen (1)	1991
Intermediate School, Killorglin (1)	1996
St Patrick's Academy, Dungannon (1)	1997
Good Counsel, New Ross (1)	1999
St Patrick's College, Navan (1)	2000

Appendix 9

SIGERSON CUP UNIVERSITIES AND HIGHER COLLEGES SENIOR FOOTBALL CHAMPIONSHIP, 1911–2000

Winning teams

UCD [NUID] (32)	1911, 1915, 1916, 1917, 1920, 1923, 1926, 1928, 1929, 1930, 1931, 1932, 1935, 1944, 1945, 1947, 1949, 1953, 1955, 1956, 1957, 1959, 1961, 1968, 1973, 1974, 1975, 1977, 1978, 1979, 1985, 1996
UCG [NUIG] (21)	1912, 1921, 1933, 1934, 1936, 1937, 1938, 1939, 1940, 1941, 1948, 1950, 1954, 1960, 1962, 1963, 1980, 1981, 1983, 1984, 1992
UCC [NUIC] (19)	1913, 1914, 1919, 1922, 1924, 1925, 1927, 1943, 1946, 1951, 1952, 1965, 1966, 1969, 1970, 1972, 1988, 1994, 1995
QUB (7)	1958, 1964, 1971, 1982, 1990, 1993, 2000
UU, Jordanstown (3)	1986, 1987, 1991
ITT, Tralee (3)	1997, 1998, 1999
St Mary's, Belfast (1)	1989
St Patrick's College, Maynooth (1)	1976

Appendix 10

ALL-IRELAND INTER-COUNTY VOCATIONAL SCHOOLS SENIOR FOOTBALL CHAMPIONSHIP, 1961–2000

Winning teams

Kerry (9)	1973, 1977, 1978, 1986, 1987, 1990, 1992, 1993, 1997
Tyrone (6)	1967, 1969, 1970, 1988, 1989, 1998
Donegal (4)	1984, 1985, 1995, 1996
Mayo (4)	1971, 1975, 1982, 1999
Derry (3)	1979, 1980, 1981
Galway (3)	1964, 1965, 1976
Dublin City (2)	1962, 1963
Wicklow (2)	1974, 1983
Cork (2)	1991, 1994
Fermanagh (1)	1966
Antrim (1)	1968
Carlow (1)	1972
Cork City (1)	1961
Dublin (1)	2000

BIBLIOGRAPHY

Barrett, J. J., *In the Name of the Game,* Bray: Dub Press 1997.

Barry, John, and Horan, Éamonn, *Years of Glory,* self-published 1977.

Breheny, Martin, *All in the Game,* Dublin: Blackwater Press 1996.

'Carbery' [Patrick Mehigan], *Carbery's Annual.*

'Carbery' [Patrick Mehigan], *Gaelic Football,* Dublin: Gaelic Publicity Services 1941.

'Carbery' [Patrick Mehigan], *Famous Captains,* Dublin: Carberry Publications 1946.

Carthy, Brian, *Football Captains: All-Ireland Winners,* Dublin: Wolfhound Press 1993.

Carthy, Brian, *The Championship 1995,* Dublin: Wolfhound Press 1995.

Carthy, Brian, *The Championship,* 1996, 1997, 1998 and 1999.editions, Dublin: Sliabh Bán Productions.

Conboy, Tony, *Ros Comáin: 101 Years of Gaelic Games in Roscommon, 1889 to 1990,* Roscomáin: Cómhairle Chontar 1990.

Corry, Eoghan, *Kildare GAA: A Centenary History,* Newbridge: Kildare Co. Board GAA 1984.

Corry, Eoghan, *Oakboys: Derry's Football Dream Come True,* Dublin: Torc 1993.

Courtney, Pat (editor), *Famous All-Irelands, Book 1,* Dublin: Canavaun Books 1984.

Courtney, Pat (editor), *Famous All-Irelands, Book 2,* Dublin: Canavaun Books 1984.

Cunningham, P., and Scully, R. (editors), *The Faithful County: Official Centenary Publication, 1884–1994,* Tullamore: Offaly Co. Board GAA 1984.

de Búrca, Marcus, *The GAA: A History,* Dublin: CLCG 1980; second edition Dublin: Gill & Macmillan 1999.

Doire: A History of the GAA in Derry, Derry: Derry Co. Board GAA 1984.

Dunne, Mick, *The Star-Spangled Final of 1947,* Dublin: Gaelsport Publications Teo 1997.

280   BIBLIOGRAPHY

Fenning, Paddy, *Offaly: The Faithful County*, Tullamore: Esker Press 1993.
Fitzgerald, Dick, *How to Play Gaelic Football*, Cork: Guy and Company 1914.
Gaelic Athletic Association, *GAA Yearbook*, Dublin: GAA 1976, 1977, 1978, 1980.
Gaelic Athletic Association, *A Century of Service, 1884–1984*, Dublin: GAA 1984.
Gaelic Athletic Association, Cork County Board, *Cork, 1990*, Cork: Gaelic Sport Publications 1990.
Gaelic Athletic Association, Cork County Board, *Cork, 1991*, Cork: Gaelic Sport Publications 1991.
Gallogly, Daniel, *Cavan's Football Story*, Cavan: Cavan Co. Committee of GAA 1979.
Hayes, Liam, *Out of Our Skins*, Dublin: Gill and Macmillan 1992.
Healy, Paul, *Gaelic Games and the GAA*, Cork: Mercier Press 1998.
Hogan Stand, 9 April 1999.
Kerryman, *Three in a Row: Kerry's 1978, 1979 and 1980 All-Irelands*, Tralee: Kerryman 1980.
McCann, Owen, *Record-Makers of Gaelic Games*, Cork: Oisín Publications 1996.
McCrohan, Owen, *Mick O'Dwyer: The Authorised Biography*, Waterville: MOD Publications 1990.
McDermott, Peter, *Gaels in the Sun*, self-published 1968.
Mahon, Jack, *The Game of My Life*, Dublin: Blackwater Press 1993.
Mahon, Jack, *For Love of Town and Village*, Dublin: Blackwater Press 1997.
Meath Chronicle, *Centenary Publication*, 1997.
Mulligan, John, *The GAA in Louth*, Dundalk: Louth Co. Board GAA 1984.
Nic an Ultaigh, Síghle, *An Dún: The GAA Story: Ó Shíol Go Bláth*, Coiste Stair: Down Co. Board GAA 1991.
O'Brien, Barry, *Macroom GAA Club History, 1886–1987*, Macroom: GAA Club 1987.
Ó Ceallacháin, Seán Óg, *Tall Tales and Banter*, Dublin: Costar Associates 1998.
Ó Ceallaigh, Séamus, *The Story of the GAA*, Limerick: 1977.
O'Connell, Mick, *A Kerry Footballer*, Cork: Mercier Press 1974.
O'Rourke, Colm, *The Final Whistle*, Dublin: Hero Books 1996.
O'Sullivan, Thomas, *The Story of the GAA*, self-published 1916.
'P.F.', *Kerry's Football Story*, Tralee: Kerryman 1945.
Puirséal, Pádhraic, *The GAA in Its Time*, Dublin: Purcell family 1982.

Quinn, Jerome, *Ulster Football and Hurling,* 1993.

Quinn, Jerome, *Ulster Gaelic Games Annual,* self-published 1994.

Quinn, Jerome, *Ulster Sports,* Belfast: Jequi Books 1995.

Reilly, Terry, and Neill, Ivan, *The Green Above the Red,* Ballina: Western People 1985.

Royal Meath Association, *Souvenir Book: All-Ireland Champions, 1954,* Dublin: Pearse Press 1954.

'Sliabh Ruadh' [Phil O'Neill], *History of the GAA 1910–1930,* Kilkenny: Kilkenny Journal 1931.

Smith, Raymond, *The Football Immortals,* Dublin: Bruce Spicer 1968.

Smith, Raymond, *The Football Immortals,* Dublin: Cityview Press 1971.

Smith, Raymond, *The Football Immortals,* Dublin: Creative Press 1973.

Smith, Raymond, *The Football Immortals,* Dublin: Madison Publishers 1995.

Smith, Raymond, *Sunday Independent Complete Handbook of Gaelic Games,* Dublin: Sunday Independent 1988, 1993, 1999.

Tyndall, Billy, *Kildare's Golden Years,* Naas: Leinster Leader 1966.

Wexford People, 'Centenary tribute to GAA in Wexford, 1884–1984' (supplement in *Wexford People*), 1984.

Young, Éamonn, *Rebels at the Double,* Edinburgh: Mainstream Publishing Co. 1990.

INDEX